MW00879305

BOOTS, BADGES & BULLETS

BOOTS, BADGES & BULLETS

TEXAS RANGER LORE

MIKE COX

First Edition

Blue Hole Press
Wimberley, Texas
Beverly Waak Cox, Managing Editor
Cover design, digital typesetting and layout by
Sargent Brothers, Printers & Typographers
Austin, Texas
sargentbrothersprinters.com
Blue Hole Press logo by Erika Marcoux

On the Cover

The pen-and-ink drawing of a mounted Texas Ranger comes from a syndicated December 1910 newspaper article, "The Texas Rangers." Illustrated by an unknown artist and written by an unknown author, the piece appeared in numerous newspapers across the U.S. While the distributor is not indicated, it likely came from the New York-based McClure Newspaper Syndicate. The syndicate paid a writer for an article, then collected $5 from any newspaper publishing it. Founded in 1884, McClure went out of business in 1951. The syndicate's most notable legacy? It introduced the world to the Batman and Robin comic strip in 1943.

FOREWORD

I first met Mike Cox in the 1970s when I was a Texas Ranger stationed in Austin and he was a reporter for the Austin American-Statesman. Later, when Mike left the newspaper to join the Texas Department of Public Safety's public information office, he assisted me in dealing with the news media during several high-profile homicide cases prior to my retirement in 1993.

Mike and I became better acquainted at the annual membership reunions of the Former Texas Rangers Association (FTRA). At the time, we held these gatherings each May on the grounds of Memorial Hall in San Antonio next to the Witte Museum. Built in 1936 during the Texas Centennial, the exhibit-filled hall honored the Rangers, pioneers and trail drivers who helped build Texas.

While I was FTRA president the board of directors voted to build a larger museum dedicated solely to Ranger history. I was then appointed president of the Former Texas Rangers Foundation which had been established in 1971 as a 501c3 non-profit organization. The foundation would begin raising money to fund a new museum. In the meantime, the Ranger artifacts displayed at the overcrowded Memorial Hall were moved to the popular Buckhorn Saloon attraction in downtown San Antonio.

I asked Mike if he'd be willing to serve on the foundation board. He said yes and we've been working together in one way or another ever since.

Not long after Mike began sitting in on board meetings the foundation began planning the Texas Ranger Heritage Center. The first phase of this 12-acre Fredericksburg complex opened in 2015. The second phase, which we're currently raising money to complete, will feature a state-of-the-art museum and Ranger archive.

Back when he was still with the DPS, the FTRA elected Mike as associate historian. Considering the corral-full of books he's written on the Rangers, by all rights he should have been voted in as the FTRA historian. But our bylaws say that only a Ranger descendant qualifies for that position.

In March 2015, shortly after Mike retired from the state, both of us joined a "posse" of former Rangers and other history-minded folks in search of a remote box canyon in Presidio County.

There, a century before, former Ranger Joe Sitter and a rookie Ranger died when ambushed by Mexican bandits. After a long, dusty ride on modern-day "mules" (aka all-terrain vehicles), our well-armed party succeeded in reaching the site. After hunting unsuccessfully for any century-old shell casings, we took photographs and noted the GPS coordinates to document its location.

The same year we shared that adventure, Mike accidentally made a discovery that caught him off guard. One day while working on his book Gunfights and Sites in Texas Ranger History, he happened to be looking at the FTRA website when something grabbed his attention. A Ranger Cross installation ceremony was scheduled at the grave of a former Ranger buried at the Wilke Family Cemetery near the old Gillespie County town of Albert.

This was of particular interest to Mike because his mother's maiden name was Wilke. He knew that his German forebears settled in Fredericksburg in the late 1840s, but he'd never heard of any of them serving as a Ranger. Even Mike's grandfather had not known of any connection between the Wilkes and the Rangers.

But to Mike's delight, after thinking for most of his life that he had no family ties to any former Ranger, he discovered that his great-great grandfather Heinrich Wilke's brother, Fritz Wilke, had ridden as a Ranger in Gillespie County during the Civil War.

So, when the then-current FTRA historian stepped down in 2020, the membership elected Mike to the position, and he's been re-elected every year since then. He also continues as an FTRA Foundation advisory board member and is currently working on a history of the FTRA to be included in a book commemorating the 125th anniversary of the organization's predecessor, the Ex-Rangers Association.

Over the decades, through his writing, his tenure as DPS Chief of Media Relations and as FTRA historian, Mike has done much to preserve the long history of the Rangers.

Boots, Badges & Bullets is Mike's eighth Ranger-related book. I've enjoyed his previous books as well as this one and believe you will, too.

Joe B. Davis, President
Former Texas Rangers Foundation
Texas Ranger, Retired
Fredericksburg, Texas

People have been fighting and killing each other in what is now Texas since long before recorded history.

American Indians fought other American Indians, followed by conflict between American Indians and a succession of other cultures seeking to claim their land.

In the vast area that would become Texas, American Indians first fought Spanish colonizers and to a lesser if still sanguinary extent, the French. Then Mexicans fought the Spanish and wrested control of much of the Southwest from them. That led to conflict between American Indians and Mexicans.

When Texas became a Mexican province in 1821, Anglo-European colonists fought American Indians and later fought to separate themselves from Mexico. After Texas became an independent republic, fighting continued with American Indians and Mexicans bent on recovering their lost territory. Next, from 1846 to 1848 the U.S. fought Mexico to assure its hold on the new state of Texas and much of the rest of the Southwest.

Less than two decades after the end of that conflict, in 1861 thousands of Texans fought for four bloody years to establish a separate pro-slavery Confederate States of America. At the same time, other Texans fought for the North to preserve the union and free enslaved people. After the Civil War, Texans continued to fight with American Indians still struggling to retain their ancestral land. Later, during the Mexican Revolution in the early 20th century, new violence between Mexicans and Texans erupted along the Rio Grande.

Right or wrong, at least since the days of the Mexican province of Coahuila y Tejas, the Texas Rangers had a role in the many conflicts that soaked much Texas soil in blood. Fortunately, no significant fighting has taken place in Texas in more than a century—at least not with arrow, blade, or bullet. Today's Texas Rangers are highly trained criminal investigators, not war fighters.

But beginning in the last quarter of the 20th century and continuing at a faster pace in this century, a different type of fighting came to the fore: A war of words over how we should view our history and how we should teach it to younger Texans. Cultural war is raging elsewhere as well, but in recent years it has grown particularly contentious in Texas—especially in regard to the history of the Rangers.

This book isn't intended as a definitive history of the Rangers. I've already endeavored to cover that in my two-volume work, Wearing the Cinco Peso and Time of the Rangers (New York, 2008-2009) and Gunfights and Sites in Texas Ranger History (Charleston, SC, 2015). Boots, Badges & Bullets is a collection of historical essays, true tales, anecdotes and legends about mostly little-known figures and incidents in the long saga of the Texas Rangers. Arranged by era, some of these stories are about Rangers who did good, some are about Rangers who didn't always do good and some are about Rangers who simply did their job. Some of the pieces are funny, some sad.

So, cinch your saddle, check your six-shooter one more time, shove your Winchester in its scabbard and mount up for a ride through more than two centuries of Ranger history.

Mike Cox
Wimberley, Texas

TWO CENTURIES OF RANGER HISTORY

Texans celebrated the bicentennial of the Texas Rangers in 2023. But should the observance have been delayed until 2035? Or 2036? Each of these years has a claim on being the Ranger's 200th birthday.

But there are more dates to consider. Even though 1823 is generally accepted as the Rangers' Big Bang year, there's room for argument over whether it happened in January, May, June, July, or August 1823.

Two years before, in 1821, Stephen F. Austin assumed his late father's contract (initially executed with Spain) to develop a colony in the new Mexican province of Coahuila y Tejas. Austin had authority to recruit settlers from the U.S. and Europe who would be given land if, among other conditions, they agreed to become Mexican citizens, adopt Catholicism, learn Spanish and not bring any slaves with them. For governing the colony, Austin's compensation for his services would be land.

The Mexican government hoped that Austin's colony, and those proposed by other empresarios (land speculators), would bolster the new republic's economy through increased trade and serve to stave off the expansionist-minded United States. Beyond that, the colony would serve as a buffer between the Comanche and other hostile tribes and existing settlements such as San Antonio de Bexar and Laredo.

Under Mexican law, Austin had the authority to form a militia to ward off Indian attacks, capture criminals and patrol against intruders. On May 5, 1823, while Austin was in Mexico City, his militia lieutenant Moses Morrison received written permission to assemble a company of men to protect the Texas coast from the Tonkawa and Karankawa tribes.

Earlier that year, on Jan. 7, 1823, John J. Tumlinson (considered THE first ranger) and newly arrived Austin colony settler Robert Kuykendall wrote Jose Felix Trespalacios, governor of the Mexican province of Coahuila y Tejas, seeking authorization to raise a 15-man volunteer company to protect the new colony. That action may have been related to a one-page broadside printed by Samuel Bangs that summer:

Gen. [Felipe de la] *Garza orders six regulations for police actions to combat the high rate of robberies and murders in Texas, Coahuila, and Tamaulipas, including the recruitment of private citizens in Texas and other areas where the militia is not stationed.*

Finally, on the back of a used land document dated Aug. 5, 1823, the 29-year-old empresario Austin wrote a 177-word passage that has come to be considered the "Magna Carta" of the Rangers:

I have determined to augment at my own private expense the company of men which was raised by order of the late Governor Trespalacios for the defense of the Colony against hostile Indians. I therefore by these presents give public notice that I will employ ten men in addition to those employed by the late Governor to act as rangers for the common defense. The said ten men will form a part of Lieut. Moses Morrison's Company and the whole will be subject to my orders.

While the colony already had a civilian, Ranger-like militia, Austin's musings marked the first use of the word "rangers" in Texas. Given the differing nomenclature regarding colonial defense forces, no wonder that late 19th and even early 20th century writers and historians viewed 1835 or 1836 as the Ranger start-up year—not 1823.

Historian Dr. Malcom D. McLean, who edited the multivolume Papers Concerning Robertson's Colony of Texas, contended that the true origin of the Rangers occurred in mid- June 1835 when Robert M. Coleman led a company of mounted riflemen against a party of Tonkawa Indians in what is now Limestone County.

In November 1835, Texas' independence-minded provisional government (formally if illogically known as the "Permanent Council") passed a resolution authorizing a "Corps of Rangers." Though its men would be paid $1.25 a day for their service, they were required to furnish their own arms, mounts and equipment. Of course, Texas still belonged to Mexico. The Rangers were as "provisional" as the delegates who voted to create such a force. Not until Texas prevailed in its rebellion against Mexico did the newly formed Republic of Texas organize a paramilitary outfit that amounted to rangers. That happened in 1836, the year the Rangers first became a legitimate arm of government.

There's even a later year that could be observed as the true start date for the Rangers—1874. That's when the Texas Legislature created a mounted force designated as the Frontier Bat- talion. But even though the word "ranger" does not appear in the measure, members of the battalion, the citizenry and the press almost always referred to them as rangers or state rangers. And for the first time, rangers were vested with law enforcement authority in addition to their duties as Indian fighters. For a few years they continued to deal with hostile Indians as well as outlaws, but by 1881 all the Frontier Battalion concerned itself with was the enforcement of the state's criminal statutes.

While 2023 saw statewide observance of the Ranger bicentennial, no one celebrated 1923 as the Rangers' 100th birthday. In fact, no one even proposed such an event.

Entering the search terms "Ranger centennial" or "Ranger anniversary" in newspapers.com (a subscription database of hundreds of digitized newspapers) did not turn up a single hit in any Texas newspaper published that year. Not only did the 100th anniversary of Austin's proposed "rangers for the common defense" go uncelebrated, that year the Rangers were about to ride into a legal ambush that would amount to a figurative gunfight over their very survival. In early 1924, a respected San Antonio citizen (backed by a well-known gambler who did not appreciate Ranger efforts to suppress gambling in the Alamo City) filed a civil suit that if it held up would effectively put the Rangers out of operation. In district court, a jury found in favor of the plaintiff and while the state appealed the verdict, essentially the Rangers had no power to enforce any laws. Fortunately for the state, a higher court reversed the district court judgment in February 1925.

Despite the absence of any centennial observance in 1923, a lengthy newspaper article published that year, following a three-paragraph introduction, reprinted a chapter devoted to the Rangers' early history from former Ranger James B. Gillett's Six Years with the Texas Rangers, 1875 to 1881. Privately published in 1921, the book stands as the best memoir by a veteran of the Frontier Battalion. Still, as readable as Gillett's recollections are, the old Ranger's version of the Ranger origin is dead wrong. This is what Gillett wrote:

"The Texas Rangers, as an organization, dates from the spring of 1836. When the Alamo had fallen before the onslaught of the Mexican troops and the frightful massacre had occurred, General Sam Houston organized among the Texan settlers in that territory a troop of 1,600 mounted riflemen. This company, formed for the defense of the Texan borders, was the original Texas Ranger unit..."

Written by Claude L. Douglas, a reporter for the long-since defunct Fort Worth Press, the first general book on the Rangers came out in 1934—The Gentlemen in White Hats. At the beginning of the book, in discussing when the Rangers came to be, Douglas invoked the old Mexican expression "¿quién sabe?" (Who knows?) Here's how he copped out: "Somewhere, among the scrap-ends that history has shuffled into the discard, the exact date of original organization has been lost."

However, in the very next paragraph, Douglas contradicts himself by reporting that empresario Austin had mentioned "rangers" in correspondence in 1821. Of course, that's two years ahead of when it actually happened. The Cowtown journalist did get it right that the provisional government created during Texas' revolt against Mexico provided for a ranger-like force in 1835.

In 1836, Rangers played a role in the struggle for Texas independence. Thirty-two volunteer Rangers died at the Alamo. Following the fall of the old Spanish mission, other Rangers covered the retreat of civilians from the Mexican army in the famous "Runaway Scrape," harassed columns of Mexican troops and provided valuable intelligence to the Texas Army. Some of those Rangers also fought in the pivotal Battle of San Jacinto on April 21 that year.

But Douglas makes no mention at all of 1836.

As Douglas' book hit the shelves, University of Texas historian Walter Prescott Webb worked to wrap up his ground-breaking 1935 history of the Rangers, The Texas Rangers: A Century of Frontier Defense. While the work stood for decades as THE Ranger history, by modern standards it is racist and lacks balance. Webb devoted a few paragraphs in his book to the 1820s, but noted, "Not until the outbreak of the Texas Revolution in 1835 do we find much evidence of the existence of an irregular corps of fighters called the Texas Rangers." The University of Texas published a slightly revised edition of Webb's book in 1965, which allowed for one major correction to the first edition. Given that in 1935 the Rangers merged with Texas' nascent Highway Patrol to create the Texas Department of Public Safety, Webb had predicted that legislative action would be the end of the Rangers. That didn't happen.

Whether investigating felony crimes or patrolling the Rio Grande, no matter their birthday and despite occasional controversy, the Rangers still work for "the common defense."

SIX BULLETS

Hundreds of books, from old-timer recollections to popular and scholarly biographies and institutional histories, have been written about the Texas Rangers. Add to that substantial body of work countless newspaper articles, magazine pieces, pamphlets, websites, blog posts and podcasts and the bibliography alone would fill a book.

But for all that, the Ranger story can be molded into six bullets:

• Dating to the 14th century, the concept of fielding mounted, non-uniformed, irregular guerilla-like fighters to "range" a given area crossed the Atlantic from England in the 17th century. The essential ranging model worked its way south along the Eastern seaboard and finally westward. In Texas, the Spanish colonial rural patrol model—under which the Crown empowered mounted irregulars to arrest, adjudicate and summarily execute cow thieves or other wrong-doers—influenced the Anglo-European ranger concept. The first rangers in the Mexican province of Coahuila and Tejas served in volunteer- or government-sanctioned paramilitary companies mustered to protect Anglo colonists.

• Not until 1835, on the eve of Texas' bloody fight for independence from Mexico, did the Rangers evolve into an arm of the Texas government. First authorized by Texas' provisional government, under new laws the Rangers later served the Republic of Texas (1836-1845) and then the state of Texas. Even so, partial reliance on volunteer companies and individual unpaid rangers continued in Texas into the early 20th century.

• For more than half the 19th century, the primary Ranger focus was to protect settlers from raiding parties of American Indians desperately fighting to retain their land and way of life. During the 1840s Rangers also periodically fought regular Mexican Army troops hoping to regain their lost province. During the 1846-1848 Mexican War, state- or federally funded Rangers engaged in vicious guerilla warfare south of the Rio Grande, earning them the label "los Diablos Tejanos," the Texas Devils.

• Though the Rangers gained legislative authority to function as prairie police officers beginning with the creation of the Frontier Battalion in 1874, not until 1877 did a directive from Frontier Battalion Maj. John B. Jones make law enforcement the Rangers' primarily focus.

• For the remainder of the 19th century and into the first three decades of the 20th century, Ranger effectiveness and integrity waxed and waned depending on state politics, legislative funding and political-organizational leadership. But throughout this period—for the most part—Rangers did their job. They captured or killed outlaws, recovered stolen livestock while arresting horse and cattle thieves, prevented lynchings, tamed rowdy oil boomtowns and interdicted bootleggers during Prohibition. But when violence associated with the Mexican Revolution spilled over into Texas, the Rangers sometimes ran roughshod over civil liberties, extrajudicially killing innocent Mexicans. Legislatively mandated reforms in 1919 additional low points occurred during the two administrations (1925-1927 and 1933-1935) of Gov. Miriam Ferguson (wife of impeached Gov. James Ferguson).

• Beginning with legislation in 1935 creating the Texas Department of Public Safety—a new agency merging the Rangers with the state's six-year-old Highway Patrol—the Rangers have continued both to professionalize and become more diverse in their makeup. While their duties have greatly expanded, modern Rangers (including men and women) have the advantage of state-of-the-art equipment, technology and training. Politics, leadership quality and funding remain as variables that can impact effectiveness, but to a much lesser extent than ever before.

Traveling in equipment-laden pickup trucks, aircraft, high-speed boats mounted with machine guns or occasionally still on horseback, the 21st century Texas Rangers continue to range the Lone Star State.

SHAPING THEIR LEGEND

While they have always had their critics, the Texas Rangers stand tall in the history and mythology of the Old West. Often compared with the Royal Canadian Mounted Police or England's Scotland Yard, the Rangers are known world-wide.

Of the thousands who've served as Rangers over the past two centuries, arguably the demeanor and actions of just ten men shaped the Ranger reputation in the 19th and early 20th century.

JOHN COFFEE HAYS

Though Stephen F. Austin generally is credited with conceptualizing the Rangers, a young, slight man from Tennessee who came to Texas in 1838 as a surveyor soon fathered their reputation.

Taking the measure of Central Texas with transit and chain, Jack Hays survived several close calls with hostile Indians who correctly understood that his instruments presaged the loss of their land. He soon mixed his surveying work with service as a volunteer Ranger, but it was not until January 1841 that the new Republic of Texas made him a Ranger captain.

On June 8, 1844, near Walker's Creek in Central Texas, Hays and his smaller Ranger contingent tangled with more than 70 Comanches and allies.

"After ascertaining that they could not decoy or lead me astray," Hays later wrote, "they came out boldly, formed themselves, and dared us to fight. I then ordered a charge; and, after discharging our rifles, closed in with them, hand to hand, with my five-shooting pistols, which did good execution. Had it not been for them, I doubt what the consequences would have been."

The Rangers killed 23 warriors, wounding another thirty. Hays lost one Ranger with three wounded in a battle that changed the history of the American West. For the first time, Rangers had fought Indians with an effective close-range weapon that didn't need reloading after each shot.

Hays didn't do his work single-handedly, but he proved a leader of men, a savvy tactician and a fierce fighter.

After further adding to his legend during the 1846-1848 Mexican War, Hays left Texas for the West Coast during the 1849 California gold rush. There, he served as sheriff of San Francisco. Later he became a successful businessman. He died in 1883 and is buried in his adopted state.

SAMUEL H. WALKER

One of the men who rode with Hays was Samuel H. Walker.

Born in Maryland, he served with the U.S. Army during Florida's Seminole War before coming to Texas in January 1842. That September he joined a volunteer company and fought an invading Mexican military force bent on reclaiming Texas. In December 1842, captured with other Texans during an attack on the Mexican town of Mier, Walker ended up in Mexico's infamous Perote Castle. He escaped that prison in 1843 and early the following year joined Hays' Ranger company.

That summer of 1844, Walker participated in the Walker's Creek battle. Though clearly disadvantaged by the Rangers' new revolvers, the Comanches still proved quite competent with arrow and lance. "In this encounter," Graham's Magazine reported, "Walker was wound- ed by a lance, and left by his adversary pinned to the ground. After remaining in this position for a long time, he was rescued by his companions when the fight was over."

His fellow Rangers took Walker to San Antonio, where he recovered. Despite the close call, Walker stayed with Hays until the company ran out of funding. In 1845, he served in another Ranger company, this one led by "Ad" Gillespie.

War with Mexico looming, in May 1846, the battle-hardened Walker formed a Ranger company and scouted for General Zachary Taylor. Once Taylor invaded Mexico, Walker joined a Ranger regiment headed by Hays. Later accepting a captaincy in the regular Army, in October 1846 Walker traveled to the northeast to procure weapons and recruit men for his new unit, the First Regiment, Texas Mounted Rifles.

When Samuel Colt learned Walker was in New York, he wrote to invite him to his shop in Paterson, New Jersey: "I have [heard] so much of [Col. Hays] & your [exploits] with the Arms of my invention that I have long desired to know you personally & get from you a true narrative of the [various] instances where my arms have proved of more than ordinary utility." Soon meeting over brandy, Walker gave Colt feedback on his invention. That led to a new, heavier, larger-caliber revolver that fired six shots instead of five. With those changes and some other improvements, the firearm was called the Walker Colt.

Before Walker returned to Mexico in the spring of 1847, the Army contracted with Colt for 1,000 of the new weapons. Colt, who had no plant of his own, subcontracted with Eli Whitney to manufacture the revolvers.

In appreciation of his input, Colt shipped Walker two of the new six-guns in early October. But Walker did not carry them long. In a battle on Oct. 9, 1847, a Mexican rifleman dropped Walker with a single shot.

When Walker was later reburied in San Antonio, his eulogist James C. Wilson compared Walker to Ad Gillespie, the late captain's close friend and fellow Ranger: "Gillespie was brave. Walker had no sense of fear. Gillespie did not shun danger ... Walker seemed to seek danger..."

JOHN H. "RIP" FORD

"Rip" Ford—doctor, lawyer, surveyor, newspaper publisher and legislator—furthered the Ranger image in the 1850s.

Born in South Carolina and raised in Tennessee, Ford came to Texas in 1836. While Texas had already won its independence from Mexico, Ford served in a couple of volunteer Ranger-like companies before turning to his medical and legal practices. He also held a seat in the Republic of Texas Congress and later published a newspaper in Austin.

In the Mexican War, he served under Hays as regimental adjutant. One of his duties involved keeping track of Ranger casualties. On each fatality report, he wrote "Rest in Peace." Later shortening that to "R.I.P." he earned his nickname.

After the war Ford served as a Ranger captain from 1849 to 1851 and participated in numerous Indian fights. He then returned to professional pursuits, but in 1858 when legislators authorized a Ranger force of 150 men Ford became senior Ranger captain.

That spring, Ford and his men splashed across the Red River in pursuit of Comanches who had been raiding in Texas. Less than two weeks later, the captain and his Rangers attacked a Comanche village in the decisive Battle of Antelope Hills.

Beyond his service in the saddle, near the end of his long life, Ford organized an association of former Rangers. Now called the Former Texas Ranger Association, it remains active today. Also, his posthumously published memoir preserved much of early Ranger history. He died in 1897.

LEANDER H. MCNELLY

Never technically a Ranger, battle-tested Civil War veteran Leander McNelly built on the exploits of Hays, Walker and Ford. In 1870 he became a captain in the newly created State Police, serving in that unpopular uniformed body until its disbandment in 1873. The following year, due to out-of-control outlawry and feuding in South Texas, he was appointed captain of the Washington County Volunteers. The outfit soon became known as the state-funded Special Force, but McNelly and his men were Rangers in function if not name.

McNelly dealt harshly with outlaws and Mexican bandits, even illegally crossing the Rio Grande to recover stolen stock. But McNelly had "galloping consumption" (tuberculosis) and began spending much of his time in San Antonio. The Adjutant General's office did not like McNeely's paltry paperwork and began to chafe at the cost of his medical expenses, which the state paid.

And McNelly sounded just about as put out with the powers that be as they were of him. In an interview with the San Antonio Herald in November 1876 the captain complained about "the utter inadequacies of the force at his disposal to the task before him."

While he commanded 50 picked men, he said it would take four times that many Rangers to rid South Texas of its "vermin." With 200 men, he said, he could get the job done.

But McNelly got neither the additional men nor much more time in the Rangers. In early February 1877, the state mustered out McNelly and his command but almost immediately created a 24-man company to replace it. On Sept. 3 that year, he died at 33.

JESSE LEE HALL

Red-headed Lt. Jesse Lee Hall, who had joined McNelly's command already having a noted reputation as a lawman, became captain following McNelly's death.

"Capt. Hall is energetic and persevering in his efforts to capture the murderers and rogues in Texas or cause them to fly to a country of safety," the Daily Fort Worth Standard pronounced on Aug. 23, 1877.

In May 1877, Hall and 16 of his men brought eight prisoners to San Antonio. They'd collected them while scouting from San Antonio to Eagle Pass and back. Among the prisoners, the Galveston Daily News of May 29, 1877, noted, "is one Murray, who, assisted by another ruffian, severely wounded a colored man and ravished his wife and daughter…" The crimes had occurred the year before in Pleasanton.

Rangers did not wear uniforms, but Hall set standards. In the summer of 1879, the San Antonio Herald reported Hall "forbid the wearing of sombreros, fancy top boots, and carrying of white-handled revolvers in his command." Why? "All these things are characteristic of the desperado, and he wishes his boys to look like civilized people."

Presumably using wooden-handled six-shooters, Hall and his men demonstrated their stand-up nature in Atascosa County. Hoping to thwart a planned robbery, the captain and his men staked out a rural store about twenty miles north of Pleasanton. Eventually, five mounted men approached. Two captured the store clerk and three began looting the store.

"Hall then appeared from his concealment and ordered them to surrender, and was answered by a shot," the Nov. 11, 1879, Marshall Tri-Weekly Herald reported. The Rangers returned fire. When the shooting stopped, one badman lay dead with two others wounded. The remaining two bandits escaped.

After numerous other successful operations involving Hall's Rangers, including Lt. John B. Armstrong's sensational capture of killer John Wesley Hardin in Florida, Hall resigned in 1880 to pursue business interests. He died in 1911.

JOHN B. JONES

If Hays and his men spurred on the Ranger legend, John B. Jones hog-tied the force's reputation as an efficient law enforcement body.

In 1874, the legislators created the Frontier Battalion, a force charged with frontier protection. The measure also vested Rangers with law enforcement authority for the first time. The battalion would be under state Adjutant General William Steele with Jones as major in command. Both men had served together during the Civil War.

The Houston Telegram in December 1877 described Jones as "...the peer of Walker, Hayes [sic], [Ben] McCulloch, and the men whose names are in history and whose exploits have illustrated the romance and daring of life on the Texas border."

The unknown journalist continued:

"By birth and education a gentleman...this daring chief...is a small man scarcely of medium height and stature, whose conventional dress of black broadcloth, spotless linen, and dainty boot on a small foot, would not distinguish him from any other citizen..."

The newspaper writer went on to say that "it would require a good deal of penetration to see in this quiet, affable gentleman the leader of the celebrated Texas Rangers and the hero of many a daring assault and wild melee, and the bulwark of the border and the terror of frontier forayers."

Despite Jones' leadership, the Frontier Battalion was always short-staffed and hamstrung with smaller-than-needed appropriations. But despite the problems they faced, the Rangers stayed in the saddle and continued to build their renown.

Having survived a bloody encounter with hostile Indians in North Texas in 1875 and the 1878 shootout with Sam Bass's train-robbing gang in Round Rock, Texas, Jones died at 47 in 1881 of complications following surgery.

JOHN R. HUGHES

John R. Hughes first exhibited moxie as a teenager. Born in Illinois and raised in Kansas, at 15 Hughes hired on with a cattle outfit in Indian Territory. When a would-be rustler tried to cull some stock from Hughes' herd, the youngster took his first stand. It ended with a funeral for the cow thief and a bullet in Hughes' right arm. After that, he never had full use of the limb, but before long he could draw as fast with his left hand as originally he could with his right.

Hughes continued cowboying until 1878, when with the trail driving earnings he'd saved he and his brother bought a ranch in Central Texas.

Now 30, Hughes preferred poetry and reading his Bible to any of the easily available vices on the frontier. His pistol stayed in its holster, hanging on the ranch house wall. Unlike many men of his time, Hughes viewed the weapon as a tool for use when needed, not an item of ornamental apparel.

As a rancher, Hughes specialized in horses, building his remuda from herds of wild mustangs still roaming to the west. He was a contented man until one morning in 1886 when he discovered that outlaws had ridden off with 16 of his best animals, including his favorite stallion. Another fifty-four horses had vanished from neighboring ranches.

"I followed them to New Mexico, got all my horses back and a lot of my neighbor's horses," Hughes later modestly related. "Two of [the horse thieves] were...sent to the New Mexico penitentiary." Hughes forgot to mention that he'd killed three of the horse thieves, leaving only two survivors to stand trial.

Meanwhile, a friend of the thieves came to Texas to settle accounts. But when the would-be assassin arrived at Hughes' ranch, he happened not to be there. Hughes did not know someone was gunning for him, nor that a Texas Ranger already was on the outlaw's trail with a murder warrant stemming from a robbery-homicide in Fredericksburg, Texas. Ranger Ira Aten located the gunman before the outlaw could get to Hughes.

"They exchanged shots," Hughes recalled. "The ranger shot the pistol out of his hand, but the man got away The ranger asked me to help catch the man."

Three weeks later, Hughes and Aten found the outlaw. "Unfortunately," as Hughes later put it, "he would not surrender and was killed. His friends then were so annoying to me that I could not go without arms, so the ranger persuaded me to enlist in the company with him." In August 1887, in Georgetown, Texas, Hughes began a Ranger career he expected to last only a few months. But months turned into years. By spring 1890 he'd been promoted to sergeant. Three years later, when Captain Frank Jones died in a gun battle with Mexican bandits near El Paso, Hughes rose to captain.

When he retired in 1915, Hughes humbly summarized his Ranger career: "Unfortunately, I have been in several engagements where desperate criminals were killed. I have never lost a battle that I was in personally, and never let a prisoner escape."

Hughes was 92 before a bullet finally ended his long and rich life. On June 3, 1947, the old Ranger's body, his .45 nearby, was found in a garage behind a relative's home in Austin. The captain's health had been failing, and he did not want to burden his family.

WILLIAM J. MCDONALD

With a background in business, ranching and county law enforcement, Bill McDonald became a Ranger captain in 1890. He's the Ranger generally credited with first uttering a line that morphed into the slogan "One Ranger, one riot," but it's never been definitely established that any Ranger ever said that.

McDonald was both big-headed and bull-headed, but he had sand. He usually got his man and was a pioneer in using forensics—crude as scientific evidence analysis was in the late 19th and early 20th centuries.

As much as he welcomed publicity, McDonald knew when to keep his mouth shut. "The captain is known to the newspapermen as 'the squirrel hunter,'" the Austin Statesman noted on June 1, 1903. "It matters not what is happening throughout the state, the newspapermen can only find out from this veteran that he is going squirrel hunting."

His gutsiest moment came in 1906, when an African American soldier stationed at Fort Brown in Brownsville was accused of raping a white woman. McDonald and several of his men took the train to the Valley with the captain determined to arrest the trooper on state charges. The military would not release him, and a battle of words ensued that came close to being a real battle between the Rangers and the Army.

McDonald did not prevail, and it's generally accepted that he was overreaching his authority. Still, the so-called Brownsville incident led one Army officer to opine that McDonald would "charge hell with a bucket of water."

The captain left the Rangers in 1907 for another state job and died in 1918. State law makers had done away with Frontier Battalion in 1901, but the Ranger service continued under a new law.

WILLIAM L. WRIGHT

Joining the Rangers in 1899, Will Wright quickly began building his reputation as an honorable man who would stand his ground.

That happened Oct. 25, 1900, in Cotulla, Texas when the young Ranger told a drunken James R. Davenport—a contentious man Wright knew had killed before—he was under arrest for unlawfully carrying a handgun.

"About six o'clock yesterday evening, Ranger [Wright] attempted to arrest...Davenport... and a fight ensued," one newspaper reported. "Davenport fired first and shot twice," one newspaper reported. "Wright knocked his pistol out and fired, hitting Davenport five times, all in the breast, killing him instantly."

As town folks gathered outside a local saloon to gaze at his riddled body, a small fire caused by the muzzle blast from Wright's revolver continued a slow burn on Davenport's vest.

Meanwhile, Wright reloaded, entered the saloon to grab a Winchester he'd pre-positioned inside and arrested J. Guy Smith, a local newspaper editor, for unlawful carrying. The Ranger relieved Davenport's drunken crony of two pistols, a dirk and a set of brass knuckles.

Wright left the Rangers in 1902 to successfully run for sheriff in his native Wilson County and spent fifteen years in office. In 1917, his reputation having continued to grow, he received a gubernatorial appointment as Ranger captain.

When the captain and his men shot it out with border bootleggers one time, a bullet whizzed by Wright's head. The story spread that the lawman later said, "After that I went down on them sights."

With the exception of a couple of politically related interruptions, Wright served until 1939. He died at 74 in 1942.

FRANCIS AUGUSTUS HAMER

One of the younger Rangers Wright rubbed shoulders with along the border (but never supervised) was another Wilson County boy—Frank Hamer.

Some saw Ranger Frank Hamer as a cold-eyed killer who fortunately worked for the good guys. The majority, however, considered him the epitome of the Texas Ranger. Not noted for ever having much to say, what he did say usually commanded attention. Though taciturn, he never shied from acting when necessary—from slapping to slugging to shooting.

He joined the Rangers in 1906 when the force still relied mostly on horses or trains for transportation. But he quickly adapted to new innovations, including automobiles.

In January 1916, for example, Hamer and a Tom Green county sheriff's deputy were hunting a felon wanted by Idaho authorities. The man had been working in a Wild West show that played at San Angelo's 1915 fall fair. When the man heard officers were on his trail, he left town immediately. "When overtaken by [the deputy] and Hamer in an automobile, he was making haste toward the north on a big stallion," the San Angelo Evening Standard reported. Hamer left the force occasionally to take other law enforcement jobs, but by 1921, he was captain of Del Rio-based Co. C. At the beginning of 1922, the state adjutant general transferred him to Austin, where he would spend the next decade as a Ranger captain. Soon newspapers began referring to the captain as Texas's most famous Ranger.

Though best known for his leadership role in taking out the cop-killing outlaw couple of Bonnie Parker and Clyde Barrow in 1934 (though he was not a Ranger at the time), Hamer's entire career was a series of notable events, from pacifying oilfield boomtowns, busting bootleggers during Prohibition, and—aside from one notable failure in Sherman, Texas, in 1930—preventing lynchings. In addition to investigating homicides and other major crimes, in 1928 he exposed a scheme in which innocent men were being set up to look like bank burglars or robbers so the perpetrators could collect an award for dead bank robbers posted by the Texas Bankers Association.

John Boessenecker, author of Hamer's definitive biography, asserted that Hamer stands as the nation's most effective lawman of the first third of the 20th century. Though he did not hesitate to use deadly force when necessary, Hamer was highly intelligent, his integrity never questioned.

Hamer left the Rangers in 1932, but the veteran Ranger still held a special Ranger commission and continued in security related work until age finally slowed him down.

Former Ranger Lee Trimble worked for Frank Hamer when the former Ranger captain during World War II was handling dock security in Houston.

Hamer told Trimble that when a Dallas sheriff's deputy whispered that it was indeed Bonnie and Clyde headed toward them on that spring day in Louisiana that made Hamer famous, Hamer stood and shot twice. Then he sat down and lit another Camel while the other officers kept shooting, riddling the car with bullets. Former Crockett County Sheriff Jim Wilson, who had known Trimble, deduced from this story that Hamer had shot each outlaw once in the head and knew that his work was done.

Over the course of his career, Hamer had been shot 17 times. On his death bed, he told his son he'd killed 52 men, all of them justified. He died at 71 in 1955.

THEY RODE FROM GONZALES

As the first elements of Gen. Antonio Lopez de Santa Anna's army marched into San Antonio de Bexar on Feb. 23, 1836, Texian Col. William Barrett Travis knew he didn't have enough men to defend the old Spanish mission known as the Alamo.

Inside the small room that constituted his headquarters and billet, Travis dipped his pen in ink and started writing letters. His first was addressed to Andrew Ponton in Gonzales, 70 miles southeast of the Alamo.

"The enemy in large force is in sight," he began. "We want men and provisions. Send them to us. We have 150 men and are determined to defend the Alamo to the last. Give us assistance."

Via courier, the letter arrived in Gonzales two days later. When Ponton read the communication publicly on the town square, men immediately began volunteering to ride to the Alamo's defense.

One of those men was Thomas R. Miller. Until recently, he'd had all a man could hope for. The 41-year-old Tennessee native, one of the wealthiest men in town, owned a productive farm and a flourishing mercantile business. And for 16 months, he'd also had the companionship of his teenage wife, a pretty young woman from Kentucky named Sidney Gaston.

But then things turned south. The couple's first-born died as an infant, and in the summer of 1833, his wife left him for John Benjamin Kellough, another Kentuckian.

Soon after Travis' plea for assistance had been read, George Kimball and Albert Martin (Martin had just arrived with a more eloquent letter from Travis) began recruiting volunteers for a newly formed Ranger company.

With nothing to lose, Miller saddled up for the ride to San Antonio. So did the teenager who'd stolen his wife.

Interestingly, Gonzales committed more than men and their weapons to the defense of the Alamo. When the Gonzales men left town, they carried as heavy a load of supplies as they could—including 52 pounds of coffee.

Before dawn on Sunday, March 6, the defenders would have no time for coffee. Mexican troops overwhelmed the Alamo and killed or executed every defender.

With the nascent Texian Army gathering in Gonzales only days after Texas' March 2, 1836, declaration of independence from Mexico, volunteer soldier Robert Eden Handy arrived to find three companies already encamped there. A native of Philadelphia who'd come to the Mexican province of Coahuila and Tejas in 1834, 30-year-old Handy was ready to join the fight.

On March 8, an aged Mexican man brought news to Gonzales that the Alamo had fallen two days before and that "every man was put to the sword." That meant that 32 men and teenage boys who had ridden from Gonzales to bolster the defense of the Alamo were dead along with the other defenders.

"My pen—no human pen—can describe the scene that these sad tidings produced…," Handy later said. "Not less than a dozen women with young and helpless children were made widows by the fall of the Alamo. Fathers had lost their sons, brother lost brother, in short, there was scarce a member of that once happy and flourishing little village that did not mourn for some murdered relative."

The men who had hurried to help defend the old Spanish mission in San Antonio were Texas Rangers, even if years would pass before they would begin to be referred to as Rangers. For decades, these men were better known simply as "the men from Gonzales."

Newspapers.com is a website containing more than 26,500 digitized and searchable newspapers from around the world. A search of Alamo and Ranger news coverage from 1836 to 1846 located no article making mention of the Gonzales Ranging Company of Mounted Volunteers or the Gonzales Mounted Ranging Company.

Initially, the most common term used in print was "the men of Gonzales" or "Gonzales men." Travis used the term in his March 3 letter from the Alamo: "…A company of thirty-two men from Gonzales made their way into us on the morning of the 1st instant, at 3 o'clock." One newspaper referred to them as "32 Texians from Gonzales." But almost all the early accounts of the Alamo focused on the siege and its overall number of victims, not the Gonzales men.

A. J. Sowell, a former Ranger and son of Revolutionary War figure Andrew Jackson Sowell, wrote an article for the San Antonio Light in 1912 that referred to the Gonzales force as "thirty-two men and boys of DeWitt's colony…" When historian Walter Prescott Webb's Ranger history—the first scholarly book devoted to their story—arrived in bookstores in 1935 he made no mention of the Gonzales Ranging Company of Mounted Volunteers. Even the large Texas Centennial monument to the Immortal 32 at the entrance of the Gonzales Memorial Museum does not mention the word "ranger" in its inscription.

A major turning point in nomenclature came in 2007 with the publication of Stephen L. Moore's groundbreaking book, Savage Frontier, Vol. I, 1835-1837 (Denton: University of North Texas Press). In it, Moore devoted a chapter to "The Alamo's 'Immortal Thirty-Two." His in-depth research into surviving early Texas records left no room for argument:

On February 23, 54-year-old Byrd Lockhart enlisted 22 men in what the muster roll he prepared identifies as the Gonzales Ranging Company of Mounted Volunteers. Today the company is more commonly referred to as the Gonzales Mounted Ranger Company. But those who joined the company on February 24 are generally listed as rangers even though there's not a final muster roll to verify this. That may be why the Sons of Dewitt Colony Texas website refers to the company as the Gonzales Alamo Relief Force. But that's a modern-day term.

Bottom line: 166 years went by before the Gonzales men began to be referred to as rangers. In another matter of nomenclature, when did the honorific "Immortal 32" first come into use in regard to the Gonzales men? The phrase could have been used locally before it entered the mainstream, but the first newspaper reference to Gonzales' Immortal 32 does not seem to have occurred until printed in the March 17, 1958, edition of the Fort Worth Star Telegram in a syndicated column by James Farber. The term did not appear in the media again until 1965. And then it disappeared from print until 1977.

The death of the Gonzales men at the Alamo stands as the largest one-day loss of Ranger lives in Ranger history. (The second-largest one-day loss occurred Nov. 10, 1837, in what is known as the Stone House battle. Ten Rangers died fighting Indians that day. Of all the Rangers listed as killed in the line of duty from 1823 to 1987, most died singly. Only 16 times, not counting the Alamo and the Stone House battle, did Ranger engagements result in two or more deaths.)

At least two questions about the Gonzales ranging company still linger:

• Did more than 32 men fight their way inside the Alamo only to die five days later? Some writers claim the records show that some 60 additional volunteers started for the Alamo but dropped out for reasons varying from being confronted by Mexican patrols before they could get to San Antonio to desertion.

• Did some of those 60 men actually make it inside the fortress? Since Travis' last letter was dispatched on March 3, we'll likely never know for sure.

Unless someone discovers a long-lost diary, a forgotten cache of authentic vintage letters or early newspaper accounts not already known, there's not much hope that historians or family history buffs will noticeably broaden our understanding of the Immortal 32. But one thing needs no further evidence: The Gonzales rangers made a choice they knew probably would cost them their lives.

IN GRATEFUL MEMORY

More than a decade before Texas celebrated a hundred years of independence from Mexico by putting up hundreds of historical markers across the state, the school children of the Central Texas town of Taylor collected money for a stone marker commemorating a little-known fight between Comanche warriors and Rangers called the Battle of Brushy Creek.

Historian Walter Prescott Webb, then doing research that would lead to his groundbreaking book on the history of the Rangers, traveled the 30 miles from Austin to present the keynote speech when Williamson County residents gathered on Nov. 5, 1925, to dedicate the monument.

Located on private property off Circle G Ranch Road just west of State Highway 195, four miles south of Taylor, the monument is a tombstone-sized slab of red granite bearing a bronze plaque that says:

In Grateful Memory
To Those Who
Gave Their Lives
In The
Battle of Brushy
1839
Erected By
Friends and Students
Of
Taylor Public School

Busy bird-dogging political news in the Capital City, neither of Austin's two daily newspapers covered Webb's talk. Had reporters been there, they would have heard him explain to those on hand that the fight on Brushy Creek had been the culmination of a series of events that began a month earlier.

On Jan. 26, 1839, La Grange plantation owner John H. Moore led 63 volunteers and nearly a score of Lipan Apache scouts on an expedition against a large party of Comanches camped on the upper San Gabriel River. A fight on February 15 proved indecisive, but like most conflicts, spilled blood soon brought more spilled blood.

In retaliation, a Comanche war party with as many as 300 warriors swept down the Colorado River into the settlements of Central Texas, killing Elizabeth Coleman and two of her children on February 24 in Bastrop County. The raiders also struck the nearby cabin of Dr. James W. Robertson. Luckily for the doctor and his family, they were not at home, but the Indians captured seven of his slaves—a woman, five children and an old man.

As word of the Indian incursion spread, 14 Bastrop county men under Capt. John J. Grumbles saddled up to pursue the raiders. They soon overtook the war party but pulled back when they realized they had bitten off more than they could chew. Following the arrival of an additional 52 men, the volunteers resumed the pursuit under the command of Jacob Burleson. Twenty-five miles from the scene of the Coleman massacre, Burleson and his volunteers overtook the Comanches on the prairie near Brushy Creek. As the Indians tried to reach a line of timber that would have afforded them a more easily defended position, Burleson ordered his men to gallop between the Indians and the trees.

Fourteen-year-old Winslow Turner and veteran Indian-fighter Samuel Highsmith abided by the command and dismounted to face the Indians. But the other volunteers, realizing they were seriously outnumbered, wheeled their horses to flee.

Knowing he could not face the Comanches with only one man and a boy, Burleson shouted to the pair that they needed to retreat. Just as Burleson started to spur his horse into a run for safety, he saw the teenager having trouble getting back astride his nervous mount. Burleson jumped out of his saddle to lend a hand and caught an Indian bullet in the back of his head. Jacob's brother Edward Burleson, a brigadier general in the militia, soon arrived with reinforcements. Assuming overall command, the general rode after the Indians who'd killed his brother.

The Houston Telegraph offered this account of the fight that followed:

General Burleson, at the head of about 70 men, recently encountered a large body of Indians on the Brushy, and, after one or two skirmishes, finding the enemy numerous, retreated to a ravine in order to engage them with more advantage; but the Indians, fearing to attack him in his new position, drew off and retreated into a neighboring thicket. Being unable to pursue them, he returned to Bastrop. It is reported that he has lost three men in this engagement; the loss of the Indians is not known; it, however, must have been considerable, as most of the men must have been considerable, as most of the men under Burleson were excellent marksmen, and had often been engaged in Indian warfare.

The newspaper had it mostly right. When the Indians fell back into the woods, Burleson and his men got what sleep they could overnight and charged the thicket early on the morning of February 25. But they found the Indians had decamped.

The warriors had left behind one of Dr. Robertson's slaves, an old man who told Burleson the Rangers had killed about 30 of the Indians. If that number was correct, Burleson's losses were minor in comparison—only three men (Ed Blakey, John Walters and James Gilleland) killed or mortally wounded.

J.W. Wilbarger devoted four-and-a-half pages to the fight in his 1889 classic, Indian Depredations of Texas. Noah Smithwick, who participated in Moore's expedition but missed the Brushy Creek fight, later termed the battle "disastrous," the result of a "badly managed pursuit."

In the end, the only accomplishment attributable to the fight on Brushy Creek was that it further fueled the animosity between the Comanche people and Texans. The bloody war would continue for decades.

THE PREACHER AND ROWDY RANGERS

Rumor can quickly get out of hand.

The Rev. John Wesley DeVilbiss found that out in 1846 in San Antonio.

DeVilbiss, born in Maryland in 1818 and raised in Ohio, came to Texas in December 1842. A circuit-riding Methodist preacher, he figured the new republic offered ample opportunities for work. While a desire for salvation was not unheard of in Texas, sinfulness abounded. In fact, someone had warned the cleric not to drink any water from the Sabine when he crossed into Texas "as it gave a person an inclination to steal."

DeVilbiss traveled from one community to another, dodging hostile Indians and bandits while striving to redirect the inclinations of Texans who had, at least in the figurative sense, drunk from the Sabine.

When DeVilbiss conducted a camp meeting on McCoy's Creek, a tributary of the Guadalupe near present Cuero in South Texas, a detachment of Capt. John C. (Jack) Hays' Texas Rangers stood guard. The rough-and-tumble frontier fighters impressed the preacher. Like most of the early men of the cloth who came to Texas, DeVilbiss preached well and wrote well. He sent letters to the Western Christian Advocate from time to time with observations on his new home country. In one of those dispatches, he wrote about the Rangers. By this time, he had settled near San Antonio, where he preached and started a Sunday school.

Though some San Antonioans relished the opportunity to learn more about the Bible, Sunday school started at the same time of day as the regular Sunday cockfight. Large crowds gathered for these violent rooster matches, and in addition to reducing the attendance of his missionary efforts, they made a lot of noise. Beyond that, the drinking, wagering and cursing attendant to the bloody sport conflicted totally with the Christian view of the Sabbath.

As if that were not enough for a preacher to worry about, a rumor got out that DeVilbiss had written some unflattering things about the Rangers.

Some of Hays' men, having stood guard while DeVilbiss sought converts, found it annoying that the preacher would write something unfavorable about them. Of course, they hadn't read the story. They were merely depending on rumor.

Word reached the preacher that a group of six Rangers planned to "duck" him on Saturday night. (Accounts of this incident don't explain exactly what "duck" meant in this particular context, but it might have had something to do with involuntary immersion in the San Antonio river.) DeVilbiss sent a messenger to tell the offended Rangers that if they would delay their planned visit with him until Sunday morning, when they were welcome at his service, he would explain the perceived insult.

Willing to turn the other cheek at least in the short term, the Rangers postponed the ducking, came to hear him preach, and left satisfied with his explanation of the writing in question. It turned out that a number of the Rangers had previously been regulars at the weekly cockfight, but were so impressed by DeVilbiss' sermons, they started coming to his church instead. Attendance eventually dropped off so much the chicken fighting stopped. After nearly four decades of spreading the Gospel in Texas, DeVilbiss retired in 1880. He had a ranch on the Medina River near Oak Island, where he died on Jan. 31, 1885.

BATTLE OF WALKER'S CREEK

While a vicious and bloody fight, it certainly does not rank as one of Texas's largest or better-known engagements. However, despite a low body count in comparison to the Alamo, San Jacinto, or the sanguinary granddaddy of them all, the 1813 Battle of Medina, the affair at Walker's Creek has a significance beyond its reported casualties.

Considering the fight's impact, ascertaining the exact details of the clash has proven frustratingly elusive. Indeed, the story of what happened that distant summer has been mired in conflicting and sometimes downright wrong information. While it's generally accepted that the engagement took place in the vicinity of present Sisterdale in Kendall County, despite extensive research and field work, historians have been unable to determine its precise location. And while the incident is generally known as the Battle of Walker's Creek, at the time no stream in the area bore that name. That came later, likely to honor one of the conflict's noted participants. Finally, since more than one Republic of Texas-era Indian fighter falsely claimed to have been in the fight, pinning down the names of the actual participants has been difficult.

Not disputed is that the fight was between a company of Texas Rangers and a much larger party of hostile Indians. No one has questioned that Jack Hays commanded the Rangers and that the leader of the Indians was a chief known as Yellow Wolf. Nor is there any doubt that the Rangers used Colt Paterson five-shot revolvers in addition to muzzle-loading rifles. Finally, that the Rangers prevailed is unequivocable.

The fog of vagueness that shrouds the incident is understandable enough considering what Texas was like during its near decade as a sovereign nation. While some records were kept back then, government officials and employees were not the sticklers for detail that they are today. Early day officials did file reports and did write and receive correspondence, but not to the extent that modern bureaucracies compile information. On top of that, in a little-known fire at the Adjutant General's Office in 1857 in Austin, many documents related to the Republic of Texas-era were lost.

Newspapers did report the battle, but surviving accounts were neither timely nor exacting. In the pre-telegraph era, news traveled only as quickly as the fastest horse. Beyond the relatively slow flow of news, production also took time. Type was set by the character and presses were hand operated. Most sheets were gotten out by an editor-publisher and maybe one or two other writers. For their out-of-town news, editors relied heavily on letters from readers or what other newspapers printed.

Finally, the books and memoirs mentioning the battle all were published well after the fact, primarily based on hearsay or memory made less accurate by the passage of time.

Here's what is known about the battle:

The Texas Congress passed an act on Jan. 23, 1844 "Authorizing John C. Hays to raise a Company of Mounted Gun-men, to act as Rangers, on the Western and South-Western Frontier." The company's lieutenant would be elected by the 40 privates Hays enlisted. The legislation charged Hays' company with ranging "from the county of Bexar to the county of Refugio, and westward as the public interest may require." The Rangers would serve for four months, though the president of the Republic could extend their enlistment in case of emergency. Each Ranger would be paid $30 a month for his services. Hays earned $75 a month as captain. Ben McCulloch, elected lieutenant, made $55 a month.

In light of recent Mexican incursions into Texas, on Jan. 31, 1844, the Congress—codifying what Hays had already done at least once—approved an act providing for the court-martialing of anyone "in arms" against the Republic. That legal process could be done instanter, with the ultimate penalty being execution.

Though not yet at full strength, Hays' company rode out of San Antonio that March in pursuit of cattle thieves. The Rangers had no statutory authority to act as law enforcement officers, but maybe they operated under the "as the public interest may require" segment of the new measure. The rustlers had driven off nearly 2,000 head of cattle and were believed headed north toward the Colorado River. If the Rangers caught up with the outlaws, the result did not make the public prints.

In early June 1844, returning from a fruitless scout for Indians between the Pedernales and Llano rivers northwest of San Antonio, Hays' rangers camped at a point he later described as "four miles east of the Pinta trace ...

nearly equally distant from Bexar, Gonzalez and Austin." The absence of Indian sign did not mean the absence of hostile Indians. Wise in the ways of the Comanche, Hays detailed one of his men to lag behind the rest of the Rangers, alert to the possibility of their being backtracked.

The Pinta Trail ran from the old Spanish missions in San Antonio northwest through what later became Fredericksburg and on to an abandoned mission near future Menard. Hays and his men had taken the trail on their scout and had not been veering too far from it on their way back to their base camp on the Medina River, about 12 miles from San Antonio.

Ironically enough, during Hays' scout, a council with representatives from most of Texas' Indian tribes had gathered at Torrey's Trading Post on the Brazos River as government officials sought to hammer out a peace treaty with them. President Sam Houston very much wanted to strike an accord with the Indians, particularly the Comanches. But not all Comanches were interested in making nice with Texans.

On June 8, with the Rangers stopped to cook lunch in a valley near where two creeks con- verged and flowed into the Guadalupe River, the rear guard galloped into camp to report he'd discovered multiple sets of Indian pony tracks following the Rangers' trail. Looking in the direction his scout had ridden in from, Hays soon made out several Indians in the distance. As he continued to watch, they nonchalantly faded into the trees.

Telling his men to mount up, the captain ordered them not to shoot until within powder-burning range of their foes. Then he spurred his horse toward the tree line. As the Rangers advanced, three or four warriors emerged from their cover and made a show of surprise at seeing the Texans. The Indians then quickly pulled back into the timber on the east bank of a creek.

"Hays, however, was too old an 'Indian fighter' to be caught by such traps and made no efforts at pursuit," the Clarksville Northern Standard later reported. "As soon as the Indians saw this strategy was of no avail, they came out of the timber and displayed their whole force in line, some 75 in number."

The Ranger captain had only 15 men under his command. But a great equalizer rested in each of their holsters—the five-shot, .36 caliber Paterson Colt revolver. Though the Indians clearly had the Rangers outnumbered, the young Ranger leader calculated his numbers differently than the

Comanches: 15 times 5 equaled 75 shots without having to reload. Some accounts have the Rangers carrying two revolvers each. Either way, in a time when most weapons still could be fired only once before being reloaded, the Texans had awesome firepower at their disposal. Also, as the North Texas newspaper soon reported, "His men were highly disciplined, of tried courage, [and] their horses well broke."

Slowly, the Rangers advanced toward the Indians. Having higher ground behind them, the Indians fell back, moving to a position that would give them even more advantage over the approaching Texans. At the crown of the hill, the Comanches dismounted. Brandishing their fearsome 14-foot, feather-draped lances and raising and lowering their tough buffalo-hide shields, some of them knew enough English to taunt the Rangers with cries of "Charge! Charge!"

Hays then demonstrated the genius for fighting that established his reputation. He knew the Indians could not see him at the base of the elevation. Rather than charge uphill, which was precisely what the Comanches wanted, Hays spurred his horse and wheeled around the rocky prominence. The Rangers followed, circling to the Comanche's exposed flank.

Now the Indians got their charge, but from an unanticipated direction. Seeing the Texians galloping toward them on level ground, the Indians remounted. The shock of the charge broke the Indian line, but only for a moment. Regrouping, they split and attacked the Rangers from two sides. On horseback, the Comanches considered themselves invincible.

"Back-to-back, the Texians received them and the close and deadly fire of their pistols emptied many a saddle," the Clarksville newspaper reported. "Thus, hand to hand the fight lasted fifteen minutes, the Indians using their spears and arrows, the Texians their repeating pistols. Scarcely a man of the brigade [sic] was not grazed . . . their gun stocks, knife handles and saddles perforated in many places."

Those Comanches still capable of sitting a horse tried to distance themselves from the Rangers, but the Texians rode after them. At the end of a two-mile running fight, the chief rallied his warriors, enjoining them to turn and face the Texans. Like the Rangers, the Indians also had a brave leader.

"He dashed backward and forward amongst his men to bring them back to the charge," the newspaper continued. "The Texians had exhausted nearly all their shot. Hays called out to learn who had a loaded gun. [Robert] Gillespie rode forward and answered he was charged. 'Dismount and shoot the chief,' was the order. At a distance of thirty steps, the ball performed its office and, madly dashing a few yards, the gallant Indian fell to rise no more."

While it's fairly certain that Yellow Wolf led the Indians that day, he did not die in the battle. It is well-documented that he took part in peace treaty negotiations more than a year later, so Gillespie's shot either only wounded Yellow Wolf or killed some other Comanche who'd been displaying leadership skills. Losing so many warriors finally broke the spirit of the Indians, who fled in every direction.

When the last white clouds of gun smoke blew away, 20 Comanches lay dead. Another 30 Indians had suffered wounds. Only three Rangers had been wounded, including slim, red-headed Samuel Walker, pinned to the ground with a Comanche lance through his body. (Amazingly, he survived.)

The Rangers remained in the area, nursing their wounded. In the distance, they could see the campfire of the Indians, who were similarly preoccupied with caring for their casualties.

Three days later, four Indians probably intent on reclaiming their dead showed up at the battleground, where the Rangers remained in camp. Hays attacked again, killing three more warriors and raising the Comanche body count to 23. During this clash, German-born Rang er Peter Fohr suffered a wound from which he died three days later, the only fatality among Hays' men.

As Hays wrote in his report a week after the fight, "The second day after the fight a party of four [Indians] made their appearance. I immediately ordered six men to give chase to them; thinking at the same time that they had embodied and presumed to give me another fight. My men, at the word, mounted their horses and pursued them about a mile, when they came upon them and killed three of them...the fourth having evinced a disposition to escape from the first."

Indian Commissioner Thomas G. Western wrote President Houston on June 16, noting that, "The Western mail arrived here last evening and brings the intelligence that Maj. Hays has had a pretty smart brush with some 60 Indians supposed to be Comanche, on the river Guadalupe, above the San Antonio Road and near the 'Pinto trail' distant about 60 miles from Bexar."

English visitor William Bollaert gave an account of the fight in his June 26 diary entry: "News arrived late at night of 2 more fights about 10 days since, 40 miles from San Antonio on the Pinta between a party of Comanche of 70 to 80 warriors and Hays and his men. He had one killed, 3 w[wounded], the enemy 20 or 30 killed and many wounded."

In his entry for June 27, Bollaert devoted a sentence to Hays' second fight: "Hays came accidentally upon his Comanches and they finding one of his men alone, Peter Foyer [sic], a Frenchman [sic], killed him."

In an account of the fight published June 29, 1844, the Houston Morning Star acknowledged an often-ignored truism of combat—bravery knows no race, uniform or flag. The newspaper, characterizing what happened near Walker's Creek as a "close and deadly struggle," called the fight between Hays' Rangers and the Comanches "unparalleled in this country for the gallantry displayed on both sides." But with that nod to the Indians, the newspaper went on to praise "the gallant partisan captain of the West" for his "triumphant success."

The Paterson Colts, as Hays wrote on June 16 in his official account of the fight, "did good execution." In fact, the Ranger captain added, "Had it not been for them, I doubt what the consequences would have been. I cannot recommend these arms too highly."

The fight at Walker's Creek represented more than a clash of two proud cultures. It demonstrated the power of 19th century technology over stone age weaponry. With the Colt repeating pistols, the Rangers had the frontier equivalent of nuclear bombs. In 15 minutes, Hays and his men had changed the history of the West, and combat in general.

"Up to this time," Samuel Walker later wrote, "these daring Indians had always supposed themselves superior to us, man to man, on horse ... the result of this engagement was such as to intimidate them and enable us to treat with them."

How long the Rangers had been carrying the Colts isn't known, but it had not been very long. On March 28, 1839, Colonel of Ordnance George Washington Hockley reported to the Texas secretary of war that he'd completed an examination and test of the Colt rifle, carbine and pistol.

Hockley, the man who'd so successfully overseen the use of the cannons called the Twin Sisters at San Jacinto, recommended against the new weapons. His six objections ranged from percussion caps being unreliable to the fact that revolvers were hard to keep clean. But President Mirabeau B. Lamar thought differently, ordering a major purchase from Colt. The Texas Navy requisitioned—on credit—180 five-shot Colt revolvers from the Patent Arms Manufacturing Co. in Paterson, New Jersey, on April 29, 1839. The order also included 180 carbines. Three months later, the Texas Army ordered 50 Colt pistols, then referred to as Patent Arms. Forty more revolvers were ordered October 5. Though surviving records make it unclear whether all of these weapons actually made it to Texas, the .36 caliber revolver soon became the Rangers' weapon of choice. On credit, the Texian government bought additional "belt pistols" and Colt eight-shot carbines in 1840. The Rangers probably received the Colts following Houston's disbandment of the Navy in 1843.

On the other hand, Bollaert noted in his diary that on Feb. 2, 1844, he had been on board the steamboat Vesta with Hays as it made its way to Galveston down the Trinity River. The Ranger, who he called major, was "going…to purchase arms etc. out of appropriations made." If some of those arms were the Colts his Rangers carried that June, they'd only had them a little more than four months.

No matter when they obtained them, the Rangers brought awesome weapons to their fight with the Comanches that summer. But even with state-of-the-art technology, leadership had been critical to the success of the outnumbered Anglos at Walker's Creek.

"I scarcely know which to admire most," wrote an anonymous person who heard the story from Hays at Washington-on-the-Brazos, "the skill and courage of [Hays] or his modesty when giving the details here narrated. Concealing his own deeds, he did ample justice to his comrades and, at the close of his narrative, blushed to find himself famous."

Chief Flacco, a Lipan warrior who scouted for the Rangers, famously said of Hays: "Me and Blue Wing not afraid to go to hell together. Captain Jack, great brave, not afraid to go to hell by himself."

Neither were the men who rode with Hays afraid to go to hell by themselves. As with most other details of this event, we only know with certainty the names of nine Rangers who were with Hays in the Walker's Creek fight. In addition to Hays, those men were Christopher B. Acklin (other sources have it as "Acklen"); John P. Erskine (usually identified as John's brother Andrew Erskine); Robert A. Gillespie (for whom Gillespie County was named); Peter Fohr, James B. Lee, Cicero Rufus (Old Rufe) Perry, Joshua Threadgill, and Samuel H. Walker.

Ranger history buff Sloan Rodgers has identified seven other men known to have served under Hays who likely were with him during the encounter: Michael H. Chevallier, Matthew Jett, Samuel H. Luckie, Pitkin Taylor, John M. Carolan, Alexander Coleman and James Dunn. In his book The Fight Along Walker's Creek (2021), Fredericksburg historian Mark B. Weiser lists the participants as Acklin, Carolan, Chevallier, Coleman, Dunn, John P. Erskine, Fohr, Gillespie, Lee, Perry, Josiah Taylor, his brother Pitkin Barnes Taylor, Threadgill, Joseph A. Tivy, and Walker.

While 14 of Hays' men lived to fight another day, fewer than half made it to old age. At least eight died violently: Gillespie and Walker died fighting together in the Mexican War only two years later; Erskine, Carolan and Dunn died during the Civil War; Luckie supposedly died from an old wound in 1852; Jett and Taylor were murdered, Jett in 1845 and Taylor in 1873. Finally, Chevallier committed suicide in 1852.

Another interesting footnote is that it was not until 1850 that Colt finally received payment for the arms it provided to the Republic of Texas. On June 27, 1850, the state of Texas approved settling with Colt for $10,010.27.

What were the consequences of the fight?

First, though more than 30 years would go by before the Rangers and Comanches had their final fight in 1878, the decisive victory near Walker's Creek showed the Comanches that they could never prevail against the growing number of Texans and the technology they could bring to bear.

Second, the fight changed Ranger tactics in dealing with Indians. While arguably a subset of the first point, Rangers now knew they could successfully take the fight to the Indians and engage them on horseback.

Third, a few years later during the Mexican War, Samuel Walker met with Samuel Colt and persuaded him to improve his revolvers by expanding the cylinders to accommodate six rounds of a higher caliber. A military contract that Walker helped make possible kept Colt in business and resulted in the prototype of the handgun that helped win the West, the six-shooter.

Fourth, muddled as its facts became, the fight near Walker's Creek went a long way toward establishing the enduring reputation of Jack Hays as an extraordinary captain and the Texas Rangers as an organization not to be underestimated.

As one surviving Comanche participant reportedly vowed, "I will never again fight Jack Hays, who has a shot for every finger on the hand."

TWO WAYS TO USE LEAD

As a pioneer newspaper editor, David E. Lawhon may have believed that the pen was mightier than the sword, but as a Ranger he never saddled up without his pistol and rifle.

Born in Tennessee in 1811, he came to Nacogdoches in November 1835 from Natchitoches, La. Like many arriving from the United States that fall, Lawhon came looking for a fight. Texas had begun to pull away from Mexico and a bloody revolution lay ahead.

A tall, barrel-chested, ham-fisted man, Lawhon signed up to serve in the nascent Texas army shortly after hitting East Texas. But when it became known he was a printer, local businessman William G. Logan talked the young Tennessean into editing a newspaper instead.

With a hand press and type that had been used in 1829 to produce a short-lived Nacogdoches newspaper called the Mexican Citizen, the 24-year-old Lawhon brought out the first issue of the Texian and Emigrant's Guide on Nov. 28, 1835.

Family legend has it that as editor of one of the province's only two newspapers, Lawhon was on the reception committee greeting former Tennessee Congressman David Crockett as he passed through Nacogdoches on his way to San Antonio and immortality.

That winter Lawhon also printed legal forms and official documents for the provisional Texas government. On Jan. 25, 1836, acting Gov. James W. Robison wrote Lawhon from San Felipe de Austin that the General Council had ordered the publication of its "ordinances & decrees & Resolutions" in "your useful newspaper" and that Lawhon should consider himself "one of the publishers of the Laws of Texas."

In addition, Lawhon printed handbills appealing to the people of New Orleans, Nashville, Cincinnati and elsewhere for money and volunteers to the Texas cause. His press announced the arrival of government agents seeking to buy horses, guns, corn and supplies for the army and distributed the lyrics to patriotic songs stoking the revolutionary flames.

Lawhon continued the newspaper through January 1836 and possibly as late as March 24. By then, having taken the Alamo, Mexican troops were marching eastward across Texas. While Sam Houston maneuvered what remained of Texas' army, most of the civilian population fled toward Louisiana in what came to be called the Runaway Scrape. After Houston defeated Santa Anna at San Jacinto on April 21, people began returning to their homes.

Whether Lawhon stayed in Nacogdoches is unclear, but if he left, he would come back. Having closed his print shop, he enlisted on Sept. 10, 1839, as a Ranger under Capt. Sam Davis. A second lieutenant, he served through that November.

Lawhon's company and others under Col. John C. Neill scouted up the Brazos River from the old port of Nashville past future Waco to a point on the Clear Fork of the Brazos southwest of present Fort Worth. In the process, the Rangers had three different Indian fights.

Not long after leaving the Rangers, Lawhon moved to newly founded Beaumont, where he married Nancy Carr, daughter of one of that area's earliest settlers. He served eight years as chief justice of Jefferson County, a position similar to today's county judge. Shortly before the Civil War he moved his family to Bastrop County.

When Lawhon visited Austin in the spring of 1878, the Daily Democratic Statesman ran a frustratingly brief article:

"David E. Lawhon, the first Editor, was in the City last week. He published in 1835 the first paper ever printed in Texas. His recollection of the stirring scenes occurring in the early history of Texas are as fresh and vivid in his memory as though they transpired only yesterday. He was associated in various capacities with General Sam Houston and was entrusted by him with some delicate and important services during the War of Independence. The name of his paper was 'Texian and Emigrants' Guide' and its publication continued nearly one year when the advance of the enemy compelled its suspension. Mr. Lawthon then enlisted to fight the

Indians and during the campaign was wounded three times. Mr. Lawhon resides near Elgin and is engaged in farming. He is 70 years old and over six feet tall."

One of Lawhon's granddaughters later wrote that about all she knew about her noted grandfather was that he had accidentally been wounded by one of his own men near Waco during his short but active Ranger service.

Another granddaughter later recalled that her mother, one of Lawhon's daughters, told her that Lawhon "had a wonderful voice and late in the evenings would take a song book and sit on the porch and sing for a while and she loved to hear him. . . ."

The Lawhons raised six boys and four girls, beginning with a daughter born in Jefferson County in 1841 and continuing with a final daughter born in Bastrop during the Civil War.

"Few families have a longer or more distinguished record in Texas history than that of the Lawhons," Francis W. Johnson wrote in his multi-volume work, A History of Texas and Texans.

Lawton died Feb. 14, 1884, and is buried in the Lawton family cemetery in Lee County.

'...A WILD, ROUGH-LOOKING SET OF MEN...'

Regardless of personal religious beliefs, all Texans owe a debt to the early-day Baptist and Methodist preachers who made their way to Texas hoping to make a dent in all the sinners. They not only saved souls, being literate in an era when many were not, they saved a lot of history in their written recollections.

One of those men was John A. Freeman, who wrote a piece published in the February 1892 issue of Texas History and Biography, a magazine devoted to Baptist history.

Freeman crossed the Red River into Texas in November 1845 north of Bonham. As he wrote, he was 25, "full of life and full of hope, and an earnest desire to preach. . .in this new and strange land."

Soon he took what he called the "direct route" to the Three Forks of the Trinity.

"Not far from the East Fork of the Trinity," he wrote, "we passed Col. Geary's place, where there was a company of Rangers stationed."

The young man clearly saw much work to be done in regard to these frontier protectors.

Here's what he wrote about them:

"At that time, they were a wild, rough looking set of men, some of them were dressed in buckskin, and some of them wore coon-skin caps; some of them were drinking bad whiskey [Freeman didn't explain how a Baptist would know the difference between good and bad whiskey] and some of them were playing cards. In this way they spent their time when not in pursuit of the Indians, who came in every now and then to commit depredations on the settlers." From the Ranger camp, Freeman and his wife traveled from Rowellet's Creek to the Elm Fork of the Trinity with "nothing to be seen but bands of wild horses and droves of deer and antelope."

They crossed the Elm Fork in mid-November. Six miles west of the river, they stopped at the cabin of James Gibson, deacon of the Baptist congregation that used his house as its meeting place.

Freeman preached his first sermon at this home-church and later organized the Lonesome Dove Baptist Church. In July 1846, he was ordained and preached at four Collin County churches before leaving for California in the mid-1850s.

REMEMBERING MR. HOBBS

Too bad Eleanor Jane Hobbs didn't set down more of her recollections, but at least she wrote what she did.

On Aug. 31, 1914, her 84th birthday, Mrs. Hobbs wrote a five-paragraph letter to the editor of the Elgin Courier. Many decades later, retired Austin police officer Norris McCord, who grew up in Bastrop County, discovered the letter plus another she'd written. He provided them to the Elgin Historical Association for inclusion in Elgin, Etc: Stories of Elgin, Texas, a book the organization published in 2008.

Mrs. Hobbs' letters are at once compelling for their description of frontier Texas and frustrating in that they don't go into more detail.

As she explained in her first letter, she came with her family to Texas from Dallas County, Ala., in 1839 when she was seven. They lived at a couple of places in Bastrop County before the family bought property on Piney Creek. A few years later, the family settled near present-day Young's Prairie.

Moving from place-to-place sounds routine, but in the late 1830s and early 1840s, little about life in Texas could be taken for granted.

"After we came back to Mike Young's [Young's Prairie], Levay Williams was killed and scalped by Indians," Mrs. Hobbs wrote. "I watched over his body while the men dug his grave."

At the time, she would have been about 16. And back then, that was practically grown.

"I was married July 1, 1847 to W.R. Hobbs," she continued, "who was then a Texas Ranger and served under Captain Jack Hays on the Texas Frontier."

She doesn't say in her letters, but William Right Hobbs joined the Rangers Sept. 15, 1845, and served under Capt. D.C. Cady. When the Mexican War broke out in 1846, he rode with Hays' regiment of volunteers, Rangers the Mexicans referred to as "los Diablos Tejanos" (the Texas Devils.)

The couple married after Hobbs came back to Bastrop County from his service in Mexico. "When Mr. Hobbs [he was seven years older than her] would go to Bastrop, I was left alone and as it took him all day and till late at night to make the trip," she wrote. "I would leave the house while he was away and stay on top of the corn in the crib for fear of the Indians."

But Indians didn't pose the only danger.

"Many times, I saw buffalo and wild cattle feeding out of the brush and watched bears catch our hogs," she continued. "Our nearest neighbor was Dickie Townsend, four miles away." In 1852 the couple settled on what came to be called the Hobbs place. At the time, their land lay in Bastrop County, but when Burleson County was organized, that part of Bastrop County went to the new county. Later still, it became part of Lee County.

"So we lived in three different counties and lived at the same place and in the same house all the time," Mrs. Hobbs wrote.

When the Civil War began, Hobbs joined the Confederate Army, but due to a medical issue received a surgeon's furlough.

By the time Mrs. Hobbs wrote the two letters published in the Elgin newspaper, she was the only survivor among her five siblings. She had come from a big family and raised a big family. "I have fourteen children and 49 grandchildren," she wrote. "I have divided all I have among my children and have never regretted it, for all have an outstretched arm of welcome wherever I go among them."

Mrs. Hobb's second letter was published Sept. 24, 1914. Her husband had come to Texas at 17, she penned.

"He has been in many battles and skirmishes with the Indians and had much hard fighting to do and has helped in [the] rescue of several children who had been captured and made prisoners," she wrote. "He was out...after Indians and was taking a dispatch to headquarters and had to run for his life. The creek was on the rise and that was all that saved him; they ran to the water's edge and shot arrows across at him."

Again, she mentioned the wildlife that had once been plentiful in Central Texas.

"I have seen herds of buffalo, deer and wild mustangs grazing near our home and have stood in my door and seen 25 or 30 run by not 50 yards from the house, which was a pretty sight," she wrote. "Bears were plentiful, and Mr. Hobbs used to hunt them often. One evening his hounds treed two bears up one tree, he killed them and brought them home and we certainly had some eating as bear meat is fine. While we lived near the Yegua [Creek], he killed alligators, panthers...and various other kinds of animals."

Hobbs lived until Dec. 21, 1902, dying at 79. His widow made it to Feb. 16, 1920. Both are buried in Lawhon Springs Cemetery near their old homestead in Lee County.

LETTERS FROM SESOM

At 62, former Ranger John Williamson Moses thought it important to capture on paper some of his early-day Texas experiences while he could still remember them.

In 1887, the San Antonio Express began publishing every Sunday a letter-like recollection penned by Moses. Reflecting an undue sense of modesty, he simply signed his columns "Sesom." That's "Moses" spelled backwards.

Born in South Carolina in 1825, he came to Texas via Florida in 1841. Not long after—the exact date is not clear from his columns—he enlisted in Capt. John S. Sutton's company of Rangers then operating between

San Antonio and Corpus Christi. When not in the field scouting for hostile Indians, Moses and his fellow Rangers camped outside San Antonio.

In the early 1840s, as Moses recalled, the Alamo stood in ruins and "the bridge which crossed the river near it was not in much better condition." The majority of the town's buildings were adobe. Streets were unpaved and at night, oil-burning lamps "only made darkness more profound."

Next, Moses described the Rangers:

The genus homo known as the Ranger…dressed in their blue, red, or gray flannel shirts and copperas pants tucked in their boots, rode or walked the streets in the daytime and never failed to be in attendance at the bailes and fandangos [dances] *at night. The chili stands on the plaza and the monte tables were liberally patronized.*

At the time, strict discipline in the Ranger force was more a concept than reality. Moses said many privates acted like officers, doing practically anything they pleased.

But not the men in Capt. Sutton's company. As Moses put it, "Rangers not willing to do their duty feared him." He said the captain had an "eagle glance" and could "detect at once any attempt at shirks [shirking]..." Offenders "never escaped being brought to the front [of the assembled company] and censured or punished as the occasion required."

Still, while a strict disciplinarian Sutton was not harsh or tyrannical. On the contrary, Moses continued, the Ranger leader was "courteous and polite."

Sutton was not a big man but he acted like one.

Once, Moses wrote, "a great big blustering Ranger" called out by the captain mumbled under his breath something to the effect that Sutton ought to be glad he was both a captain and a small man.

"Never mind my size," the captain responded, "and as to my position, I will give you your discharge, and you can have an equal showing with me. I will meet you with any weapon in… camp, and you can choose what suits you best."

What the out-of-line Ranger chose instead was a hasty apology. Looking piercingly at the cowed private, the captain said, "I will overlook your conduct this time. Go to your tent and remember that the duty of a solider is to obey the commands of his officers." Moses said the man went on to be one of the best Rangers in the company "from that day until the company was mustered out."

During Moses' time in the Rangers, Comanches and Lipan Apaches raided at will across South Texas. But for whatever reason, in his recollections he did not dwell on his company's activities, only occasionally referring to "engagements" in which he participated.

Moses did, however, offer insight into Ranger weaponry. They carried five-shot Colt revolvers, each chamber hand-loaded and primed with a percussion cap.

"Some of the old percussion caps were indeed inferior in quality and if they got damp they were as likely to miss fire [misfire] as not," Moses observed. "When we Rangers were in camp, if it rained or if the atmosphere was humid, we always recapped every morning. If we expected an engagement, and the circumstances permitted, we discharged our arms, wiped out and reloaded them."

But the Rangers weren't the only men toting revolvers back then. There being no law on the books against carrying a gun, Moses said most male-born San Antonio residents and visitors alike strode the streets armed with revolvers "or some [other] weapon of offense or defense." One of the Rangers in Sutton's company was "a good Indian fighter and a first-rate fellow" named Mitchell. His colleagues knew him as Mitch. Personable as he was, Mitch was "overly fond of his glass." When he got drunk, Moses said the Ranger changed into "a morose and dangerous man, ready to fight at the drop of a hat and to drop it himself with the least provocation." That's probably why, even nearly three decades later, Moses did not reveal the Ranger's last name.

When Mitch "got on a high lonesome" [drunk] in a saloon near Main Plaza, Capt. Sutton dispatched a corporal and several privates to escort the rowdy Ranger back to camp. Inside the cantina, the squad found Mitch standing on the bar holding a cabesto [rope] that led outside to his horse, Blue Dick. Periodically, Mitch pulled on the rope just to make sure someone hadn't stolen his fine mount.

While the corporal tried to talk Mitch into dismounting the countertop, some of the Rangers slipped outside to have a little fun at their fellow ranger's expense. When they'd first reached the saloon, they'd noticed an old ox standing nearby. Carefully removing the rope from around Blue Dick's neck, one of the pranksters slipped the drunk Ranger's makeshift halter over the ox's head.

Meanwhile the corporal had managed to get Mitch's pistol out of its holster without him noticing. Equally unaware that he now held a rope attached to an ox, Mitch continued to pull on the rope. But unlike Blue Dick, the ox responded to the pulls by moving ever closer to the saloon. Before long, the beast of burden stuck his head inside.

"Words are inadequate to describe the surprise and rage of Mitchell when, in place of the handsome Blue Dick, he saw the old…ox.," Moses wrote. However, a moment later the drunk Ranger broke into laughter and did not resist as his fellow Rangers escorted him back to camp to sleep it off.

"About this time, there was an order to muster out of service, or discharge the Rangers," Moses wrote. "[Our company] was one of the first companies to be mustered out. What made it worse, and proved a real hardship, was that we got our discharges but not our pay. Just where the hitch was, I don't now remember, if I ever knew, but so it was."

That left the Rangers, officers and privates, "without one cent in their pockets to take them home, and some of their homes were at a considerable distance from San Antonio." On top of everything else, he added, "This was during the coldest winter I've ever experienced in this state."

Moses said a few of the Rangers "were able to borrow on their certificates of honorable discharge, which had the amount due to each for the time and capacity in which he had served attached." But that money cost "a ruinous percentage." Other Rangers sold their certificates "at a fearful discount, greatly to the advantage of Mr. Lockwood and some other merchants who speculated on their necessities and made the Ranger loses their gain."

Col. Peter Hansborough Bell, the state's ranking Ranger captain and soon to become governor, loaned the discharged Rangers money from his personal account for "as long as his funds held out." But Bell couldn't accommodate every Ranger.

A number of the men opted to sell their horses and got fair prices for them. As Moses explained, "The U.S. government was buying horses to mount one or two infantry companies, who were to take the place of the defunct Rangers. Many of the Rangers' horses went to Uncle Sam's government yard."

Not every former Ranger sold his horse. According to Moses, at least a dozen men still had their mounts. When a regular Army company of U.S. Dragoons came riding into San Antonio one day, having nothing else to do, this Ranger cabal followed the soldiers into town.

"Just as the soldiers crossed the bridge, the Rangers broke into a fast gallop, increasing their speed to a run, yelling like Comanches as they passed the company," Moses recalled. "Many of the soldiers' horses had been in the ranging service, and they joined the chase. Many dragoon saddles were emptied that day, and several of Uncle Sam's horses ran riderless through the streets of San Antonio or thundered back over the bridge to the government yard at the Alamo, seeking their stables."

A RANGER HERO DIES HARD

The full story of former Ranger John (folks called him Johnny) Williams may never be known.

Born in Alabama, as one brief account puts it, he "moved several times before reaching Cherokee Creek country about 1854." Well into his 50s by the time he settled in San Saba County, he must have had some interesting experiences before then. At his age, he may have been in Texas since the days of the Republic. Question marks aside, Williams had at least one shining moment. It came during his service as a Ranger captain.

On Oct. 22, 1858, Mose Jackson, his wife and four of their seven children set out in their wagon to gather pecans along Pecan Bayou, a tributary of the Colorado River in what is now Mills County. The family would be meeting two other neighboring families and setting up camp.

As the wagon rolled along under the trees about four miles from their homestead, Jackson saw figures in the distance. Drawing closer, he realized they were Comanches, not the friends he planned to rendezvous with. Turning the wagon, he tried to outdistance the Indians, but on horseback they easily overtook the family.

Jackson and his 18-year-old daughter Louisa absorbed a barrage of arrows. With Jackson mortally wounded, the wagon careened into a tree. The Indians tore Mrs. Jackson's screaming baby, I. J., from her arms and tossed him around before smashing his head on a log. Seeing this, ten-year-old Joshua began yelling at the Indians. His mother, desperately hoping to save someone in her family, told him to be quiet. Her whispered warning ended in an agonal gurgle as an Indian came up from behind and slashed her throat.

Seizing Joshua and his screaming eight-year-old sister Rebecca, the Indians rode off. In addition to their terrified captives, the warriors also took the Jacksons' wagon team to add to a herd of horses stolen earlier in Brown and Coryell counties.

A company of Rangers under Williams on routine patrol rode up on the scene shortly after it happened. None of the men recognized the victims but learned who they were when one of the families the Jacksons were supposed to have met arrived. The Rangers buried Jackson and his wife in one grave and their children in another.

After a hasty funeral, Williams and his men took up the trail of the Indians and the two captured children. The Rangers rode until they ran low on supplies but resumed their hunt as soon as they had reprovisioned.

Fifteen days after the massacre, the Rangers discovered a newly deserted Indian camp. Finding the fresh footprints of children, the men began searching around the camp site. Before long, two Rangers saw a little face and two large, frightened eyes peeping from a tangle of thorny brush and vines. Scratched and bleeding, their feet swollen and blistered, the children had managed to escape their captives. Rebecca said when they saw horsemen approaching they'd hidden in fear that the Indians were still looking for them.

Even though the children had succeeded in getting away from their captors, they hadn't eaten in eight days. Alone out in the middle of nowhere, they would have died if Williams and his men had not found them.

Two months later, Ranger N.D. McMillin, one of Williamson's lieutenants, sent the captain a letter outlining a fight he'd just had with Indians he believed responsible for the Jackson family deaths.

On the evening of December 19, McMillin wrote, he and his men "came in sight of the Indians." He continued, "Eight in number after a hot pursuit of ¾ of a mile overtook them and in a…running fight killed two and wounded three others. I had the good luck to kill the chief who had in his possession the scalp of Miss Jackson…Night coming on the others escaped." Despite that encounter, and others, the Indians continued to be a problem along the Texas frontier. On Feb. 20, 1860, Williams wrote Gov. Sam Houston requesting assistance. Houston replied four days later, noting that he "greatly commiserates [with] your distressed condition." Had the Legislature provided any means, he continued, "I would, ere now, have afforded you protection."

After the Civil War began, Williams' part of Texas became even more "distressed." Too old to join the rebel army, he continued to saddle up anytime Indians were reported in the area.

During the early days of the war, Williams also helped feed the Confederacy. In the summer of 1862, he, David S. Hanna and others from the area drove a thousand "fine fat beeves" from San Saba County to Little Rock, Ark. Presumably with money in their saddlebags, they headed back to Central Texas in September.

Near Babyhead Mountain in Llano County, Indians attacked. Whether Williams was alone at the time or with others didn't make it into any of the San Saba County history books, but the former Ranger did not survive the experience.

Did he get caught out alone, dying hard because he faced more Indians than he had bullets? Did he try to outrun them only to have his horse stumble or go lame? No one ever knew. They buried him on land in San Saba County near Cherokee that he'd earlier donated for use as a cemetery.

Sometime later, friends and relatives placed a granite marker on his grave. For as long as igneous rock will last, these are the words on the monument:

CAPT. JOHNNY WILLIAMS
BORN 1798
KILLED BY INDIANS
OCT. 2, 1862

CIVIL WAR & RECONSTRUCTION: 1861-1873

THE BEAR HUNT DIDN'T GO WELL

T.J. Vantine enlisted as a Ranger in the spring of 1860 to do his part to help clear the country of Comanches and other hostile tribes that liked to steal Texas horses and scalp and kill their owners.

Nearly a half-century later, Vantine looked back on his days as a Ranger, writing his recollections for inclusion in a book called Pioneer Days in the Southwest from 1850-1879: Thrilling Descriptions of Buffalo Hunting, Indian Fighting, Cowboy Life and Home Building. Published in 1909, it has long been out of print, the stories it contained now virtually unknown.

While scouting in Northwest Texas, Vantine wrote, he and fellow Ranger Dave Wash found a deep rock crevice, at the end of which they discovered a bear den. Since they were after Indians, not bear, the rangers returned to camp.

"...Our colonel, M.T. Johnson, gave us orders for no one to leave camp without orders," Vantine recalled. "But I wanted to kill a bear..., so the next morning about the break of day I slipped out through the guards and struck out for the bear den about four miles away."

On his way, Vantine listened to the morning yelping of coyotes and the howling of wolves. Suddenly, he realized one howl sounded different from the rest. Reining his horse to ride in the direction of the odd-sounding howl, he spotted an Indian standing on the bank of East Otter Creek.

Forgetting about bear hunting, he dismounted, tied his horse and began stalking his new quarry.

"I drew my gun to fire," he wrote. "I thought I could hit him, but I missed, the ball striking right at the left of where he stood."

Vantine hastily reloaded but decided against a second shot. Reasoning that where there's one Indian there likely were more, the young Ranger ran back toward his horse.

"When I looked back I struck my foot against a rock, but I lost no time in the fall," he wrote. "I ran against my lariat pin and knocked it out and done my rope up as I ran and jumped on my horse and went back to camp. I didn't let any grass grow under his feet."

Back at camp, Vantine was still astride his horse when his captain stormed up, grabbed the bridle and asked him what he'd been doing outside of camp by himself.

"I told him I shot at an Indian," Vantine wrote. "He said I might consider myself under arrest and he took me to the colonel's headquarters, and they assessed my fine at 10 days on guard duty, two hours on, four hours off."

Vantine kept that regimen for two days before fatigue caught up with him. When an officer found him asleep at his post, the Ranger was ordered to perform another 10 days of around- the-clock duty.

Some of the men in his company eventually did shoot a bear, but Vantine's early morning adventure marked the end of his bear-hunting days while riding as a Ranger.

VOLLIE'S RIDE

Before, during and for more than a decade after the Civil War, relative safety could not be taken for granted on the Texas frontier. All that stood between the early settlers and Plains Indians fighting viciously to retain their land were men with guns. Some of those men rode as Texas Rangers.

Nearly a century after the fratricidal clash between North and South, Marilyn Johanson had just graduated from Texas Woman's University in Denton. Traveling with her grandparents from San Saba to Austin in the late spring of 1960, she discovered that while she had succeeded in getting a college education, she still had much to learn about her own family and early day West Texas.

"I was driving, and my grandfather was sitting next to me," Johanson recalled decades later. "Somewhere between Lampasas and Briggs, my grandfather looked out at the prairie there where it seems like you can see forever and said, 'I never come to Austin without thinking about how your great-great grandmother rode by herself from Travis County to San Saba with her two little children.'"

It's roughly 120 miles from the Capital City to San Saba, a two-and-a-half-hour drive at most. But that's today, along paved highways. When Vollie Ann Warren made her ride in 1863, she followed only a winding, two-rut road. She also had to cross numerous creeks and ford both the South and North forks of the San Gabriel River. On top of being a difficult trip in riding alone through that stretch of the state in that era, she risked her life and the well-being of her children.

Born Dec. 9, 1841, in Hardeman County, Tenn., Vollie came with her family to Texas in 1847. They first settled in Travis County, but in 1855 her parents decided to move to the frontier in San Saba County.

Then 14, Vollie had her own ideas. She stayed behind, marrying a young man named Jerry Robinson. They set up housekeeping in Bastrop County and within six years had two children, a boy and girl.

When Texas joined other Southern states in seceding from the Union following the election of Abraham Lincoln as president, Robinson and many other able-bodied men from Bastrop County signed up for Confederate military service and marched off to war in 1861. Most of the volunteers, including Vollie's husband, never returned. They died in camp not from Yankee bullets, but from an outbreak of measles.

After learning of his son-in-law's demise, Jeff Warren wrote to his daughter to tell her that he'd send her a good horse so she could come home with her children. Her father expected Vollie to join others in making the trip, but for reasons not known to her descendants, she either decided to go it alone or the larger traveling party did not materialize.

Holding her 18-month-old daughter on the saddle in front of her while her three-year-old son sat behind her, the new widow left Austin for her parents' home. A rider working a horse hard can make roughly 30 miles a day. But a young woman with two young children could not possibly have kept that pace. Even at 30 miles a day, Vollie faced a four-day ride. Likely her trip took a week or more.

"The story I heard was that she would ride until she came to someone's cabin and then ask to stay the night," Johanson said. "In the morning, they'd tell her, 'Ride yonder way to the next place and you can spend tonight there.'"

Clearly one tough Tennessee-born, Texas-raised woman, Vollie had undertaken a ride even an armed man would've been reluctant to make alone. With most able-bodied men still away at war, hostile Indians enjoyed near free reign along the state's frontier. And in 1863, little law enforcement existed. Beyond avoiding Indians who would happily take her honor, life and scalp while making her children theirs, Vollie also had to be wary of outlaws, conscription dodgers and Union sympathizers.

With so many men off fighting the North, the Rangers afforded what protection frontier settlers had from Indians. But their lines of patrol were not impenetrable.

Newton Dickens McMillin, originally from Tennessee, was one of those Rangers. He'd come to what is now San Saba County in 1855 about the time the Warren family put down roots along the upper Colorado River. In 1858, McMillan served in the Ranger company that chased a Comanche war party and recovered two small children the Indians had kidnapped after killing their parents and older siblings. The event in what is now Mills County came to be known as the Jackson Massacre.

Not long after Vollie and her children made it safely to San Saba, she met "the Captain," as he was called. He surely admired her pluck as well as her beauty. Within a year, he asked her to marry him.

"When he proposed," Johanson said, "he was 48 and Vollie was 23. He told her, 'If we have no children I will love and take care of yours as if they were my own.'"

They married at her parents' home on July 26, 1864.

McMillin honored his pledge. While he was at it, he helped raise the other nine children he and Vollie went on to have. (Two others died in infancy, for a total of 13 children born to Vollie.)

The old Ranger died at 87 on July 4, 1903. Vollie would live for another dozen years. On the evening of July 16, 1915, home after attending a revival, Vollie sat with one of her daughters and her son-in-law on the porch of their house. A light south wind felt good, and the stars shined nearly bright enough to read by. Finally excusing herself for bed, Vollie told her daughter: "I don't believe I will be with you much longer." Before falling asleep that night, maybe she thought about the long, perilous ride she made as a young mother, and the tough but kind-hearted Ranger she married. In the morning, her family found her dead.

'I HAVE BEEN OUT RANGERING...'

The nation barely a year away from the beginning of its cataclysmic Civil War, in the spring of 1860 folks along Texas' frontier had a more immediate problem on their minds—incursions by hostile Indians.

Two weeks out of each month, 23-year-old Isaac Gann volunteered to serve with a home- grown ranging company in Hamilton County. The other two weeks, he tended to his farming and stock raising. While not on the state payroll as a regular Texas Ranger, Gann and his comrades-in-arms were rangers in function. In a way, they had a better incentive than money to scout the countryside. They rode to protect their families and neighbors.

Gann, having heard that Hamilton County offered good grazing, had driven his cattle there from his home in Angelina County in 1858. He planned to have his family join him as soon as he felt it safe to do so. But two years after he moved there from East Texas, Hamilton County was not safe. Indians raided frequently, settlers losing livestock at a minimum, their lives at worst.

On March 5, 1860, while on scout somewhere in Hamilton County, Gann found time to sit down and write his wife "a few lines to let you know that I am yet in the land of the living and I hope that you are in better health than I am." He continued: "I have been out Rangering an taken the flux and it jerked me down mightily." (Flux was the 19th century term for diarrhea.)

But that was enough about health issues.

"I want you to get someone to attend to my mares in the spring if you can," he went on, obviously just putting things down on paper as he thought of them.

The matter of his horses off his mind, Gann got sentimental and noted he'd "like to see you and the children mighty well." Until then, he continued, "you must write me as often as you can." After adding that his father Solomon, who also rode with his company, was doing well, Gann returned to his wife's honey-do list:

"Tell mother. . .to take care of what corn she's got for I don't expect to make much here [at the Hamilton County place] and well if anybody is attending to the place [in Angelina County], let them work the oxens and if they ain't I want you to turn the oxens out. I want them to be as fat as they can agin we move. Send me a pair of pantaloons and a shirt as quick as you can."

And the list went on. Gann wanted to know where his brother and nephew were as well as his brother-in-law. He wanted his mother to write him "what the times is there."

"Times is very hard here," he pointed out. "Corn is from 10 to 11 dollars [a bushel.]" Finally, he wrote, he didn't know when he'd get home. "So I must come to a close by remaining your husband until death," he concluded.

Somber as that sounded, his end lay a long way off. Gann survived his "Rangering" and also made it through Confederate military service. By the time he died on March 4, 1906, he and his wife had raised seven children (five living to adulthood). On top of that, the Ganns took in three of their grandchildren when one of their daughters died in childbirth.

The oldest of those children was Vernie March Walker. When her mother died, the 10-year- old Vernie, a younger brother and a sister went to live with the Ganns in 1902. Eight years later Vernie married and went on to have five children. Fortunately for posterity, she acquired the letter her grandfather had written as a young home guard ranger in 1860 and later made it available for inclusion in a sketch of her family published in a history of Hamilton County. By 1924, when Frontier Times magazine published an article on a birthday celebration for Mrs. Gann that included some of her recollections of early days in Hamilton County, she had 50 grandchildren, seven great-grandchildren and two great-great-grandchildren. She lived another eight years, joining her husband in death on March 3, 1932.

F. M. PEVELER'S KEEPSAKE

At 93, former Ranger Franz Peveler still owned a sharp, mean-looking piece of iron that more than six decades before had come close to killing him—a Comanche arrowhead.

Francis Marion Peveler's parents came from Kentucky to Texas, where he was born April 10, 1843, in Fannin County. His father, David Peveler, settled in Fannin County on a land grant he'd received in 1838 for service during the Texas revolution. In 1857, Peveler moved his family to Parker County on the western frontier of the young state. The following summer the Pevelers moved even farther west, this time to Young County.

The Pevelers built a cabin near Fort Belknap, but as they soon learned the presence of a military garrison did not guarantee protection from hostile Comanches. As one 21st century Peveler family chronicler would put it, "relations with the Indians were not stable."

In 1860, Franz and four brothers (John, William R., James M., and Samuel H.) joined the legislatively authorized Ranger company of Capt. John Cochran for a 12-month enlistment. During that time, they skirmished several times with warriors who still considered northwest Texas as their land.

While Peveler—despite his later claims—was not a direct participant when Rangers under Capt. Sul Ross recaptured Cynthia Ann Parker, he did escort Isaac Parker, Cynthia Ann and her infant daughter from his father's ranch about 40 miles west of Young County to the Army post of Camp Cooper in present-day Throckmorton County.

When Texas seceded from the Union in 1861 just before the Civil War, the situation on this remote section of the frontier grew only more dangerous. Under Capt. J.J. Cureton, Peveler and his brothers joined a Ranger-like frontier defense force funded by Texas's Confederate state government to keep the Indians from depredating even deeper into Texas.

Early one morning in 1862 the Rangers ran into a band of Comanches on the Brazos River. Peveler peeled off from the others and rode toward one of the warriors until he was close enough to use his revolver. But the Comanche was ready. His upper body making a half-turn on his pony, he let fly with an arrow.

Arrows travel swiftly, but not as fast as a bullet. Peveler saw the deadly missile headed his way and jerked his head. That probably saved his life, but the shaft still sunk into the young Ranger's shoulder.

Painfully wounded, he somehow managed to stay in the saddle. After the Comanches fled, one of Peveler's fellow Rangers tried to pull the arrow from his body but the blade had penetrated too deeply. Instead, the Ranger tending to Peveler broke off the shaft. A day and a half passed before a doctor finally extracted the blade and the rest of the shaft.

On Sept. 1, 1864, Franz' older brother Bill Peveler and four other men encountered some 50 Indians about 10 miles north of Graham near Flag Springs in Young County. In the running fight that followed, a warrior killed Sheriff Harvey Staten "State" Cox and Bill Peveler suffered a mortal wound.

As a newspaper writer in 1933 told the story, "Peveler's horse gave out and an Indian rode up as Peveler was crossing a…ravine and tried to pull him off his horse." But Peveler stayed in the saddle and shooting and killing his attacker. The warrior's body fell across the trail and his fellow tribesmen would not ride over his corpse.

That allowed Bill Peveler, having only one bullet left in his gun, to ride to safety. But he'd suffered 19 wounds ranging from minor to severe and died 20 days later.

The following month, Franz saw even more widespread fighting as hundreds of Comanches swept across Young County on October 13 in what came to be called the Elm Creek Raid. Eleven settlers died in the raid, and the Comanches took seven captives.

Peveler later recalled that fall day:

"I was at Belknap a-getting' up some oxen and wagons to take to Fort Murrah [a private fortification near present Newcastle in Young County] to go to mill with grain for about 10 families. On the 13th my brother's

[hand] and I were on the way with the wagons. I was on horseback, and he with the oxen."

After passing an abandoned ranch on California Creek, the two men noticed "smoke away toward Belknap...We went on into Fort Murrah and were eating dinner, when [Ranger] Lt. Carson came running in, said he had 5 or 6 men killed and that the country was alive with Indians."

Peveler wanted to join the fight, but he soon discovered that the raiders had made away with all the horses that had been grazing near the fort. Peveler and another man climbed on top of their cabin and "...with a spyglass we could see the whole country for two miles away alive with Indians."

Peering through the glass, from about one and a half miles away they saw the raiders killing "old man McCoy and his son." Rangers and volunteers held off the raiders until Mrs. McCoy and her niece could be brought to safety inside the fort.

Frantz continued his Ranger service until the end of the war. With Young County still vulnerable to the Comanche, Peveler moved east to Hood County. He married there in 1869 and spent most of the rest of his long life in and around Granbury.

In April 1936—the year Texas celebrated 100 years of independence from Mexico—Peveler's family and friends honored him on his 83rd birthday. Born when Texas was still a republic, the weathered pioneer by then lived in Weatherford with one of his daughters. His eyesight had faded, but that did not dim his memories of life, and death, on the frontier.

Peveler died Dec. 18, 1936. He's buried in Hood County's Granbury Cemetery. What became of his souvenir arrowhead is not known.

VOICES IN THE DARK

Hard as life could be in the 19th century, old-time Texans almost always found something to laugh about.

In the early 1900s, as an old man living in the state Confederate Home in Austin, Civil War veteran and former Texas Ranger Taylor Thompson regaled his friends with tales of his experiences. He also wrote up some of his stories for the old Fort Worth Record. One of those tales must have brought smiles to his readers.

It grew out of something deadly serious, trailing Indians.

Leading 14 men, Thompson followed a party of Indians up the Medina River to near the stream's head. Realizing they were not going to catch up with the Indians, the Rangers quit the pursuit and split up. Thompson sent 10 men, under his corporal, down Hondo Creek while he and three others rode east toward Bandera. His plan was for them to meet up on the lower Hondo.

Before rendezvousing with the rest of his command, Thompson and his fellow Rangers rode up on three men camping near the Medina.

"They were strangers to us," Thompson wrote, "but we camped with them for the night." The trio, who had been traveling in a wagon, told the Rangers they hailed from Atascosa County. They said they'd been in the Hill Country gathering honey from wild beehives.

The small talk out of the way, the Rangers took the standard frontier precautions. Being at least 10 miles from the closest settlement, Thompson knew they had to keep a careful lookout for Indians. Between the Rangers and the bee hunters, they had around a dozen horses. That many mounts would be an attractive prize for any raiding parties that might be on the prowl. "We all prepared to sleep with one eye open that night, though of course the sentinel was posted before we retired," Thompson continued.

He took the second watch himself, going on guard at 11 o'clock that night. Sitting with rifle in hand, Thompson gazed out into the darkness beyond their dying campfire.

Maybe he'd downed a cup of coffee to stay awake, maybe he hadn't and fought sleep. Either way, a voice from the darkness startled him to alertness.

"Come out here, I want to show you something," the voice said.

Thompson did not answer but slipped back to camp to see if one of the men had been calling him. The Ranger found all were lying on their blankets, sound asleep.

Moving cautiously back to his post, Thompson heard a different voice. This time it was in Spanish and coming from the opposite direction of the first voice he'd heard:

"Look out, you damned Rangers, we'll get all your horses tonight, and maybe some of your scalps."

Knowing many Comanches spoke Spanish, Thompson crept back to camp again, his rifle at the ready, to wake the other men. They carefully searched all around their camp, losing sleep but finding nothing.

"We began to think the place was haunted," Thompson recalled. "I slept no more that night, but nothing untoward occurred."

Weighing the incident over his morning coffee, the red-eyed Ranger noticed that one of the Atascosa County men "could scarcely control his risibilities."

Unable to contain himself any longer, the man exploded into laughter and revealed that he was a trained ventriloquist. His was the voice that had cost the Rangers a good night's sleep.

"We took the matter good naturedly," Thompson wrote, but when they got to Castroville, the drinks were on the man who could throw his voice.

AS RANCE MOORE LAY DYING

Shot through his kidneys, as former Ranger Rance Moore lay dying, it's not hard to imagine he almost looked forward to it. Not so much to end his agony, but in atonement for what he'd done eight years before.

Moore first came to the Texas Hill Country during the Civil War. Living in Milam County when the rebellion began in 1861, about a year later Moore enlisted in state service to protect the frontier from hostile Indians. Originally considered more of a military force, the men who guarded the far settlements during the war between the states are today generally regarded as Texas Rangers. While they conducted regular patrols and had a military-style command structure, they wore no uniforms and furnished their own weapons and mounts.

Scouting the Edwards Plateau country, Moore liked the land he saw. Later, in what is now Kimble County, he bought some acreage along Bear Creek. Despite the ongoing Indian threat, after his enlistment, Moore moved his family to his new property in West Texas. With a wife and six children, he raised cattle and most of the food his family needed. What couldn't be grown could be harvested with a rifle or a baited hook dropped into the creek.

An assortment of friends joined the Moore family along or near Bear Creek. More settlers gave a heightened sense of safety, but more horses, cattle and people made for a more attractive target for raiding Comanches and Kiowas. Depredations increased to the point that in 1867, for their safety, Moore decided to move his family to Mason County.

Even so, his new home still lay on the on the edge of the frontier.

On the night of February 5, a noise from the stable awakened Moore. His horses sounded agitated. It could be wolves, a mountain lion or bear, but the former Ranger thought it more likely that Indians were trying to make off with his stock. Grabbing his rifle, Moore looked out into the dark.

At first he saw nothing. But as his eyes adjusted, he made out a human silhouette standing near the corral, an Indian. Squeezing the trigger, Moore put a rifle ball in the center of the Indian's chest and the figure toppled to the ground.

As he stood grimly waiting for more Indians to appear, he realized something wasn't right. No arrows or bullets flew in his direction. No cries of mourning came from the dead Indian's fellow warriors. Rushing outside, Moore found to his horror that he had just killed his teenage son, Danie. The boy would have turned 15 on February 10.

Why the youngster had ventured out while everyone else in their cabin slept was not explained in the primary recounting of this story. Of course, the reason would have meant nothing to Moore. What mattered, and would remain with him like a festering, embedded iron arrowhead, was that he had mistakenly shot down his own flesh and blood.

The boy's simple and misspelled grave maker, carved into local stone, makes no mention of the heartbreaking circumstances of his death. All it say is:

> Danie More, Son of Permelia And Rance More.
> Born February 10, 1852—Died Feb. 5, 1867

The grieving family moved back to their Bear Creek ranch in Kimble County not long after the tragedy. They stayed there until 1873 when Moore had an opportunity to sell the place along with all his cattle. Using the profit from that transaction, he acquired a tract of irrigated farmland on a fork of the Llano River.

While Moore did well as a farmer, the change of location did nothing to alleviate the enduring pain he lived with. After about a year, Moore sold out and moved again, this time to a place on Saline Creek.

Salt in the unhealed wound for Moore was a harsh reality: Indians continued to prey on the people living in Texas's western-most counties. Two days before Christmas in 1874, nine warriors swept across Moore's ranch and herded away several horses.

Knowing that a company of Rangers was camped only five miles from his ranch, Moore dispatched one of his other sons to alert the state lawmen. Under command of Capt. Dan Roberts, the Rangers followed the Indians' trail up Saline Creek but never encountered the raiders or recovered the stolen horses.

Meanwhile, Moore continued to have to make a living for his family. He made a deal with two men named Jim Mason and Henry Sharp to brand his calves and otherwise manage his cattle. That fall, they settled up and Moore got ready to drive his share of the herd to market. In the process, Moore and Mason had a profanity-laced disagreement over some of Moore's camp equipment that Mason and Sharp had used. They men eventually parted company but Moore continued to stew over the matter.

On Dec. 12, 1875, Mason and one Wes Johnson showed up at Moore's place. While warming their hands in front of his fireplace, Mason vented over the earlier incident as Moore heard him out. Finally appearing satisfied, Mason walked outside.

The unarmed Moore followed, and the argument rekindled. Accounts of how things unfolded varied, but Mason shot and mortally wounded Moore. His family buried in him in the Koockville Cemetery next to the son he had mistakenly killed.

Johnson spent four years in prison following his conviction as an accomplice in the killing.

A grand jury indicted Mason for murder but the Rangers never found him.

WRITIN' RANGER

Andrew Jackson Sowell easily could have held himself out as a third-generation Texan. But while his family already had deep ties to the Lone

Star State, he and an older sister were the first two members of the Sowell clan actually born in Texas.

John Sowell, his grandfather, came to Texas from Tennessee to join Green DeWitt's colonists in 1829. He did his share in Texas' fight for independence from Mexico by making and repairing firearms. He also fashioned a wide-bladed knife for fellow Southerner James Bowie, a distinctive edged weapon that would bear Bowie's name. Sowell's father, Asa J.L. Sowell, was too young to take part in the Texas Revolution, but he later rode with Capt. Jack Hays' Rangers and was a pioneer settler of Guadalupe County.

Asa Sowell and his wife, Mary Mildred Turner Sowell, had nine children—five girls and four boys. Born Aug. 2, 1848, near Seguin in Guadalupe County, Andrew Jackson, given his father's initials and a former President's name, was the oldest of the boys. In the 1850s, the family moved to Hays County and settled in what became known as Sowell's Valley. But Guadalupe County remained the family's heartland.

Hearing tales of his father's Ranger days must have spurred young Sowell—he went by Jack—into saddling up for service to the state. On Nov. 5, 1870, Sowell joined Co. F of the newly created Frontier Force under Capt. David P. Baker. He soon participated in the Wichita Campaign, an Indian suppression effort in Northwest Texas.

Sowell's company disbanded in Austin on June 15, 1871. When he mustered out, the young Ranger was due $350 in pay, less $135 for one horse, $50 for another horse, $30 for a Winchester carbine, $10 for a McClellan saddle, $12 for an overcoat, $3.50 for a blanket and $58 for "goods." That left him $51.50 in cash to show for a long, hard winter and several Indian fights.

By the fall of 1871, Sowell was back in Guadalupe County. When he'd ridden off with the Rangers, he'd left behind a sweetheart, Mary Lillian Tinsley. She'd waited for his return, and they were married the day after Valentine's Day, 1872. The couple started raising crops and a family.

As new Sowells were born (the couple had five children), others in the family died. The former Ranger's mother died in the spring of 1873, followed in death by his father on Dec. 21, 1877.

Though still a young man, Sowell was well aware of his family's proud history. Perhaps the loss of his parents and the death of other family members, compounding the death he had seen during his Ranger service, made him aware that while humans were mortal, their stories could live on—providing someone went to the trouble to preserve them.

At some point in the early 1880s, Sowell began writing down stories he'd heard and interviewing old-timers to collect additional material. Too, he began writing an account of his Ranger adventures, though he may have kept a journal during the campaign. That resulted in the 1884 publication of his first book, Rangers and Pioneers of Texas.

With his parents gone, Sowell decided to move west. He and his brother Pleamon left Seguin to look for real estate in the Sabinal Canyon country southwest of San Antonio. The rugged canyon land had been one of the last refuges of hostile Indians in Texas, but by 1887, only the memory of the clash between the two cultures remained.

Pleamon bought 17 lots in the new town of Montana, later renamed Utopia. On Dec. 3, 1887, brother Jack joined him as a property owner there, buying three lots for $100. In 1892 and again two years later, A. J. Sowell bought acreage outside town at a place called Conception Losoya. By 1896, Sowell owned two more lots in Utopia.

Despite the modest prosperity that enabled him to buy land, there was one thing he could not buy—the health of his family. His wife Mary and two of their daughters had chronic respiratory problems. On April 23, 1899, Sowell's oldest daughter Almedia Mildred Sowell died. Three years later, with his wife and daughter Emma's condition worsening, Sowell decided to follow conventional medical wisdom and seek a higher, dryer climate.

The family only got as far as Uvalde on a planned journey to New Mexico Territory when Emma died on April 16, 1902. After her burial, Sowell and Mary continued to Del Rio, still intending to put down roots in New Mexico. But two months to the day after Emma's death, Mary Sowell died in Del Rio. The 54-year-old widower had her body shipped to Uvalde for burial next to her first-born daughter. No longer needing to go to New Mexico, Sowell returned to Center Point to live in a house next to his only remaining daughter, Adeline Willis Rogers.

Sowell wrote three other books, Early Settlers and Indian Fighters of Southwest Texas (1890); The Life of Big Foot Wallace (1899); and History of Fort Bend County (1904).

In addition to his books, from 1904 to 1918 Sowell penned Texas history-related feature stories for the San Antonio Light, the San Antonio Express, the El Paso Times and other publications. Approaching his 70th birthday, Sowell sent a story to the Express about the Big Bend region, the last semblance of wild country in Texas.

Sowell wrote in the article that he'd been in the Big Bend for three years, but he traveled quite a bit to get there: "I came up the Rio Grande from Laredo to the mouth of Green River, Old Mexico, to New Mexico, the plains of Texas and other places."

When he wrote the article, Sowell sat in camp on the Pool Ranch in the Chianti Mountains. In his piece, he explained that the ranch had recently sold and that the new owners had a problem. Running 700 head of cattle, including 200 fat calves, they'd discovered their herd count being diminished by mountain lions.

To cope with the predator problem, the owners hired Sowell's son, Fountain Lee (he went by Lee), to hunt down the offending cats. "As it was an exposed place bordering the Rio Grande, I came with him," Sowell wrote.

Sowell's Big Bend trip turned out to be his last big adventure. As the desert bloomed with spring wildflowers, the old Ranger headed home for Central Texas in his small spring wagon. He stopped at Del Rio to see his son and at Uvalde to visit his wife's grave before taking the well-worn mail and military road up to San Antonio. From there, he returned to Center Point.

Early in July 1921 Sowell suffered a stroke and was driven to Santa Rosa Hospital in San Antonio. On Independence Day morning, Melvin Sowell (son of the former Ranger's brother Leroy) got a telephone call from Sowell's daughter Adeline. She told her uncle that his brother lay gravely ill and that he should come immediately.

"My father took me with him," Melvin's son Russell Sowell later recalled. "We had to dart through the Fourth of July parade that was passing the hospital when we got there. We could see his daughter standing in the front door...crying. Andrew Jackson Sowell had passed away."

NO MEAT AND NOT MUCH BREAD

The few photographs of A.J. Sowell show him as a trim man of normal weight. But he easily could have spent the rest of his life overeating and putting on pounds to compensate for his days as a Ranger.

Sowell's days in the saddle for the State of Texas came in the early 1870s. Predating the Frontier Battalion, the Rangers of 1870-71 doubtless saved some lives along the frontier even though they never had sufficient funds or adequate leadership at the top. Compounded by an undependable supply chain, Sowell and his comrades never seemed to have enough to eat. "This morning," he later wrote in his book Rangers and Pioneers of Texas, (1884), "we had nothing to eat, as our supply of meat had given out, and we had sighted no game since that we could get a shot at; and it always seems the case."

One of many instances of lean rations that Sowell recalled came after he and his comrades got thoroughly soaked one night in a thunderstorm that left them unable to move on. High water in a nearby creek and the river that it flowed into forced them to stay in their soggy camp.

"The rain was over," he wrote. "The next thing now was something to eat. We had a little bread; not more than enough for one man, and no meat at all."

The Rangers grabbed their rifles and moved up their side of the creek, expecting to find game. Meanwhile, the company sergeant produced a hook, some line and declared that he'd try his luck at fishing.

"We had no doubt but what we could get plenty to eat," Sowell wrote, "but our amazement was great as, one by one, the hunters returned empty-handed, not even finding a quail or rabbit. Well, here we were: no breakfast, no dinner (as early Texans referred to the noon meal), the sun sinking in the west with but little prospect for supper (as early Texas referred to what modern Texans call dinner.)

The boys must have been in quite a funk until their sergeant walked back into camp toting a catfish they guessed weighed about a pound and a half. Good as that blue-backed fish looked, it was still a little lean for seven hungry young men. Even so, the Rangers were not about to look a gift catfish in the mouth. They soon had the fish roasting over the coals. Sowell remembered that it tasted pretty good, even divided by seven.

In the morning, with nothing for breakfast and still trapped by the flooding, the Rangers headed out for another day of hunting. Once again, the sergeant went to the creek with his fishing line.

"But," Sowell continued, "as the day before, one at a time they came in with no better fortune, and in vain the sergeant whipped the stream with his line, until he gave it up with disgust."

As the Rangers looked around camp, they realized one of their number had not returned.

Surely bugler John Fitzgerald, the best hunter in their unit, had meat. But as the shadows grew longer, he still hadn't shown.

Concerned, the sergeant had one of his men fire two shots in case Fitzgerald had gotten lost. The shooting was answered with a single round, and soon Fitzgerald, hungry and tired, trudged into view. And he had something in his hand—a turkey hen.

Fitzgerald stretched out to get some rest while the other boys got a fire ready and cooked the bird.

"It was soon ready and the boys gathered around," Sowell concluded. Shortly, "There was nothing left of that turkey but the slick bones and feathers."

Unfortunately, Sowell's story did not have a happy ending. As he put it, "Next morning we were all hungry again."

'THE...MINUTE MEN DO THEIR BUSINESS'

Only 16, French-born Charles Armand Schreiner became a Texas Ranger in 1854, joining the company of Capt. John W. Sampson.

Born in 1838 in the mountains of Alsace-Lorraine, he had come with his family to Texas in September 1852. The Schreiners settled in San Antonio, where his father soon died. Four years later, his mother died from a rattlesnake bite. Except for his siblings—three brothers and a sister—the young Ranger was on his own.

While scouting for Indians with the Rangers, he saw the Hill Country for the first time. As historian J. Evetts Haley later wrote, "[H]e must have reasoned that a man was foolish to range and rove, and thirst and starve, in such a bountifully attractive land...."

In 1857, Schreiner left the Rangers to take up ranching with his brother-in-law, Caspar Real. He lived with his sister Emilie and Real in a log cabin on Turtle Creek in the vicinity of Camp Verde. Not quite six months after the outbreak of the Civil War, on Oct. 1, 1861, Schreiner married Mary Magdalene Enderle. Soon after, he enlisted in the Confederate army at San Antonio. After service throughout the rest of the conflict, Schreiner was mustered out in San Antonio in 1865. One story has it that he walked from San Antonio back to Turtle Creek in Kerr County with only five gold dollars to his name.

On Christmas Eve 1869—with $10,000 put up by August Faltin of Comfort—Schreiner opened a general store in a cypress plank building in Kerrville. Before closing for the day, the store had sold (on credit) 7.5 pounds of coffee and two quarts of whiskey. Whoever bought that liquor probably intended to enjoy eggnog and toast the arrival of a new year, but whiskey also dulled the ongoing pain of Reconstruction and the terrible memories that haunted many Texans who had fought in the Civil War.

Texas—never successfully invaded by the North—had escaped most of the physical devastation of the bloody conflict. Unlike Georgia and other Southern states, its cities did not lay in smoke-stained ruin, but Texas' economy had nearly been destroyed.

After the war, to hitch supply to demand, Texas ranchers began rounding up longhorns and walking them north to the railheads, first to Sedalia, Missouri, and starting in 1867 to Abilene, Kansas. One of the major routes, known initially as the Dodge City Trail and soon simply as the Western Trail, passed through Kerrville.

Schreiner soon acquired a financial interest in the trail and built shipping pens in Kerrville. The captain also moved tens of thousands of his own longhorns up the trail. And Kerrville's emergence in the mid-1870s as a cow town did nothing to harm the bottom line at his general store.

But cattle were not the only animals that could get by on the semi-arid land of Southwest Texas. Schreiner and Caspar Real had pioneered sheep raising in the area, successfully breeding Delaines to his flock to produce better wool. Soon he also began raising goats.

Schreiner's three-pronged approach to ranching not only enhanced his success, it helped transform Kerrville from a town with a courthouse and a few businesses into a regional agricultural center. Ranchers came to Kerrville for their supplies, giving Schreiner's store a steady business, and freight wagons hauled wool and mohair from there to San Antonio and the state's coastal bend. Before long, the astute Alsatian-Texan had enough cash to begin loaning money to others, the beginning of Schreiner's soon-to-be quite profitable banking business.

While an increasingly successful young capitalist, Schreiner had not forgotten how to lever a Winchester. On June 30, 1873, a rowdy-looking group of cowboys walked into his store, ostensibly to have a drink or two. But what they really had in mind was relieving Schreiner of any money he had on hand. Unluckily for them, the captain had been tipped off as to their true intentions and members of the local volunteer minuteman company that he commanded had been strategically positioned outside Schreiner's store.

One of the strangers unwisely shot at a local resident inside the store and the minutemen opened up on the party. When the smoke cleared, five of the outlaws were dead and several lay moaning in spreading pools of blood or staggering around wounded to various extents. The survivors had mounted their horses and galloped out of town, the minutemen in hot pursuit. The Kerrville men caught up with the robbers about eight miles from town and surrounded a house where they had holed up. Newspaper accounts are sketchy as to what happened next, but the Galveston News reported later in July that some 20 outlaws had been killed in the area recently.

Two years later, when five horse thieves hit town and built a herd from other people's stock, Schreiner led a group of his minutemen in pursuit. Thirty miles upriver, the Ranger-like unit and their tracking hounds caught up with the thieves and mortally wounded one of them. Ten horses had been recovered, with another accidentally killed in the exchange of gunfire. Even though the minutemen had recovered the stolen stock, they rode on after the other thieves. "The Highwaymen Come to Grief!" the San Antonio Express reported on June 16, 1875. "Captain Schreiner and the Kerrville Minute Men Do Their Business."

Schreiner went on to establish the famous YO Ranch in 1880. He lived until 1927, dying in Kerrville at 89.

Born less than a month before the captain's death, grandson Charles Schreiner III (locals and others who knew him well just called him "Charlie Three" or sometimes simply "Three") took over operation of the YO in 1949. While he continued to operate it as a working ranch, in the drought years of the early 1950s "Three" expanded its long-time business model through commercial hunting for whitetail deer, turkeys and exotic wildlife. Offering both hunting opportunities and outdoor adventure in general, the YO became a popular destination known worldwide.

In 1966, "Three"—an avid collector of guns with particular emphasis on firearms once owned by Rangers—began acquiring vintage Ranger photographs and biographical material for inclusion in the now-scarce A Pictorial History of the Texas Rangers, published in 1969. He also built a significant collection of Ranger-related artifacts.

Schreiner periodically hosted Texas Ranger company meetings (for training and firearms qualification) at the YO. He also served on the board of directors of the Former Texas Rangers Association Foundation as it worked to raise funds for the Texas Ranger Heritage Center in Fredericksburg. He died in 2001 and was buried in the YO Ranch Cemetery.

PRAIRIE POLICEMEN: 1874 - 1901

RANGER BRIDE

The lanky young Ranger faced a choice that seemed worse than life or death: Resign or lose the woman he loved.

Unfortunately, Co. D Lt. Dan W. Roberts loved rangering as deeply as he cared for his be- trothed. He liked the freedom of riding the West Texas frontier, scouting for hostile Indians and outlaws on the dodge, making camp in one trouble spot until things settled down and then moving on when all hell broke loose somewhere else. He liked the camaraderie with the other Rangers in his company, as sturdy a group of men as he ever hoped to ride the river with. He liked the notion that he was making Texas a safer place to live and work. And if he stayed with the Rangers, he knew he'd soon be promoted to captain.

Sitting around the campfire, Roberts drank coffee and continued to ponder his predicament while the other Rangers told stories and pulled pranks. The idea of giving up the prettiest girl in Columbus left a heavier feeling in his stomach than the company cook's biscuits. His only choice, it seemed, was quitting the Rangers.

When Frontier Battalion Maj. John B. Jones rode into camp that August day in 1875, he also had a problem—one of his best officers leaned toward submitting his resignation on account of a woman.

Well respected by his men and the grateful residents of Texas, Jones took Roberts aside for a private parlay. Marriage was no reason to end a promising Ranger career, he said. He would approve a leave of absence for as long as the lieutenant needed, and then he could bring his new bride to the field with him.

The matrimonially minded Ranger may have wondered if he had heard right, but he took Jones up on his offer. He had about decided to give up state service for his bride-to-be. Now, thanks to the major, he could embark on a new life as a married man without leaving the Rangers.

But after his initial elation wore off, the lieutenant worried anew. He had cavalierly accepted the major's offer without consulting his intended. What would she think about leaving the comforts of home to camp beyond the edge of settlement, where Indians still left arrow-studded bodies strewn around smoldering cabins and wagons, and where outlaws felt they could do as they pleased, so long as they could shoot better and ride faster than anyone who disagreed?

Nervously, Roberts saddled up and rode east to Columbus, a town of stately ante-bellum homes shaded by ancient oaks and sweet-smelling magnolias, a place where Indians had not been a danger for decades. Meeting with his beautiful fiancée, who had never even ridden a horse, the lieutenant outlined Jones' offer.

Luvenia "Lou" Conway had already told the Ranger "yes" once when he asked her to marry him. She did not hesitate when she heard his second proposal.

"My friends thought that I was courageous; in fact, quite nervy to leave civilization and go into Indian country," she recalled. "But it did not require either; I was much in love with my gallant captain [actually, a lieutenant at the time] and willing to share his fate wherever it might be. Besides the romantic side of it appealed to me strongly. I was thrilled with the idea of going to the frontier"

The young couple married Sept. 13, 1875, in Columbus. The conductor on the Houston-to-Austin line obligingly held the train at the depot until the ceremonies ended so the newlyweds could leave immediately on their honeymoon—a trip to Indian and outlaw country.

In Austin, the newlyweds awaited the arrival of the Rangers who would travel with them back to their Menard County camp. Before the wedding, the bride-to-be had sewn herself a riding habit after learning the lieutenant had selected a horse for her. Now she busied herself assembling the rest of the wardrobe she would need for frontier living.

Escorted by two well-armed Rangers, "we set out on our bridal tour," she wrote. "I'm sure there was never a more delightful one, and there can never be another just like it."

Before long, Roberts and his Rangers waded into the so-called "Hoodoo War," a feud born of cattle thievery and fanned by ethnic tension between German settlers and Anglo ranchers then raging in Mason County, a hundred miles northwest of Austin. The honeymooning lieutenant soon found himself helping the local sheriff stand off a lynch mob outside the courthouse. At least a dozen men died in the war before Roberts and his men settled things down. Throughout it all, Luvenia hardly left her husband's side.

At first the couple lived in a white canvas tent with gunny sacks spread on the ground for flooring. Eventually, Co. D got a second tent and wood for real flooring. For winter camp, the Rangers built a log cookhouse with a canvas roof. Adding a touch of elegance to an otherwise rustic setting, a brush fence with a whitewashed wooden gate ringed the camp.

Her surroundings hardly what she was accustomed to, Mrs. Roberts never complained. Her husband, freshly promoted to captain, taught her to shoot and fish. Often, with the captain and most of his men out on a scout, she stayed around camp with the remaining men, reading, sewing, hunting, or fishing. Occasionally, a female relative of one of the other Rangers visited camp, but the captain's devoted wife had little female companionship.

To fill the void, the Rangers brought her pets and otherwise pampered her, and she in turn "mothered" them. Ever the Southern gentlemen, Maj. Jones occasionally sent her candy and fresh fruit, addressing the box to "Assistant Commander, Company D."

That joke notwithstanding, in practicality, Mrs. Roberts did assume some authority, particularly in her husband's absence.

Married only a year, Roberts resigned in September 1876. He offered no reason other than to say he and Luvenia planned on moving to Houston. Fourteen months later, Jones again used his persuasive skills on Roberts, offering Roberts his old job back. Roberts took him up on it, and by November was back in the saddle.

For nearly six years, Mrs. Roberts stayed in camp with her husband and his men. But she had begun to suffer from health problems. Finally, on Oct.

12, 1881, after numerous scrapes with Indians and outlaws, the captain resigned his commission so he could move his wife to another frontier—higher and dryer New Mexico Territory.

Returning to Texas in 1914, the couple lived in San Antonio for a time, then moved to Driftwood in Hays County. In 1917, they relocated to Austin, where they spent the rest of their lives.

Well into his 80s, Roberts still regaled friends and newspaper writers with stories of his Ranger days–if pressed. A quiet and unassuming man, he died in Austin on Feb. 6, 1935. Gov. James V. Allred ordered the Texas flag flown at half-staff above the Capitol and approved Roberts' burial in the State Cemetery.

"Though he sleeps," the officiating pastor said, "he is not dead, because when Captain Dan W. Roberts dies, all Texas will die."

One of the few 19th century Rangers who ever bothered to write a memoir, in a way the captain did live on. His wife also wrote of her experiences as a bride on the frontier.

"It was with regret I parted from the Ranger camp where I had spent so many happy days," Mrs. Roberts wrote. "Camp life afforded many pleasures, which, coupled with duty and a determination to serve the people of Texas well and honestly, have caused us to treasure the memory of those years."

"I HAD GOOD LUCK THIS MORNING"

The Rangers sat digesting their noon meal one fall day in 1876 when they saw a wagon pulled by a yoke of oxen headed toward their camp. They recognized the man holding the reins as John Delong. A saddle pony and several dogs trailed behind his wagon.

"Howdy boys," Delong said.

Then, turning to Co. E Lt. N.O. Reynolds, he got more specific. "I had good luck this morning."

The Ranger lieutenant looked in the bed of Delong's wagon and saw it loaded with fresh venison, hides and dripping honeycombs.

"So I see," he said.

"Not that," Delong said. "I killed two Indians this morning."

Hearing that snapped the Rangers from their early-afternoon drowsiness.

"That is our business, killing Indians," one of the Rangers said as the company gathered around to hear what had happened. "But we have not been able to find any lately."

Indeed, Texas' half-century war with Indians was nearly over. The Rangers and the U.S. Cavalry finally had the situation pretty well in hand.

Delong then told his story.

The night before, he began, he had camped about six miles up the North Llano River from the Rangers. A cautious frontiersman, he had put his bedding down some distance from his wagon and pony, just in case. He hobbled the oxen so they could graze during the night.

His dogs, of course, slept with him. During the night, they growled and barked and made several charges toward the wagon. The notion of Indians crossed his mind, but Delong decided some prowling animal, maybe a raccoon looking for food, was what had his dogs agitated.

But when he got up the next morning, his oxen were missing. Delong saddled his pony and set out with his dogs to find them.

Searching out that stretch of the river valley without success, he climbed a hill to get a better view. He sat down on the sunny side of a big rock formation and looked up and down the valley for his missing animals.

Then he heard pebbles falling. Something was moving on the rocks behind him.

Delong peeped over the boulder and saw an Indian slowly moving in his direction. He put a copper shell in his single-shot .50 caliber rifle and aimed at the Indian. When the Indian went down and didn't move, Delong loaded another shell in his rifle and stayed put to await developments.

Another Indian soon appeared, running toward his fallen comrade. He looked wildly in each direction, trying to figure where the shot had come from. When he stood still for a second, Delong pulled the trigger.

He waited awhile to see if there were more Indians. Finally convinced there had only been two, he went to where they had fallen to see if they were both dead. Satisfied that they were, he got his pony, found his oxen and headed down river toward the Ranger camp.

Lt. Reynolds wanted to see where all this had happened and check the area for any other Indian sign. Delong led him back to the spot.

The Rangers concluded the Indians had stolen Delong's oxen with the intention of ambushing him when he set out to look for them. The Texans collected the Indians' bows and arrows and other possessions and left the bodies where they had fallen. The man who saved this story for posterity was A.J. Sowell, a former Ranger who had known Reynolds and many other early-day Texans. Sowell wrote an account of Delong's close call for one of the San Antonio newspapers in 1903. By that time, even whitetail deer were becoming scarce in the Hill Country.

LOVE LETTERS FROM AN OUTLAW

Back in the 1870s, the Rangers had more than Bowie knives, six-shooters and Winchesters to choose from when it came to bringing justice to the frontier.

Sometimes, passing a little information along to a reporter—in today's jargon that would be called "leaking" something—could serve the ends of justice quite well. One example of a Ranger resorting to street justice began one day in early 1877 when a young man named Donaho took pen in hand to write a love letter to his sweetheart in Dallas, a young lady named Anna Parson.

"Dear Darling," he began, off to an affectionate start. "'Tis with pleasure that I seat my self on the Banks of Llano River a Beautiful stream Rippling its way through the Western firmament and on each side...far as the eye Can behold is Mountains and prairies which vast herds of Buffalo roam...the lean Cyote Can be seen skulking around and all is lovely to the eye of one sad Boy..."

Clearly, Donaho couldn't claim to be the world's best speller and he apparently missed class the day they talked about capitalization, comma usage and run-on sentences, but as spring settled on Texas, he obviously had an eye for nature's beauty. He also had an eye for beautiful women, which was why he was "one sad Boy..." (Ellipses have been inserted to make his epistle easier to read.)

No less longingly than Romeo for Juliet, Donaho pined for his lovely Anna in faraway North Texas.

"Could Anna But know the sad and shocking feelings that exist in my bosom," Donaho went on. "When I think of my Anna....Yes the Rose...the day star of my life I am winding my way through this barren Country to Mexico for my idea is to be a Western Warrior..."

Did Donaho intend to join the cavalry or saddle up with the Texas Rangers? Obviously, he knew the days ahead would be dangerous.

"We may never see each other again," he lamented, "but live with hope. My desire is that we shall both pass the short but treacherous hours away willing and well...Darling to dream of you by night and sigh for you by day."

Then, serenaded by the river, he really lets it flow: "What a luxury for me it would be to behold your illustrious imige [image]...Yes Anna your eyes burn Liquid fire so flaming to my heart that [it] is irresistible."

Poor Donaho felt so lonely, so much longing for his darling Anna. Too, the road stretched on and on.

"As I travel along the Western horizon I seldom meet anyone except the old hunter who is as grave as the Wind," he despaired in his awful solitude. "My only companion is three young men...we have a lonsime [lonesome] Time of it."

Finally, Donaho cut to the chase. He had not signed up as a "Western Warrior" to protect the frontier while wearing the blue uniform of a horse soldier or a Ranger's white hat.

In truth, Donaho rode the Owl Hoot Trail as an outlaw, having recently robbed the stagecoach between Austin and Fredericksburg. Now he was on the lam.

But like many young men, Donaho had hope for the future, a desire to make a good living at his chosen vocation and a comfortable home for the girl he wanted to marry.

"We inhabit the Western Country and will Continue until we get Rich which I most emphatickly [emphatically] think we will and when we do I am Coming Back to dallas," he wrote. (Clearly, this was before the city earned its Big D status.)

"Wait for me Anna for I am solid with you...God is my witness I do love you...I am held to no Locality...Bound to no personal object except yourself...Yes wait for me and I will make you a jenerous [generous] husband."

Alas, Anna never received the letter. But she did learn of its contents when the Galveston News gleefully published it for all to enjoy after a Gillespie County ranging company captured Donaho and his fellow robbers in early March 1877. When the Rangers went through his things, they found his unfinished love letter and cheerfully passed it on to the press.

The missive from the sad, bad Donaho caught the attention of readers in Texas and across the nation. Even the serious-minded New York Times considered Donaho's letter interesting enough to merit inclusion in its pages, publishing it on March 11, 1877.

The newspaper concluded: "The young man will have to serve five or ten years in the Penitentiary before he can lay his fortune at the feet of gentle Anna...and claim her hand."

'OFTEN DISTRESSING THINGS TO BE DONE'

Sometime in the 1890s, a former Texas Ranger long interested in the state's history sat down with former Ranger Neal Coldwell to interview him about his days on the frontier.

A.J. Sowell, who'd ridden as a Ranger only a few years before Coldwell enlisted in the newly created Frontier Battalion in 1874 ended up devoting a little over 11 pages to Coldwell in his classic Early Settlers and Indian Fighters of Southwest Texas (1900).

First, Sowell spent a couple of pages on Coldwell's early life. Born May 2, 1844 in Dade County, Missouri, Coldwell at the age of six traveled overland with his family to California during the gold rush. After Coldwell's father died there in 1852, his widow took the family back East to her native Tennessee. In 1859, the Coldwell family headed west again, settling in Kerr County in 1860. A year later the Civil War began. Coldwell joined the Confederate army and went on to take part in 32 skirmishes or battles. Returning to Kerr County after the defeat of the South, he took up the more peaceful vocation of farming and stock raising.

In May 1874—likely due to the reputation he gained during the Civil War—the just turned 30-year-old Coldwell was appointed one of the six original Frontier Battalion company captains. Though the law creating the Frontier Battalion vested the Rangers with law enforcement authority, as captain of Company F Coldwell spent the first part of his Ranger service chasing hostile Indians. However, the battle-hardened captain and his company never fired a shot at a warrior. That said, during one arduous scout in rough Hill Country terrain, Coldwell's company did succeed in preventing a war party from committing any serious depredations.

Sowell's chapter primarily focuses on Coldwell's efforts to protect Texas from hostile Indians and only covers two of his law enforcement cases: the famous Kimbell County outlaw roundup of 1877 and Coldwell's experiences at Fort Davis in 1880 when the Jesse Evans gang ran rampant in that part of the state.

With the Texas Indian problem finally fading after a half-century of off-and-on warfare, in 1877 Coldwell's command and the other five companies under Maj. John B. Jones turned their attention to law enforcement.

In doing his job, Coldwell gained the respect of citizens and comrades alike. "He was more than any captain in ability and one of the best officers in the service," former Ranger Capt. Dan Roberts later observed. Historian Walter Prescott Webb, in his 1935 history of the Rangers called Coldwell "an active and zealous man who showed a disposition to discipline and control his men."

Yet, other than the chapter on Coldwell in Sowell's book, little else has been written about the captain. While some insight into his time as a peace officer can be derived at the state archives by going over the handwritten monthly scouting reports and correspondence that were a part of his job as a Frontier Battalion officer, as far as is known Coldwell never penned any recollections concerning his days in the Frontier Battalion.

Beyond the lack of any private correspondence or autobiographical jottings, during his Ranger captaincy and after becoming Frontier

Battalion quartermaster in 1879 Coldwell— unlike more garrulous Rangers—never got much ink in the press. In fact, a search of one subscription website that contains hundreds of digitized Texas newspapers turned up only three articles mentioning the captain between 1874 and 1882. Both were just routine news items.

And for the decades following Coldwell's Ranger service, the pace never picked up. From 1884 to 1904, Coldwell's name appears in only a couple of articles: A brief account of a deer hunt he took with three friends on the Devil's River in 1890 (during which they killed 24 deer and one antelope) and a piece listing livestock award winners in the annual fair put on by the Guadalupe Valley Stockman's Association. From 1905 to 1915, there are no newspaper mentions of Coldwell. Finally, during the last decade of his life, from 1916 to 1925, the captain's name made the newspapers only three times.

Of course, this database does not include every old Texas newspaper. There may have been a few additional news items about him over the years, but these numbers clearly show that Coldwell was not a seeker of publicity.

Then came J.E. Grinstead. At 33, he moved to Kerrville in 1899 from Oklahoma Territory for his wife's health. She suffered from tuberculosis, but the drier climate and higher altitude did not save her. She died soon after.

However, the widower Grinstead chose to stay in Kerr County where he became a popular citizen, an enthusiastic promoter of the Hill Country and a Mason. In 1900 he began publishing a newspaper called The Kerrville Paper, which he renamed The Mountain Sun. During his 17 years of newspaper ownership, he also served for a while as Kerrville's mayor and as a member of the state legislature. After selling his newspaper in 1917, he turned to freelance writing, specializing in Western pulp fiction. In addition to producing numerous short stories and more than 30 novels, from 1921 through 1925 he edited a magazine he called Grinstead's Graphic.

At some point in 1921, Grinstead met with the captain to interview him about his career. While he was at it, he took several photos of Coldwell at his ranch, "Fairland." The result was a full-page feature story on the cover of the Fort Worth Star-Telegram Sunday Magazine.

Most former Rangers, then as now, tend to look back on their glory days with fondness. While surely the captain felt proud of his accomplishments and doubtless relished some of his experiences, Coldwell told Grinstead that "the Ranger service was never a pleasant duty."

Beyond the dangers faced by Rangers, the 70-something Coldwell continued, "there were often distressing things to be done."

Still, in an era when most Rangers served less than a year and seldom more than two or three years, with one hiatus due to funding issues Coldwell stuck with the Rangers from May 4, 1874 to Feb. 15, 1883. (However, some documents show he left the Frontier Battalion effective Dec. 31, 1882.) Since Ranger pay was nothing to get excited about, even for officers, the only logical conclusion to be drawn from his long Ranger service is that he saw his role in protecting the people of Texas as a duty he would not shirk.

One example of a difficult thing Coldwell had to do as a Ranger involved a routine arrest. "We carried warrants and arrested men who were wanted in other parts of the state," he told Grinstead. Also, he continued, "When some situation arose that was too heavy for the county peace officers we assisted them."

Coldwell went on to tell the Kerr County writer about "a most pathetic case" in which official duty had to transcend personal feelings.

Here's what the captain related:

"At Bandera we got information that [a fugitive] was with a gang camped near the head of the Medina River. As I recall it now, his name was Sapp, and he was wanted for some crime committed in one of the North Texas counties."

As was often the case with Ranger scouts, he continued, in their search for Sapp, "Most of our riding was done at night. It was useless to ride in the daytime. Runners would go ahead of us and warn the outlaws."

The hunt for Sapp took place in late fall or winter. Coldwell did not say what year. Whenever it was, the night was bitterly cold. In crossing and recrossing the Medina, the Rangers' boots got wet and soon had a coating of ice.

Coldwell and his men reached the outlaw camp at daybreak, "only to find that our man was not in the outfit." Clearly happy the Rangers had no business with them, the men said Sapp was not a member of their gang. Beyond that, in the spirit of justice for all the men readily divulged that Sapp lived in a canyon "a few miles further down the country and gave us directions to the place."

The still-cold Rangers, not even having taken time to build a fire and boil coffee, rode on to the canyon.

"Just after turning into the canyon," the captain continued, "...we met two little boys coming down the trail on one horse."

When they saw the Rangers, one of the boys slipped off the horse while the other "turned about and rode under whip and spur" toward their house. Realizing the boy intended to warn his father, the Rangers galloped after him. Just as they caught up with him, they saw Sapp hobbling a horse in a nearby glade.

"We got our man, but when the family saw that we were going to take him away the woman and children set up a wail that was heartrending," Coldwell went on. "They knew that he would be taken back, tried and either hanged or sentenced to a long term in prison."

While the captain and his men were duty-bound to arrest Sapp, Coldwell said it had been "a most distressing duty." He continued: "The man was the head of a house. ...To his wife and children he was doubtless as dear, according to their lights, as other men are to their families."

The old Ranger told Grinstead he never learned how the matter turned out. Whoever Sapp was, if that was his name, he must not have been too desperate a desperado. A check of Texas newspapers between 1874 and 1880 did not turn up any notorious outlaw with that surname. But if Mr. Sapp was just a common lawbreaker living in the shadow of an unserved warrant, Texas had no shortage of sure enough hardcases in the 1870s. Indeed, especially in the less-settled regions of west and south Texas, outlaws reigned supreme.

"For a time," Caldwell told Grinstead, "the outlaws simply had this section of Texas at their mercy. They were thoroughly organized and carried on horse stealing systematically."

He said gangs stole horses in Texas and sold them to other less than savory characters until the stolen stock ended up in Kansas. Often, Coldwell said, the horses were stolen again in the Sunflower State driven back to Texas to be sold in Texas. "It was a regular shuttle arrangement," the captain said.

In 1876, Coldwell got orders to take his Rangers to Oakville, then the rough-and-tumble Live Oak County seat.

"Thieves and cutthroats in that part of the country had reached the point where they took what they wanted, openly, and settlers and ranchmen were powerless," the captain told Grinstead.

While camped at Oakville, the Rangers got word that a group of local citizens had "arrested" a party of men they'd found with a string of horses lacking provenance. The men then turned the suspected thieves over to the sheriff.

"The sheriff…, having learned that the animals were stolen near San Diego, in Duval County, started to San Diego with the thieves and the stolen property." Coldwell said.

But a well-armed posse of concerned Duval County citizens met the sheriff at the county line to say they'd be taking the thieves off his hands. After all, the lawman already had plenty on his plate in Live Oak County. Given the overwhelming odds against him, the sheriff decided it was in the best interest of justice—and his continuing good health—to head back to Oakville.

"Duval County never had any expense of trying the thieves, and they never stole any more horses," Coldwell told Grinstead. "I suppose the [grave] mounds, if they took the trouble to bury them, have long since disappeared, and there is nothing to mark the spot where the sheriff of Live Oak County met the citizens of Duval."

This incident may have occurred in February 1876, when a week or so later the Marshall Tri-Weekly Herald in East Texas expended all of three lines of type to blasély report: "Nine men—six white and three colored—are reported to have been hung near Oakville last week." Technically, the extra-judicial execution of a group of suspected horse thieves—constitutionally innocent until proven guilty—should have triggered an investigation on the part of the Rangers. But that didn't happen. Coldwell and his men must have had more pressing issues elsewhere.

While Coldwell's evident modesty is admirable, it can only be imagined what other stories the captain could have told. Surely he must have passed on certain of his other recollections to family, friends, or his fellow Masons, but only Sowell's and Grinstead's interviews are known.

Less than five years after Grinstead's article appeared, on Nov. 7, 1925, the old captain died at Fairlands and soon joined his fellow former Rangers at the Center Point Cemetery.

EARNING SOME EXTRA CASH

The Trans-Pecos country of West Texas seemed positively tame in 1883 compared with only a few years earlier.

The Ranger's last Indian fight had been in January 1881, the worst of the man-killing outlaws were either in the ground or prison and only a few stray buffalo survived on the east side of the Pecos. But a couple of entrepreneurially minded Rangers still found something to shoot at: quail.

While their Ranger outfit (Co. A, under Capt. George Baylor) was stationed at Ysleta, down river from El Paso, Rangers Joe Deaver and August Fransel noticed the area, as Deaver later put it, was "overflowing" with wild game. Farms in the valley of the Rio Grande below Ysleta and Socorro "were simply swarming with wild quail."

To frontier tastes, and to many gourmands today, a quail may as well be a miniature chicken. As opposed to the dark meat of dove, grilled or fried quail amounts to several tasty bites of white meat.

Back then, in the booming railroad town of El Paso, local butcher Jack Carter happily paid $1.50 a dozen for fresh-from-the-field quail. Given that the state paid its Ranger privates only $30 a month, a man handy with a shotgun could supplement his income substantially by providing Carter quail.

The 24-year-old Deaver, whose parents brought him to Erath County from his native Tennessee when he was a youngster, was a fine shot. His apprenticeship as a marksman came in hunting buffalo before he turned to rangering in 1881.

Dropping a big bison for its hide took a high-powered rifle, but Deaver knew how to work a scatter gun, too. As a part-time meat hunter, on a good day, the dead-eye Ranger killed as many as 10 dozen quail–half a month's pay.

Not that his day job did not afford Deaver the opportunity to shoot at something other than wild game. One on occasion, wild cowboys became Ranger targets.

That happened when Deaver and the rest of his company were camped at Toyah, a tough new-born railroad town to the west of Pecos.

One day the Rangers received a telegram that read: "To the Rangers at Toyah: We understand you have come to take care of the town. We are coming up tonight to take her in. [Signed] Cowboys."

Deaver said the Rangers figured the wire was just a prank on someone's part and, as he put it, "made no plans to receive the rowdies."

Later that day, he recalled, "We were standing about 300 yards from the station when the train from Pecos pulled in. Suddenly a volley of shots belched forth from the windows."

Still the lawmen paid no serious attention to the shooting, figuring the cowboys were just letting off a little steam. But later, when a freight train was about to depart for Pecos, Deaver heard that the cowboys, apparently having had their fun, had taken over the caboose.

Running to the train, Deaver yelled, "Boys, we don't want to have to shoot anyone. Unbuckle your guns and leave them on the seats and come out."

Unfortunately, the cowboys had consumed too much alcohol.

"Someone fired and glass splattered everywhere," Deaver recalled in an interview with the El Paso Herald Post years later. "It was pitch dark and Rangers on both sides of the caboose poured fire into the car."

Deaver said the leader of the party was killed by Ranger fire, but if that was the case, the news does not seem to have made it into print.

Despite the pounding his shoulder took in firing his shotgun 120-plus times a day (surely he missed every once in a while), the young state lawman and his business partner saw hunting quail as far preferable to disarming drunks or making long horseback scouts along the Rio Grande. On Oct. 31, 1883, Deaver and his older partner, who had first come West as a stagecoach driver, left state service and became full-time meat hunters.

In addition to providing El Paso consumers with fresh quail, the two former Rangers used the Winchester rifles they bought from the state to bring down mule deer. Happily for the hunters, most folks back then enjoyed venison just about as much as they did beef. Deaver and Fransel worked out an agreement with another El Paso meat house to provide them fresh venison.

To harvest deer, the two professional hunters had to ride down river to the Quitman, Eagle and Carrizo mountains, not long before the disputed province of Texas' last band of hostile Apache.

For every deer carcass they put on the train to El Paso, they were paid eight cents a pound.

The buyer even picked up the freight charges.

"We often shipped from 10 to 15 head a day, and seldom less than three to five," Deaver later recalled.

The average weight per deer was 85 pounds, but occasionally they brought in a big buck weighing 250 pounds.

Back in Austin, Texas lawmakers had not yet realized the importance of game conservation and few, if any, statutes were in the books to prevent the wholesale slaughter of quail, deer or other wildlife. In time, conservation laws did get passed, but by the early 20th century much of the state had been hunted out. Deer, pronghorn antelope, wild turkey and quail were scarce. It took decades for the state's game animals to recover from the era of unregulated hunting.

Deaver later defended his meat hunting with the argument that wild animals would be detrimental to farm crops, but both quail and mule deer prefer rough country, not agricultural land. (He was closer to being correct in regard to white tail deer, which love to graze oat crops and people's gardens.)

The two ex-Rangers continued their meat hunting for two years. When Deaver's partner heard that gold and silver could be found near Sierra Blanca, they stored their guns and took up prospecting.

Indeed, back then the mountain country of West Texas was believed to hold rich veins of precious metals. A reasonable amount of silver ore was found by others near what became Shafter, but the dream that Texas would equal New Mexico or Arizona in mining never materialized.

Deaver and Fransel would have made a lot more money if they had stuck to hunting quail and deer, not gold and silver.

Both men later turned to ranch work. Fransel died at 83 in 1927 and is buried at Sierra Blanca. His former partner made it until 1940, dying in Nueces County. He's buried in Robstown.

BUCK BARRY WRITES HIS GRANDSON

Newly arrived in Austin from Bosque County, former Texas Ranger James Buckner "Buck" Barry grabbed a sheet of House of Representatives stationery and began scratching out a letter to his 12-year-old grandson.

Elected to the House the previous year, in January 1883 Barry traveled to Austin to serve in the 12th Legislature. In the largely ceremonial early days of the session, the 61-year-old's constituents had presented him with what he called "the finest gun that could be bought" in recognition of his Ranger service along the frontier during the Civil War.

Once the two chambers finally got down to business, Barry proved as good a lawmaker as he'd been an Indian fighter. The North Carolina native, who'd come to Texas in 1845 as a young man of 24, had a way with words even if he couldn't spell all those words. Nor did he seem to have any awareness of what a period is used for in composition. His missive consisted essentially of only two giant run-on sentences. Even so, Barry penned a meaty letter.

Texas's 1850s-vintage limestone Capitol had been gutted by fire in November 1881 and the Legislature was conducting its business in a hastily built temporary brick state house at 11th and Congress. Reading between the lines, Barry likely wrote his letter while sitting in the House chamber. Meanwhile, a permanent red granite Capitol slowly took shape across the street, construction having begun in February 1882.

"Dear son," he began, "I hardly know what to write you unless I knew what would please you most…." After that, the old Ranger dispensed with any "I'm fine, how are you?" sentiments and went right to the most interesting thing he could think of, the recent death of former Gov. E.J. Davis.

"[H]e died 7th Feb of something like Pneumonia Called pleurisy[.] Yesterday the 9th he was buried in the state Cemetery[.] The weather was bad and there was not [a] great many that turned out maybe five hundred with the Colored folks," he wrote. Barry said Davis had lain in state in the House for four hours.

"His face was left bare that all who wanted…could see him[.] He looked very natural though his beard was much whiter than when I last saw him," Barry wrote. "He was a man that all rebels hated very much, but the Legislature bothe [sic] the House and Senate were all rebels…paid a great tribute of respect to him when he died, as [his] History…will constitute a part of the great state of Texas history and consequently the tribute of respect paid to him after his death by his political enemies will also be a matter of history."

Davis had served as a Union officer during the Civil War, and as the state's chief executive during Reconstruction he'd been seen as a near-despot by most of his constituents. The respect Barry described for the former governor more likely masked the near elation many Texans experienced at his passing.

But almost 18 years since the war ended, Texas faced new problems.

The invention of barbed wire, and its growing popularity in the state, pitted large landowners (ranchers) against small landowners (cattle operators or farmers.) Those opposed to fencing what for years had been free range took every opportunity to cut wire fences, often in the dead of night. Fence cutting had led to violence, and Barry's successors in the Rangers had been tasked with stopping the costly practice.

"Johnny," the freshman representative from Bosque County continued, "I am trying now to get a law passed to indict [indiscernible] and all others who do not put pole or rail on their wire fence so that we will not have so many horses to doctor for worms." (The result of parasites entering wounds caused by barbed wire.)

However, Barry was having trouble with the measure.

"The stock men on the Rio Grande and the Panhandle Country oppose me[.] They have 20 to 40 miles [of] wire fence without pole and do all they can against me as they don't want to pay money for [poles] and they have no poles out there," the Ranger-turned-lawmaker wrote.

While Davis's death and the barbed wire problem had been the main topics of his letter, Barry did dispense a bit of fatherly advice to his son:

"You must try to write well which you do very well for a boy of your age," the elder Barry said. "You must not forget it no boy or man can get a position in any Department of state unless he writes a smooth, clear. . .hand."

His election to "a position" in the Legislature didn't happen because of his penmanship, but Barry practiced what he preached. His script was readable (at least by those familiar with the handwriting of the day) and with no scratch-outs.

Barry would live to be an old man, dying on his 85th birthday on Dec. 16, 1906. But even in his early 60s, he seems to have had a sense of posterity.

"When you read this [letter] and all the rest," he enjoined his son, "file it [away] with your old papers as rellicks."

THE DISAPPEARANCE OF RANGER WOODS

It's the coldest cold case in the history of the Rangers—the disappearance and suspected murder of one of their own.

James W. Woods first joined the Frontier Battalion at Colorado City on Dec. 1, 1882, enlisting in Capt. Sam McMurry's Co. B. When McMurry filled out the simple paperwork that transformed Woods into a Ranger, the captain noted that Woods was 24, stood 5 feet 11 inches, had grey eyes and light hair. Born in Texas, Woods' occupation was listed simply as "farmer."

Earning $30 a month, Woods served as a Ranger through May 1884. During that time, McMurry concentrated most of his efforts in keeping the peace in the wild and wooly new towns and rail gang construction camps along the route of the westward-bound Texas and Pacific. A quiet man not given to self-promotion, McMurry had a reputation as a captain who got the job done, particularly when it came to corralling cattle thieves.

Nearly a decade after his Co. B hitch, on Jan. 31, 1893, a seasoned 34-year-old Woods joined the Rangers a second time. By then, Texas had grown considerably tamer than it had been the decade before, but one law enforcement problem persisted—cattle rustling.

Capt. McMurry having left the Rangers in 1891, Woods' new boss was Capt. John H. Rogers, commander of Alice-based Co. E. Though stationed in South Texas, thanks to Legislative budget cuts that had the Frontier Battalion stretched thinner than a senator's hatband, Rogers and his men covered a lot of country. The captain soon assigned Woods upstate to Menard County to work with Sheriff R.R. Russell in, as later correspondence put it, "procuring evidence against cattle thieves in that county."

More specifically, Woods rode into the Menard area in what today would be called an undercover capacity. His job was to somehow ingratiate himself with those with no regard for brands and funnel whatever information he could collect about their operations to Sheriff Russell and, sooner or later, to the district grand jury.

But in July 1893, less than six months after rejoining the Rangers, Woods simply vanished. Capt. Rogers sent Sgt. Tupper Harris and Private James J. Callan to Menard in search of the missing lawman, but they turned up nothing.

In late November, still not having heard from Woods, Rogers sent Adjutant General W.H. Mabry letters from the sergeant and Callan in regard to their investigation into the Ranger's disappearance. On November 29, based on those reports, Mabry wrote Rogers instructing him to drop Woods from the state payroll as of November 30, "with remarks that he mysteriously disappeared from Menard Co. while on duty there assisting Sheriff Russell...in that county in July 1893."

Mabry further ordered Rogers to have Sgt. Harris "push the investigation in the undoubted killing of Woods."

With the sergeant still not coming up with any leads in the case, on December 12 Mabry wrote Rogers that Gov. James Stephen Hogg had authorized a $200 reward "for the arrest and conviction of the murderer of Private Woods."

Though the surviving official paperwork offers few details, the Rangers seem to have had a suspect in mind in connection with Woods' disappearance. Mabry authorized Capt. Rogers to "enlist a man to be placed in prison with Goins [no first name given], & as an inducement, you can offer such a man something more than private's pay, while employed by yourself for such purpose."

In other words, the Rangers must have thought someone behind bars in Huntsville knew something about the case. But if the plant ever came up with anything of interest, it is not noted in the records of the Adjutant General's Department in the Texas State Library and Archives. Two days after informing Rogers of the reward posted by the governor, Mabry wrote the sheriffs of Menard, Edwards, Uvalde and Kimble counties to advise them of the reward and urge them to keep it quiet "as I do not want it known we are after the murderer."

Everyone involved in the case seems to have succeeded in keeping it quiet. No mention of Wood's disappearance ever surfaced in the newspapers of the day. But an Aug. 25, 1893, report published under a Menardville (as Menard was then called) dateline indicates something was going on in the area. Four men had been jailed for cattle theft, 59 head of "burnt cattle" having been found in the pasture of one of the suspects and 47 head "in adjoining pastures." One of the men, the short article continued, "attempted to suicide…by cutting an artery in his arm."

Meanwhile, Sgt. Harris and Private Callan spent the winter of 1893-94 in and around the communities of Fort McKavett and Menard. In early March, Harris mailed Captain Rogers a letter offering a startling new twist on Woods' disappearance: He might have deserted. For sure, not every private in the Frontier Battalion ended his career honorably. Good captains would fire bad drunks or plainly bad men, but it didn't happen often. Desertion seems an even more remote possibility.

Rogers forwarded Harris' report to the adjutant general. On March 10, 1894, Mabry instructed Harris to withdraw from Menard County. "But" he added, "if subsequent information points otherwise you may remain some time longer & follow up any clue which may present itself."

It could be that Woods became convinced that a thief could realize more than the $30 a month the state paid Ranger privates and decided to throw in with the outlaws. Or maybe he came to understand that his work had placed his life in danger and opted in the interest of longevity simply to disappear. But the odds are that the gang he had infiltrated figured out he was a Ranger and killed him.

Harris asked for a little more time on the case and Mabry granted his request, but the Archives contain no more correspondence on the matter. No one ever claimed Woods' pay checks, which totaled $180. On March 1, 1899, someone with the Adjutant General's Department in Austin made this notation in the payroll records of Company E Ranger J.W. Woods:

"Pay accts for Aug 30 & Nov 30, 1893 filed by Capt. J.H. Rogers. These pay certificates were never cashed because Woods was murdered somewhere at Ft. McKavitt [sic] and his body was never found and never heard from."

CASE CLOSED...MAYBE

The story of Ranger James Woods' disappearance and presumed murder didn't make the public prints for more than a quarter century.

The first known account of the mystery appeared on Oct. 23, 1925, when a reporter for the Dallas Morning News interviewed Ira L. Wheat, who'd served as Edwards County sheriff from 1883 to 1896.

Wheat, in Big D to attend the State Fair, said he and other sheriffs had tried for years to break up a large gang of horse thieves who operated from west of Austin all the way down the Balcones Fault to the Rio Grande.

"They covered a territory about 300 miles in length by 100 to 150 miles in width," Wheat said. "The gang in each county passed its roundups to the gang in the adjoining county. They operated by night and were back home by daylight."

Though Wheat said the outlaws stole horses, it's hard to imagine they did not occasionally appropriate cattle that did not belong to them. Bold as they were as thieves, Wheat continued, "It was not their idea to fight the rangers and the sheriffs. They depended on outwitting us, and this they succeeded in doing for about 12 years."

Finally, Wheat and fellow sheriffs W.H. Baylor of Uvalde County and Dick Russell of Menard County "decided to put among the thieves a man of our own."

They had a hard time finding someone willing to take the chance, he continued, but "a volunteer came forward, one of those fellows who are born without the fear bump, who live on excitement and set little value on their own lives."

The undercover Ranger, Wheat said, "Put us in possession of evidence on which we secured 37 convictions and made things so unsafe for the rest of the horse thieves that they disbanded. But, as we predicted, they got our man. We never heard exactly what befell him, but it was easy to conjecture."

While Wheat did not say who the "man of our own" had been, his old friend former Sheriff Baylor did so a few years later: Ranger Woods.

Baylor recalled in a 1930 article that in about 1888 a man walked into his Uvalde office saying he would like to help catch stock thieves. The man gave his name as J.W. Woods but declined to discuss his past. Though suspicious he might be a horse thief himself, Baylor decided to give him a chance. When Woods brought him information that led to several indictments, the sheriff realized he had made a good choice and eventually lobbied the Adjutant General to commission Woods as a Ranger.

Woods worked undercover in Uvalde, Edwards, Kimble and Menard counties and probably others, helping make numerous cases. Playing his role as a gang member to the hilt, the Ranger even rode a train to Chicago with a shipment of stolen cattle. He returned via the Atchison, Topeka and Santa Fe to Ballinger, but no one ever saw him again, Baylor wrote.

The old sheriff's story does not entirely track Wheat's recollection, or the scenario hinted at in the sketchy records in the Archives, but his version seems plausible enough. Ballinger is only 59 miles from Menard, where the Rangers last had any contact with Woods.

Baylor went to his grave believing that the disappearance of the undercover lawman had been the handiwork of a suspected horse thief named James Lafferty.

On Sept. 20, 1892, Lafferty shot and killed one Benjamin Maples in Uvalde County. A grand jury indicted him for second-degree murder, but he made a $5,000 bond and was on the ground during the time frame of Woods' disappearance. Lafferty stood trial in mid-July 1893 and on August 1 received a 75-year prison sentence. Baylor later said that one "Jim L." wrote him from Huntsville with an offer to lead him to Woods' remains if the sheriff could arrange for his release from prison. However, neither the district attorney nor the governor would go for the deal. Eventually, once Lafferty understood he had no hope of getting out of the joint, Baylor sweet-talked the inmate into drawing a map showing where Woods' body could be found.

The sheriff didn't find anything and wrote Lafferty to ask for more details. The inmate replied that Woods' body must have been moved from where it had originally been dumped. Not long after writing that letter, Lafferty died Sept. 12, 1896, of heart failure.

Baylor continued the story: "Several years passed and I was notified that a skull and one leg bone had been found some 10 miles from where Woods' remains were supposed to be. The leg bone had a boot and spur on it."

Someone carried the booted femur to Rocksprings, where the Edwards County sheriff contacted Baylor. Baylor traveled to Rocksprings to examine the grisly find and recognized the boot and spur as having belonged to Woods.

Though Baylor believed others had been involved in the case, he wrote: "I am sure L. killed Woods."

Leakey cowgirl poet, writer and lay historian Linda Kirkpatrick grew up hearing stories about a Ranger having been killed and dropped into a geologic feature in Real County that not surprisingly came to be called Dead Man's Cave. Unfortunately, the Dry Frio Canyon country is full of caves and sinkholes, and she has not yet pinned down where Woods' bones were found. Nor has she been able to find any record of Woods' remains being buried at Rocksprings.

And while she has no reason to doubt Baylor's story of Woods' demise and his belief that Lafferty was the triggerman, Kirkpatrick offers up another possible suspect—Sarge Cummings. Another character who threw a long loop, Sarge once dodged a Ranger by riding his horse across the Pecos River High Bridge.

No matter who killed Woods, Kirkpatrick hopes to someday find where Woods' remains ended up and see a Former Texas Rangers Association memorial cross placed at the site. She figures a Ranger "born without the fear bump" deserves some recognition after all these years.

JUSTIFIABLE HOMICIDE OR JUST PLAIN MURDER?

John Leakey went to his grave believing a Texas Ranger murdered his father.

No one ever disputed that it was a bullet fired by Ranger Charles Trentham that killed Mack Leakey in Marfa. The issue was whether the death was a justifiable homicide or just plain murder.

"So far as I could ever find out," Leakey's still bitter son said years later, "[my father] was killed because he had talked too much about the failure of the government and the Rangers to stop the rustling of livestock north of the border...After the killing Trentham simply rode across the border. Tom Patterson, also living in Marfa at the time, then complained about that. The next day another Ranger killed him. Neither man was ever arrested—they just rode across the Rio Grande and stayed until things cooled off."

Leakey had been a sheriff's deputy in Uvalde County, serving under outlaw-turned-lawman King Fisher. When someone shot and killed Fisher and his friend Ben Thompson in a San Antonio theater, Leakey was out of a job and moved west to Marfa.

Even in 1884, a Ranger could not get away with killing someone because they held an opinion, unless their line of thinking involved gunplay.

If Leakey was correct in remembering that his father's death occurred in 1884, Trentham was not even a Ranger at the time. Trentham joined the Rangers Sept. 1, 1881, serving for a year in Co. E under Capt. C.L. Nevill. But his old boss was elected sheriff of Presidio County in November 1882, so Trentham might have been a deputy at the time.

Years later, Presidio County old-timer Robert Ellison remembered that "Only one man was killed in Marfa in those days (the mid-1880s)—a Texas Ranger killed a...bartender named Leakey." No other details are found in a near-encyclopedic two-volume history of Presidio County by Cecilia Thompson.

The Masonic Lodge in the Uvalde County community of Leakey buried the former deputy and presented his widow with $600. The man's son claimed he got a photograph of the Ranger and carried it for years. "I hoped to meet up with him someday—and when I did I meant to see that justice was done."

Leakey's vow to kill the Ranger who killed his father, a variation of a common plot line in Western fiction, never came to pass. Whatever the true circumstances of Mack Leakey's death, his son's reaction showed that not everyone bought into the image of Texas' Rangers always being straight shooters in both senses of the term.

"There were two kinds of Texas Rangers," Leakey told Nellie Snyder Yost, the author who helped him with his 1958 autobiography, The West That Was, From Texas to Montana. "One breed was not a credit to Texas. I'll always be sorry I wasn't lucky enough to meet up with the one who killed my father."

'DON'T SHOOT NO MORE. I'M DEAD!'

On May 6, 1886, an Austin Daily Statesman reporter made his daily news-gathering rounds in the temporary capitol at 11th and Congress, just across the street from the present red granite Capitol then under construction.

One of the journalist's everyday stops was the office of Adjutant General Wilburn H. King. At the time, the Adjutant General's Department oversaw the operation of the state's militia (forerunner of the Texas National Guard) and the Rangers of the Frontier Battalion.

When the unnamed Statesman scribe walked into the Adjutant General's office he asked King if anything was going on.

"No, there is nothing today," the general replied. "But stop a moment and look at this testimony of the prowess and efficiency of the Frontier Battalion."

Then King handed the journalist a Colt double-action .44. When the reporter examined the firearm, he saw that the grips had been shattered into several fragments.

As the reporter hefted the handgun, King told him that the weapon had belonged to an accused killer that Company D Private Ira Aten and other Rangers had been trailing for months. In the gunfight that erupted when Aten finally caught up with the man, the Ranger shot the pistol out of the suspect's hand. The slug that disintegrated the weapon's handle also removed one of the wanted man's fingers. Despite his wound, the man had managed to escape on horseback. Then King showed the doubtless wide-eyed reporter a sweat-stained cowboy hat that the suspect also lost in his hasty departure.

When the reporter completed his rounds and returned to the newspaper, he devoted only 19 lines of type to his recent show-and-tell experience.

But there's a much bigger tale to tell.

The story begins in the Hill Country town of Fredericksburg on Sept. 3, 1884, and almost two years would pass before the final chapter ended in gunfire. In the process, the chain of events that began that September day would significantly influence Ranger history.

In 1884, only 38 years after the first German immigrants arrived, Fredericksburg residents—or visitors—had no shortage of beer-drinking venues to choose from. The last-chance beer stop for outbound travelers stood just off the unpaved two-rut road that is now U.S. 290 and just west of the old north-south trace known as the Pinta Trail. It was a combination biergarten, arbor-covered dance floor and grocery owned by John Wolfgang Braeutigam, a much-liked first generation German Texan. Born in Germany on March 17, 1829, Braeutigam was 55 years old. He and his wife Christine had been married 34 years and had eight living children.

Braeutigam purchased the 640-acre tract where in 1848 the military had established Fort Martin Scott. The army had abandoned the post in 1853 and after that the acreage lay fallow until Braeutigam bought the property. The new owner turned the old post guardhouse, a stone structure which still stands, into his family home and made a living farming the land.

Starting in 1881, Braeutigam gave the newly organized Gillespie County Fair permission to use his property for the annual gathering. The fair also featured horse races and other crowd-pleasing activities. At about the same time, he opened what became known as Braeutigam's Garten. Soon it was one of the most popular places in the county to enjoy conviviality and a brew.

On the third day of September 1884 four men who appeared to be cowboys rode up to the biergarten, tied their horses and walked in to order drinks. When they finished their beer, instead of asking for another round, one of the men drew a pistol and told Braeutigam they wanted his money.

The proprietor might have been willing to let the men run a tab, but he wasn't about to hand over his proceeds. Instead, he grabbed a rifle. But before Braeutigam could get off a shot, the man who'd done the talking put a bullet into the German's head. After emptying the cash box, the robbers rushed to their horses and galloped off.

Braeutigam's 10-year-old son Henry heard the gunshot and ran to the bar, finding his father lying in a pool of blood, already dead.

Someone notified four-term Sheriff John Walter, who hurried to the scene. While it was plain enough what had happened, the only evidence the robbers left behind other than the victim's body were their empty mugs, boot prints and horse tracks. Deep impressions indicative of fast-running horses led from the biergarten to the nearby Pedernales River.

The sheriff quickly assembled a posse and wired Austin seeking Ranger assistance. Then local officers followed the suspect's trail along the Pedernales to its junction with the Colorado River about 10 miles east of Johnson City. From there, the river flows into Travis County. And judging from the tracks, it looked like that's where the fugitives had gone to ground.

Fredericksburg is only 65 miles from San Antonio, but news of the murder did not make the San Antonio Light until September 27.

The Alamo City newspaper said authorities believed a man named Jim Fannin and two others it identified only as "Collier" and "Sylvester" had perpetrated the crime. The short article also reported that the state had offered a $200 reward for anyone who brought the suspects to the Gillespie County Jail. The county had sweetened the pot by offering an additional $1,500 for the trio. The name "Sylvester" never appeared again in connection with the case. In all likelihood no such person had been involved in the robbery-murder.

Scouting sparsely populated northwestern Travis County, Rangers began asking area ranchers if they knew any men who could have been involved in the Fredericksburg crime. Soon lawmen had the names of three characters—known habitues of horse-racing venues—said to be perfectly capable of the crime: William (Bill) Allison, Jackson (Jack) Beam and C.W. (Wesley) Collier.

Ranger Ira Aten, destined to become one of Texas' most famous lawmen, soon reported to headquarters: "We rounded up their houses at night at two different places and caught them in bed." Aten later described the trio as "just bad country boys, starting out being bad."

On Oct. 5, 1884, ranger Corporal P.C. Baird lodged the three suspects in the Gillespie County Jail, a sturdy limestone lockup with a wooden interior and cells made of locally forged iron. At their arraignment, the judge denied bond and bound Allison, Beam and Collier over to the grand jury.

But given the aroused state of the locals, the Rangers thought it best to take the prisoners to San Antonio, where Bexar County had recently opened what elected officials bragged was an "escape proof jail." To the embarrassment of Bexar County officials, the trio of murder suspects soon dug their way out of the Alamo City's not-so-escape-proof lockup.

Back on their trail again, Ranger Aten soon found Allison in Oatmanville, a small community west of Austin on the Fredericksburg road. This time, rather than take him back to San Antonio, Aten returned the suspect to the Gillespie County jail.

About daybreak the following morning, fire gutted the 10-year-old jail, killing its only occupant—the accused murderer. Whether the fire was accidental, caused by Allison during an escape attempt or was set by a person or persons unknown has never been determined. Years later, when Aten wrote his memoir, he noted, "This building almost immediately and mysteriously burned down upon the prisoner." In a newspaper article published only 22 months after the murder, Aten theorized that the fire had been set by Allison's fellow defendants "so that it would be impossible for him to weaken and turn state's evidence."

A history of Fredericksburg published in 1896 noted, "The real cause of the fire is not known, but it is assumed that somehow while the prisoner was reading the oil lamp caused the conflagration."

In late September, a year after Braeutigam's murder, Rangers recaptured Collier and Beam near Flatonia in Fayette County. Sheriff Walton picked them up in New Braunfels and took them back to Gillespie County. But since he didn't have a jail, he booked them into the Mason County Jail. Unfortunately, in January 1886, the two murder suspects succeeded in breaking out of that lockup.

Once again, the Rangers started beating the brush for the pair. And soon politics entered the picture. Gov. John Ireland was popular with German Texan voters, and he wanted to keep it that way. The governor ordered the young Ranger to concentrate solely on capturing the two escapees.

To that end, Aten learned as much as he could about the fugitives. He reasoned that Beam intended to leave the state but first would want to say goodbye to his sister, who lived in northwestern Travis County. With two citizen volunteers, Aten staked out the house, observing it with binoculars from a nearby hill.

On the second day, Beam rode up and hitched his horse outside the house. When night fell, Aten and the other two men crept closer to the residence. The Ranger concealed himself in the barn while his two helpers took positions outside.

Around 9 p.m., a man carrying a saddle walked into the dark barn. Aten kept still as the figure drew closer. Suddenly the Ranger stood, poked the barrel of his revolver into the man's belly and said, "Hands up, Jack."

Not of a mind to surrender, Beam dropped the saddle and made a play for his six-shooter. Aten described what happened next in his memoir:

"...I threw my left hand over...his right wrist and pushed down... hard as I could to keep him from pulling his six-shooter, at the same time saying, 'If you pull it, Jack, I'll kill you. I'll kill you if you pull it."

Hearing this, Aten's two posse men rushed into the barn and helped the Ranger subdue and handcuff the suspect.

The next day, March 24, 1886, Aten returned Beam to Gillespie County. On the way, the prisoner admitted he had indeed planned to rendezvous with Collier and leave Texas. Beam also confirmed that the fourth participant in the robbery-murder had indeed been Jim Fannin.

For the next month, Aten focused on finding Collier and Fannin. He had no luck with Fannin but made progress in his quest for Collier. On April 29, Aten stopped at the George Wells ranch in Travis County. Wells was casually acquainted with Collier but happy to help Aten in finding the fugitive.

While the Ranger and Wells sat on the rancher's front porch discussing the matter, a rider appeared in the distance. "I believe that's your man," Wells said. Through his binoculars Aten saw that the horseman wore a large red bandana which he appeared to be using as a sling for his right arm.

As the rider drew closer, Aten recognized Collier. The Ranger had already ducked inside the ranch house and stood waiting for the fugitive to ride up. As the horseman asked Wells for directions to another ranch, the Ranger bolted through the door and yelled, "Hands up, Wesley Collier!"

Still not inclined to give up, Collier quickly withdrew his arm from what turned out to be a fake sling and revealed the revolver he'd concealed. The suspect fired at Aten but missed. The Ranger got off a shot that hit the outlaw's gun and wounded his hand. Then Collier spurred his horse to flee. Not taking time to mount up, Aten ran after him and fired again. The bullet would have hit the fugitive if he hadn't ducked to miss a low-hanging limb. Instead, the Ranger's .44 slug tore into the tree and Collier galloped away, having lost his hat in the process.

By then too late in the day to trail the outlaw, Aten spent the night at Wells' place. The rancher told Aten that a fellow who owned a horse ranch near Liberty Hill might be able to assist him in the search. His name was John Hughes.

Many a Western lawman got into what today is referred to as an "officer-involved shooting." However, an officer engaging in a gunfight with the same person twice was practically unheard of and still is. But on May 25, 1886, Ranger Aten got a rematch with Wesley Collier. As the Austin Daily Statesman reported the following day:

Adjutant General King received a telephone message from Liberty Hill yesterday morning, Private Ira Aten, Company D, Frontier Battalion, sending the message to the effect that [Aten], *in attempting to arrest a man named Collier, the supposed murderer of old man Braeutigam, at Fredericksburg, killed Collier, while forcibly resisting arrest.*

That's a long, poorly constructed sentence with scant details. Frontier Battalion records, Aten's memoir and other sources tell the story better.

Per Wells' suggestion, Aten had ridden to Hughes' ranch and Hughes agreed to assist him in his search. Believing he'd wounded Collier with the shot that hit the fugitive's six-shooter, Aten and Hughes rode to interrogate the nearest physician. At first reluctant to discuss a patient's medical history, the doc finally admitted he'd treated Collier's injured gun hand. But he didn't know where Collier had gone after leaving his office.

Hughes returned to his ranch work while Aten continued to scout the area. On May 22, Aten learned that Collier, no matter that he was married, had been seeing a young lady who lived with her parents in the area. He had told her, and her family, that his name was Wes Martin. And they had believed him.

Aten re-recruited Hughes and they began watching the house. On the third day of their stakeout, they saw Collier riding toward the residence. Having spent the night in the brush, early the next morning (May 25) Aten sneaked into the house through the back door while Hughes guarded the front door.

Amazingly, before Collier's girlfriend and her parents realized what was happening, Aten found Collier sitting on a bed putting his boots on. Seeing Aten, Collier pulled a six-shooter from beneath his pillow and raised it with both hands. Unfortunately for the wanted man, Aten was quicker. "Knowing that the game was death for one of us, I fired," the Ranger later reported. His shot hit the fugitive in the heart.

"Not knowing the effect of my shot," he continued, "as Collier still held to his pistol, I was cocking my own to fire again when he called out in a faint tone, 'Oh! Oh! Don't shoot no more. I'm dead!' " And indeed, he was.

Aten left Hughes at the scene and rode to Liberty Hill to notify Austin that the case against Collier had been referred to a higher court. Not long after this incident, Hughes trailed a gang of horse thieves from his ranch in Williamson County to New Mexico. He returned with his horses, having killed two of the rustlers and capturing the others.

Gillespie County authorities and the Rangers believed Collier had been the one who shot Braeutigam. With Allison and Collier dead, and Beam in jail, only Jim Fannin remained at large. But the Rangers never found him.

What impact did this case have on the Rangers? Aten was so impressed with the way Hughes had conducted himself, not to mention his exploits in New Mexico, he suggested that the 31-year-old rancher join the Rangers.

Hughes took him up on it and within the decade rose from private to corporal to sergeant and finally, captain. He went on to become one of the so-called Four Great Ranger Captains of the late 19th century and early 20th century. Not only was Hughes a skilled tracker, he was good with a gun. (Something he proved several times during his law-enforcement career.) And he was a straight shooter in the moral since. Beyond that, he was smart and tenacious. Revered by his men, Hughes did his job well and fairly. In the process, he enhanced the reputation of the Rangers, a force he saw transition from horseback Rangers to Rangers who rode in automobiles.

Much is known about Hughes, but questions linger concerning Braeutigam's murder:

- What happened to Jack Beam? Regardless of how his case played out, one thing is for sure: He did not hang for the crime. In fact, Gillespie County never had a legal hanging.
- How much money did the robbers escape with? Was any of it ever recovered?
- What specifically led officers to believe that Allison, Beam, Collier and Fannin were the killers?

Beyond following their tracks, it may have been their propensity for gambling. In his book Hard-Riding Ranger, a biography of Aten, Bob Alexander mentions a manuscript by an unknown author that is owned by Western historian Chuck Parsons. That document says Collier and his associates were known racetrack bettors. There's also a suggestion in the manuscript that Collier had lost big the day before he killed Braeutigam and that in robbing him he was merely trying to get his money back.

• What happened to the handgun Collier lost in his first gunfight with Aten? Not only would the revolver make for an interesting museum piece, more than likely it was the murder weapon.

• What about Jim Fannin? Given that only one of the other prime suspects had adopted an alias—Collier going by "Martin"—Jim Fannin well could have been the fugitive's righteous name.

If the wanted man stuck with his real name, a short article published in the Fort Worth Daily Gazette Dec. 19, 1888—more than four years after the Fredericksburg murder—offers at least circumstantial evidence that Fannin remained in Texas, unreformed. Here's what the newspaper reported:

For several months… a party of desperate characters have been terrorizing the citizens of the northern part of [Fannin County] *along Red River. They have been going armed, threatening violence to peaceable citizens and defying the officers. A posse of officers met a part of the gang last night, among whom were Jim Fannin and Ennis Dixon, two well-known characters, and attempted their arrest. The hoodlums fled.*

An outlaw named Jim Fannin did make the newspapers one more time, a decade after Braeutigam's murder. That came in an item the Galveston Daily News reprinted from the Austin Evening News. The Capital City newspaper had noted that the city had recently extended Sabine Street through a wagon yard that had been in business since 1876. Routine as that sounds, the article's unknown writer had tried to inject a bit of humor that even then must have seemed pretty lame:

Wesley Hardin [notorious outlaw John Wesley Hardin] *never saw the* [wagon] *yard in his life, nor did the wild and woolly desperado Scott Cooley* [a former Ranger] *and Jim Fannin—whoever the mischief they are—ever squat behind a poker hand in the yard.*

While this was written in 1894, a decade after the Braeutigam murder, whoever wrote the piece may have remembered the

Fredericksburg case. That or Fannin had continued his lawless ways into the 1890s. But if he did, his exploits were not reported in Texas.

Findagrave.com lists a James David Fannin who died in Anderson County Feb. 14, 1931, and was buried in Palestine, the county seat. He was born on Christmas Day 1855 in Alabama, which would have made him 29 at the time of the robbery-murder. On the other hand, in 1884 he was already married and had three children. So, while possible, this Jim Fannin having had anything to do with the Gillespie County case is a long shot.

As big a deal as it was in Gillespie County, from a statewide perspective the murder of Braeutigam was just another of many major crimes committed in Texas in 1884. Still, the case reveals a lot about the late 19th century Texas Rangers.

• First, it shows that the Rangers, especially when they enjoyed the full cooperation of local citizens, other officers, and the judiciary, had become pretty effective in bringing bad guys to justice, especially considering that the force operated without the availability of even rudimentary forensic technology.

• Second, it demonstrates that the taxpayers of Texas got their money's worth in other ways when it came to the Rangers. Members of the Frontier Battalion worked hard for their $30 or so a month. They rode hundreds of miles (often alone), worked long hours and occasionally, some got shot at. And sometimes, they got killed.

• Third, this case certainly shows that in the 19th century there existed ample room for improvement in regard to the state's county jails. Two different jails proved unreliable—the lockups in San Antonio and Mason—and one ended up being a fire trap. Amazingly, 91 years passed before the Legislature created the Texas Commission on Jail Standards in 1975.

• Finally, the facts of this case make it plain that taking on a Ranger in a gunfight is never smart.

HE WASN'T A COWARD AFTER ALL

O. H. Finch first saw the Texas Panhandle in 1892 from the caboose of a freight train hauling two cars of bulls from Burlingame, Kansas, to his father's ranch in Donley County, the Bar Ninety-Six.

Reaching Panhandle City on the Atchison, Topeka & Santa Fe, the 12-year-old Finch and his father took the Fort Worth and Denver train to Washburn. From there, they rode to Salisbury, the nearest post office to the vast Finch ranch.

More than a half century later, the younger Finch wrote about his experiences in a now scarce, self-published family history, The Lives and Times of a Family Named Finch. In his book, he told of an incident that convinced him Texas remained the Wild West.

When their train stopped for breakfast at Clarendon, Finch and his father walked from the depot to a restaurant across the street. As they ate, Finch recalled, "My eyes popped open wide when a man stepped out of this place with two guns, one hanging on either side. It was Jim Green, sheriff of the county." (Elected Nov. 4, 1890, Green actually served as Precinct 2 constable.)

Finch had never seen, as he put it, "a wild and woolly Texan." Then 36, Green had dark hair, brown eyes and a dark complexion. He stood 6 feet. His hat, boots and the fact that he had once ridden as a Texas Ranger made him seem ever taller to the boy from Kansas.

But Green's career as a state lawman had gotten off to a shaky start.

"When he with other Rangers got into his first encounter with law breakers, and the shooting started, he could not stand the gaff, and he broke and ran," Finch wrote, crediting the story to Will Beverly, the 1890s foreman of the Rowe Ranch in Donley County. "His fellow Rangers chided him, but they knew he wasn't a coward."

Indeed, Green asked for another chance to "show that he could take it." When that next opportunity came, the young Ranger "shut both his eyes and began to shoot."

To what extent shooting blind affected his marksmanship went unsaid, but the Ranger survived the encounter and "proved his mettle many times afterwards."

Green served in the Rangers for 18 months, leaving effective Aug. 31, 1882. He had worked under Co. B Capt. George Washington Arrington and later for Co. C Capt. Sam McMurry. After leaving the Rangers, he stayed in law enforcement, though it's unclear where he wore a badge prior to his election in Clarendon.

Finch didn't recall the date in his book, but on July 5, 1892, the former Ranger got one last chance to prove that he had long since stiffened his backbone when it came to doing his job as a peace officer.

That came when the Bell boys—Bob, Gene and Wally—arrived in Clarendon on the morning train. The three brothers were, as Finch characterized them, "notorious gamblers in Amarillo." And they had a standing grudge against the former Ranger.

In a scene later repeated in many a Western movie, the three hardcases removed themselves to one of the town's saloons and began boozing it up. The boys made no attempt to conceal their identity. In fact, they let it be known, as county singer Marty Robbins sang decades later in his classic ballad "Big Iron," there was an ex-Ranger who "wouldn't be too long in town."

When Green walked into the saloon that morning, Finch wrote, "the shooting began."

The ex-Ranger, no longer needing to work his pistol with his eyes closed, put a bullet into one of the Bells before another of the brothers shot him. From the wooden floor, the dying Green shot again and killed another of the brothers. Now only Wally still stood, and he found it expedient to vacate the saloon.

"This caused a lot of excitement since three men were killed before breakfast," Finch understated.

A Donley County history published in 1975 devotes only two paragraphs to the shooting but tells the story a little differently:

"Green and the Bells had some trouble over Green's shooting Bill Bell in May of that year and the brothers called his hand. All three drew and fired. Robert Bell fell dead, but Eugene shot Green. Another unforeseen fatality occurred when a stranger who had just arrived on the early morning train entered the swinging doors of the saloon just in time to catch a stray bullet and was killed instantly."

That man was George Bingham Grissom, a Texas and Southwestern Cattle Raisers Association inspector. Born in Tennessee in 1858,

Grissom came with his family to Denton County as a youngster. Following his death in Clarendon, his body was shipped to Denton County for burial in the Bolivar Cemetery at Sanger.

The final resting place of the ex-Ranger who overcame his fear of gun play only to die with his boots on has not been located. Neither has the grave of the man he killed.

AT LEAST HE GOT A NICE FUNERAL

Whoever he was, he got a nice funeral.

Texas Ranger James W. Fulgham and Reeves County sheriff's deputy George P. Leakey left Pecos, Texas, in the summer of 1893 for a ride down the Pecos River to look for horse thieves or fugitives.

After an easy-paced 13-mile scout, the two lawmen camped for the night near Emigrant's Crossing, one of the river's two principal fords. The next morning, August 24, they continued their trek southward along the snake-like river.

Not long after swinging into their saddles, Fulgham and Leakey noticed a solitary cowboy leading a packhorse following them at some distance. Wanting a closer look at the man, the officers slowed their horses to a walk, assuming the rider would overtake them. But when they slowed, the cowboy behind them slowed as well.

Wondering why the rider didn't seem interested in company, the officers reined their horses, dismounted and waited for the stranger to catch up. When he did, he rode right by with not so much as a "Howdy, gents," or a tug of his hat brim.

At that, Fulgham and Leakey quickly remounted and trotted to catch up, flanking him on both sides. Observing that the unfriendly horseman wore a pistol, the deputy identified himself and asked the man if he was an officer.

"I have been," he said, not elaborating.

Leakey shot a few more questions in his direction.

"He answered all questions…in an abrupt and surly manner," the Pecos News reported a few days later. "His actions were those of a fugitive from justice."

If nothing else, the man was breaking the law by openly carrying a pistol. On top of that, the stranger's demeanor was suspicious.

"Jim," the deputy told the Ranger, "we will go to Pecos and take this man with us."

Hearing that, the solitary rider dropped the reins on his packhorse and reached for his revolver. The two officers yelled for the rider to throw up his hands but instead he raised his six-shooter.

The Ranger must have focused on the cowboy's Colt, because his first bullet pierced the non-communicative rider's gun hand. White smoke from that round blew into Fulgham's eyes, but aiming by instinct, he pulled the trigger again. This time a .45 slug slammed into the stranger's chest and knocked him off his horse.

"By God, boys," the cowboy said, raising up on one arm. Then he slumped down, dead. The officers left the body where it lay and rode to Pecos to summon Reeves County Sheriff G.A. Frazier. The sheriff and Ranger Lon Oden accompanied the other two officers back to the scene, where Oden picked up the dead cowboy's gun and found it only half-cocked. Then they loaded the body on the dead man's horse and brought him back to Pecos.

About all the cowpoke had to his name was a Colt revolver (one black grip, one white grip), a letter with the signature torn off and a memorandum book bearing the name Charles Carral, Suggs, I.T. (Indian Territory) and the date May 3, 1893.

"Started to work for the flying E. Cow Co.," one entry in his notebook said. Reading the letter they'd found, the officers noted one line giving credence to the officers' belief that the cowboy had been a wanted man: "I would like to be back on the old creek, but you know I can't come."

The doctor who examined the body measured him at 5 feet, 10 inches, guessed his weight at about 160 pounds and noted he had grey eyes. The man looked to be about 23.

"Messrs. Fulgham and Lackey [sic] regret the occurrence very much," the Pecos newspaper continued, "but from what we can learn from the facts of the case, we feel certain that they did nothing more than their duty required."

The El Paso Times on September 10 published a six-line report contradicting the Pecos newspaper's statement:

"It is now said that the young man killed near Pecos City by Ranger J.W. Fulgham was... an innocent cowboy well known and liked about Fort Stockton."

While "Corral" is a legitimate—if unusual surname—it also could have been a rustler's clever alias. Still not absolutely certain that Corral was the man's righteous last name, Sheriff Frazier saw to it that the unknown rider got "a nice suit of clothes" and had him "buried in a quiet and genteel way, Rev. J.E. Sawders officiating."

Meanwhile, as per routine, the district attorney filed on the Ranger for murder with the deputy charged as an accessory. Tried November 3 that year, Fulgham was acquitted by the jury after only 12 minutes' deliberation. Leakey was acquitted the following day.

Despite his acquittal, establishing his innocence cost the Ranger $250 in legal fees—roughly half his annual salary. His lawyer wanted some of that money upfront, compelling Fulgham to borrow $75 with his horse as collateral. He signed a $150 personal note for the rest of the money. Even though killing the cowboy had been done in the line of duty, the Adjutant General's department would not reimburse the Ranger for his legal bill.

The mystery cowboy was dead and buried and the two officers exonerated, but 15 months after the shooting the case briefly came back to life. The occasion was an indignant editorial in the Capital City's afternoon paper, the Daily Statesman.

"IS CIVIL OR MILITARY LAW PARAMOUNT IN TEXAS?" read a one-column headline over a wordy and not well organized six-paragraph screed published in February 1895. The piece began by quoting the 52-word summary of the Reeves County shooting that had been included in the Adjutant General's Department just-released biennial report.

Calling the state's brief account of the killing "very unsatisfactory," the nameless writer opened fire on the Rangers with lead type.

"The inquiry is natural, after reading this [summary]..., whether military or civil law is dominant in Texas," the Statesman scribe began. "It is very evident that this deputy sheriff and Private Fulgham...had no warrant for the arrest of [the] man...killed by Fulgham, nor does it appear that this man knew they were officers."

Obviously unaware that the Ranger had been acquitted, the writer said it would be interesting to know if Fulgham had been tried for homicide "of one degree or another" in connection with Pecos River shooting. Had the case gone to court, the writer opined, "a jury would in all probability conclude that it was murder in the first degree."

MISTLETOE FOR THE LADY

With four years' service as a Frontier Battalion Ranger under his belt, Jefferson Davis (Jeff) Milton for a time rode the rails as a Southern Pacific passenger train conductor.

One day in 1889, when his train stopped downriver from El Paso at Ysleta, Milton stepped off to stretch his legs. As he looked around, he noticed an attractive young woman. He'd caught her eye as well.

Sashaying in his direction, she pointed to a tall mesquite tree with a cluster of desert mistletoe at the top.

"Oh," she flirted, "I wish I could have some of that mistletoe."

A bachelor ever open to female companionship, Milton looked where she pointed. Sure enough, he saw a clump of the parasitic berry-bearing plant clinging to a high branch.

"Why, ma'am, if I had my gun, I'd shoot it out of there for you," the conductor said politely. Nearby stood Co. D Ranger John H. Hughes, only two years into his long and distinguished career as a state lawman. He often checked arriving trains to see if any wanted person or suspicious looking character alighted.

"Here, use my gun," the Ranger said to the railroad man. Clearly, he figured the conductor either would decline his offer or proceed to make a fool of himself by blasting away and missing.

Milton said much obliged, took the six-shooter and with one quick shot dropped the mistletoe onto the dusty hardpack.

"Why, son, you ought to be a Texas Ranger," the impressed lawman said. "I've been a Ranger already," Milton replied.

He sure had. Serving in the Frontier Battalion from 1878 to 1882, he'd killed one man in the line of duty and as a lawman of various stripes would kill again. Five years after the trackside mistletoe incident, Milton took the oath of office as El Paso's police chief. He and Hughes, by then Co. D captain, worked together almost daily and became lifelong friends.

The teller of the mistletoe tale was longtime Hudspeth County Sheriff Dogie Wright, one of legendary Capt. Will Wright's six sons. The recently retired West Texas sheriff, who served as a Ranger from 1918 to 1924 had known both men well.

"Jeff Milton was the most polite fellow you'd ever meet anywhere," Wright said in an interview not long after his retirement. "He'd just bow and scrape." But if necessary, Wright added, "He'd kill you in a minute." Or shoot down some mistletoe for a young lady.

THE POISONING PARSON

Six-foot, six-inch W.S.J. Sullivan made an excellent choice as the man to spend the night with the Rev. George E. Morrison.

For sure, the tall ex-Ranger and the preacher would have plenty to talk about. Sullivan believed in God and knew the scriptures. But newly elected Wilbarger County Sheriff J.T. Williams had a second consideration in mind when he asked for Sullivan's help: Having the big lawman in Morrison's cell would prevent any further trouble prior to the disgraced cleric's scheduled execution.

Sullivan, who served as a Frontier Battalion Ranger variously from 1889 to 1896, arrived in Vernon by train the morning of Oct. 26, 1899. The following day, the sheriff intended to carry out the district court's order that Morrison "hang by the neck until dead" for the murder of his wife.

Tried in Vernon on a change of venue from Carson County, the preacher had been convicted of poisoning his wife with strychnine on Oct. 10, 1897, so that he could take up with another woman. A few hours before killing his wife Morrison had delivered to his Panhandle City congregation an impassioned sermon based on the Biblical injunction that, "For the wages of sin is death."

A few days before Sullivan arrived at the county seat, the condemned preacher—who had steadfastly proclaimed his innocence—tried with two other prisoners to break out of jail. As one of the would-be escapees struggled with the jailer, who'd been attacked while serving the prisoners food, Morrison yelled: "Kill the jailer!"

Unfortunately for the preacher, news of his violent attempted escape reached Austin just as Morrison's sister knelt before the governor begging for commutation of her brother's death sentence. Sayers believed that a man of the cloth capable of breaking the most important of the 10 Commandments stood beyond redemption. Sheriff Williams soon received a telegram directing him to proceed with the execution.

Sullivan stood in the cell with Morrison when the sheriff read the prisoner the message from Austin. When Williams finished the telegram, Morrison accepted that "all had been done that was possible" and said he "guessed" he "would have to take it."

The condemned preacher had taken a liking to the lanky former Ranger. He told Sullivan he could have his suspenders and a matchbox as keepsakes. Also, at Sullivan's request, Morrison wrote him a letter.

Admitting he did not know quite what to say, Morrison nevertheless endeavored to be accommodating. He wrote out a four-paragraph letter, expressing his belief in an afterlife and noting that while "men are punished for the sins of this life" they "are rewarded for the good things." The preacher's second major point was that "though God allow man's law to take my life, yet he saves me, and of the future I have no fears whatever."

Though comfortable that he had made his peace with God, the next morning Morrison requested something he figured would make the transition to his "future life" a bit easier: A quart of whiskey.

At noon, with a prayer on his lips and liquor on his breath, Morrison stood on the trap- door of the scaffold erected for the occasion outside the county jail and addressed the large crowd which had come from miles around to see him hang. Sullivan stood nearby, looking on approvingly.

"A few minutes later [at 12:45 p.m.] his body dropped through the trapdoor and his neck was broken," Sullivan later wrote.

A doctor pronounced Morrison dead at 1:08 p.m. Six minutes later a deputy cut down his body for burial at the expense of the county. Though the preacher went to an unmarked grave, he had the distinction of being the first and last man ever legally hanged in Wilbarger County. Sullivan had left the Rangers shortly before the Panhandle murder, but he knew the details well. "The world is full of tragedies," the former

Ranger philosophized. "Having been a state officer for over twelve years, I have witnessed many of them myself."

Actually, Sullivan's service did not quite add up to a dozen years, unless he was counting the time he'd served as a deputy under various sheriffs. He joined Frontier Battalion Co. B under Capt. Sam McMurry on April 16, 1889. Sullivan left the force for several months in 1890 but reenlisted December 1 that year. On July 1, 1893, he was promoted to corporal of Co. B, then commanded by Captain W.D. (Bill) McDonald. Eight months later Sullivan rose to sergeant.

After leaving the Rangers, Sullivan worked as a deputy under various sheriffs. Using his political connections, he eventually got a job as a Capitol doorkeeper. He spent the last few years of his life living with his nephew, Will Warren, and his family in Round Rock. On May 21, 1911, they found him dead in his room, apparently of a heart attack.

The Austin Statesman noted Sullivan's death in a two-paragraph page-one story. "His death removes a familiar figure in the Legislature for the past several sessions," the story said. "He had many stirring adventures during his long service with the State Rangers."

The Warrens and Sullivan's old friends gathered in the Old Round Rock Cemetery for his burial, but no one ever got around to putting up a tombstone.

FOULLY ASSASSINATED

It can't atone for his murder, or even the apparent contempt of those who buried him, but at least James W. King lies in a beautiful cemetery.

Coyotes barked in the distance and a covey of quail flushed from the brush as a visitor walked up the red-dirt road to find King's grave in Loma Vista Cemetery, south of Batesville in Zavala County. Three mourning doves shot past overhead toward the sunset, flying to roost. In the two-acre graveyard on top of the hill, grass grew high, and bees buzzed around the sweet-smelling blooming sage.

The present could hardly have been more pleasant, the past scarcely any uglier: They buried King facing west, a strong insult. Especially for a former Texas Ranger.

Not much is known about King. A fair hand with a fiddle, and presumably with six-shooters and Winchesters, he joined the Frontier Battalion in 1882. He served under various officers in two different companies before enlisting in Capt. Frank Jones' Co. D in 1887.

When fence-cutting got out of hand in Navarro County, the Rangers sent privates Ira Aten and the younger King to work undercover. The two Rangers found catching "nippers" (as wire-cutters sometimes were referred to) tough work, but Aten proposed a solution that quickly became famous if not practicable. His idea involved attaching dynamite bombs to fences. If set up properly, Aten theorized in a letter to headquarters, the bomb would explode when someone cut a fence wire. The felony offense would be instantly adjudicated and as word spread, Aten believed, the fence-cutting problem would disappear along with perpetrators.

By return mail Aten got orders to drop the bomb idea and soon he and King were back on other duty elsewhere in the state. At least for King, it had been a chance to work with an older, more experienced Ranger.

Based on King's Navarro County work, in 1888 Jones ordered King to sparsely populated Zavala County in South Texas. Posing as a dishonorably discharged Ranger, King worked to make cases against cattle thieves.

King made inroads with the locals with his fiddle-playing abilities, but no criminal cases. His mission having proved fruitless, the Ranger returned to his company and other duties. He reenlisted on Sept. 1, 1889, but three days later, Capt. Jones fired him for drunkenness. This time his discharge was for real.

For whatever reason, with only four dollars in his pocket, King decided to go back to Zavala County. Maybe he figured on hiring on as a sheriff's deputy or working as a cowhand. Again, King told folks he'd been let go by the Rangers. But that's what he'd said before. Certain par- ties in the county both were annoyed at his reappearance and doubtful of his story.

Details are sketchy, but records say the former Ranger was slain on the W.L. Gates ranch near Loma Vista on Feb. 11, 1890. A history of Zavala County does not even say how he was killed, but in the brush country it's hard to imagine King died from any other cause than gunshots. Another source is more specific: He'd been shot seven times.

King, Capt. Jones reported to headquarters 11 days later, had been "foully assassinated...by parties who I am thoroughly convinced thought King was yet a Ranger and on detective work." The captain went on to assure the Adjutant General: "I shall do my best to ferret out the murderers and see that they are punished."

Adjutant Gen. W.H. King (apparently no relation to the dead former Ranger) wrote Jones March 25, 1890 to inform him that the governor had authorized a $250 reward for the "apprehension and conviction of the murderers of J.W. King." On April 4, three men, Fox Adams, George Rumfield and Will Speer were charged with King's murder on the docket of Justice of the Peace C.C. McKinney. Following their arraignment, Judge McKinney released the defendants on $1,000 bond each.

Tried in nearby Frio County, the three accused killers were found not guilty and presumably went on to live normal lives. George Washington Rumfield died Feb. 18, 1934, at 78 and is buried in Frio County's Covey Chapel Cemetery. The fate of Adams and Speer has not been determined.

For years, only a mesquite stump marked the former Ranger's lonesome burial spot. At some point in the late 20th or early 21st century, someone had a flat gray granite stone placed on the grave. The modern marker makes no mention of the Ranger's violent demise, merely recording for posterity these words:

James W. King
Feb. 11, 1890
Texas Ranger

Co. D

HAPPY TRAILS, SUNDAY

Nothing's perfect, but occasionally a good writer manages to arrange the literary building blocks we call words, sentences and paragraphs in such a way as to surprise and please the reader.

An excellent example is a 198-word item that appeared in the Meridian Tribune at some point in 1902—the month and day of publication were not given in a later reprinting of the piece. While the old news story raises some unanswered questions, it's hard to quarrel with the work of a clever wordsmith.

Here's the article:

Thursday afternoon as some boys were crossing the pasture belonging to Col. Ramsey Cox, they came across the dead body of one of Bosque County's oldest residents.

The find was at once reported to the proper authorities and preparations were made to give the poor old fellow a decent burial.

He has quite a history, having been raised in this country since his early youth and has seen service in many bloody battles between the Indian and the white man.

He has been faithful and true to every trust, and his many friends will grieve to hear of his death.

He took a quite prominent part in the Old Settlers Reunion at this place a few weeks ago and seemed to enjoy the day as much as anyone present.

At a late hour in the afternoon sorrowing friends took the corpse up near the hill commonly known as Hat-Top, dug a grave and consigned to the dust the dead body of Sunday, that faithful old horse who has served our friend, Col. Buck Barry, for 40 long years. If we can get a biographical sketch of his life we will give some to our readers sometime in the future.

To start at the bottom and work up, James Buckner "Buck" Barry was one of Texas' best-known frontiersmen. He had ridden as a Texas Ranger, and when he posed for a photographer in 1853, he unknowingly became the first true Ranger ever known to have his picture taken. Three years later he came to Bosque County and spent the rest of his long life there, dying in 1906.

While there's plenty of information on Barry, his memoir does not mention a horse saddled with such an unusual name for a steed as Sunday or even make any reference to having a favorite mount. If the Meridian newspaper ever came up with a "biographical sketch" of Sunday, it hasn't come to light.

There's one likely boo-boo in the piece, at least as it was reprinted. The Web site www. mountainzone.com lists 36 high spots in hilly

Bosque County, but no prominence called Hat-Top. That's probably because whoever transcribed the article mistook Flat Top for Hat Top. Look at "Fl" just right and it could easily be misread for an "H."

Actually, there are two Flat Tops in the county. One is a mountain that rises 1,178 feet above sea level 3.4 miles from Walnut Springs, which is Barry's old stomping grounds, and the other is a 1,161-foot-above-sea-level feature located 3.6 miles from Cranfills Gap. If old Sunday is buried near either location, no reference to a marker appears on any Bosque County-related Web sites or in books dealing with the county's colorful history.

Ramsey Cox proved easier to find. In the spring of 1898, a Waco newspaper listed him as a traveling freight agent for the Texas Central Railroad. He continued to move up the management ladder and by 1911 had become assistant general manager of the line, working out of Waco. Cox also happened to be married to Barry's daughter.

To get back to Barry, he didn't weigh more than 145 pounds, kept his hair long and liked to wear buckskin. An old Southerner full of energy and possessing what one contemporary described as a "militant, decisive bearing," he had a reputation of being mighty tough on Indians. Over the years, he gave away scores of captive horses to those who had lost stock to Indians or Anglo rustlers.

"He could never tolerate theft, or cowardice, or attacks on the weak, and he believed in upholding the law, even in the absence of law," the acquaintance recalled.

Ironically, his reputation and a pile of official paperwork sent to Washington never resulted in Barry getting any government compensation for all the horses he'd lost to Indians over the years. At least he held on to old Sunday.

EX-RANGERS READY TO FIGHT OVER A GRAVE

The old Texas Rangers who gathered in Austin for a reunion in the early fall of 1897 surely figured they had fought their last fight. After all, they had battled and survived Mexican soldiers, Comanches and outlaws. But that's before they heard what some folks in Tennessee were up to.

Meeting in the Capital City on the night of October 8, the aging rangers of the newly organized Ex-Rangers Association got word that certain parties in the Volunteer State were agitating for the removal of Sam Houston's remains from Texas to his old stomping grounds in Tennessee. Some of the old rangers then meeting in Austin had known Houston. The others all knew of his place in their state's history.

Houston came to Texas in 1832 following a drunken sabbatical among the Cherokees in what is now Oklahoma. Before then, he had served as governor of Tennessee, his political career there ending concurrently with his short-lived first marriage. Only four years after crossing the Red River, having assured Texas' independence from Mexico by defeating Gen. Antonio Lopez de Santa Anna at San Jacinto, Houston became the first president of the new Republic of Texas.

He lived to see Texas admitted as the 28th state in 1845, dying at 70 of natural causes on July 26, 1863 during the bloody Civil War he had tried to avert. His family abided by his wishes and buried him in Oakwood Cemetery in Huntsville, the Walker County town he and his wife Margaret had settled in because it reminded him of his boyhood home in Tennessee.

But 33 years after his death, the sentiment had risen in Tennessee that Houston should be exhumed from his Texas grave and shipped "home" to the hills of his youth. The former rangers gathered for comradery in Austin learned of this idea in a letter from Marie Bennet Urwitz, president of the Cuero-based San Jacinto Chapter of the Daughters of the Republic of Texas and the daughter of a former ranger.

Mrs. Urwitz wrote that "a proposition has been made the family of Gen. Houston for the removal of the remains of that immortal chieftain from Texas to Tennessee."

She continued, "I hope your patriotic and venerable body will offer a strong protest against any such proposition. A state which would allow [Houston's removal] is not worthy of the grave of [Ben] Milam, Bowie, Travis or the memory of such a man as your [former Ranger captain] Jack Hays."

The aging rangers, used to saddling up and riding hard at a moment's notice, acted quickly after hearing Mrs. Urwitz' letter. Voting unanimously, the veterans approved this resolution:

Whereas, we have learned that there is a proposition to remove the remains of Gen. Houston from this state to Tennessee; be it

Resolved, that we, the ex-rangers of Texas, are unalterably opposed to the removal of the remains of that hero from the land of his choice and the field of his illustrious and imperishable fame.

Resolved, that the remains of our immortal chieftain should abide in their final rest in the sacred soil of Texas, which he successfully defended and that an appropriate monument worthy of Texas should mark the grave which will be sought by patriotic pilgrims in increasing numbers through future ages.

The ex-Rangers were not the only ones dead set against the removal of Houston's grave from the state he helped build. A few days later, the Austin daily published a three-paragraph editorial, "Sam Houston's Remains Belong in Texas."

"...[E]very patriotic citizen of Texas [is] opposed to the removal of the remains of the warrior-statesman Sam Houston, from Texas soil to that of Tennessee," the opinion piece began. "Gen. Houston abandoned Tennessee for some cause in the very acme of his greatness and became more identified with and interested in Texas than in any other state."

The editorial writer then turned to Shakespeare to further his point: "[Moving the remains] would be like giving the play of Hamlet without Hamlet..."

Texas newspapers of the day are silent on how it all played out, but Houston's remains stayed put in Huntsville. Doubtless, most of the veteran rangers who voted for the resolution to keep the hero of San Jacinto in Texas would have defended Houston's burial place with force of arms had the movement to relocate him progressed further.

As for the former rangers' recommendation that "an appropriate monument" be placed over Houston's final resting place, that took a little longer. Not until the spring of 1907 did the Texas Legislature pass a joint resolution authorizing a monument above Houston's final resting place. On April 21, 1911—the 65th anniversary of San

Jacinto—assorted dignitaries showed up for the dedication of a large granite monument at Houston's grave.

Sharing the limelight with Alonzo Steele, the battle's last survivor, the "Great Commoner" William Jennings Bryan gave the keynote speech at the unveiling of the massive stone, which features a trio of bas reliefs of Houston by sculptor Pompeo Coppini.

"It is [the] willingness to die for what one believes is right," Bryan said that spring day, "that makes civilization possible."

PHOTO GALLERY

He didn't live to see them become legendary, but Texas colonizer Stephen F. Austin is generally considered the father of the Texas Rangers. In August 1823, in the log cabin of settler Sylvanus Castleman, Austin scratched out a document proposing a group of Rangers "for the common defense." (Author's collection)

Near the Colorado River upstream from present LaGrange, this is believed to be where Austin penned what has come to be viewed as the Rangers' "Magna Carta". Early in the 20th century a sharecropper family razed the old Castleman cabin and built a farmhouse in its place. While even the "new" structure now stands in ruins, two Texas Archaeological Society stewards believe chiseled rocks and some hand-cut timber visible in the dilapidated farmhouse were cannibalized from the original cabin. (Mike Cox photo)

Capt. John Coffee Hays, a young surveyor originally from Tennessee helped forge the Ranger reputation. (Author's collection)

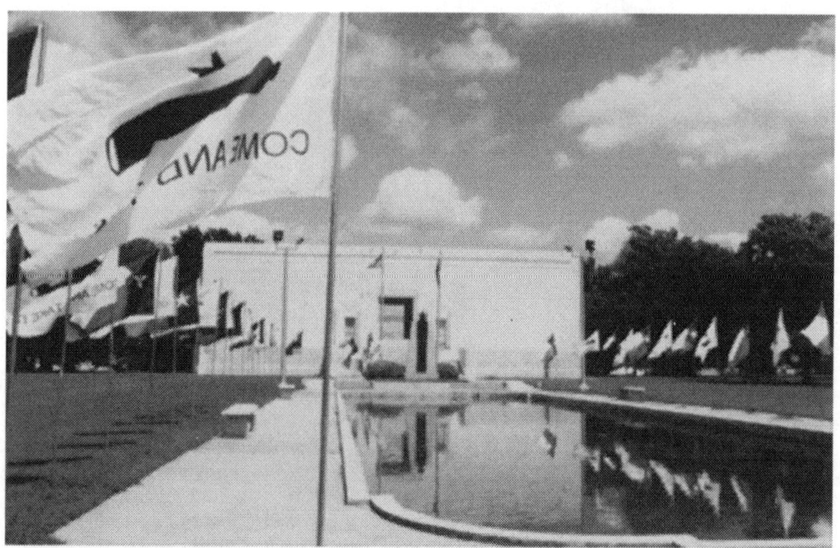

Built in 1937 just after Texas' Centennial celebration, the Gonzales Memorial Museum is dedicated to the 32 Rangers who died at the Alamo in 1836.
(Author's collection)

COMANCHE WARRIOR.

Rangers contended with the fierce Comanches and other tribes in a clash of cultures that lasted more than half a century.
(Author's collection)

JACK HAYS AND CHIEF FLACCO CHARGE THE COMANCHES.

In the 1844 Battle of Walker's Creek, for the first time in the history of the West Jack Hays and his Rangers used Colt revolvers against hostile Indians.
(Author's collection)

Newspaper drawing from 1930 depicting the 1864 Elm Creek raid, which Francis Peveler witnessed.
(Author's collection)

A.J. Sowell rode as a Ranger in the early 1870s and later chronicled his experiences and those of other Rangers.
(Author's collection)

Kerr County pioneer Charles Schreiner served as a Ranger in the 1850s and again in the 1870s. He went on to establish the YO Ranch and build a West Texas business empire. (Findagrave.com)

As a Frontier Battalion Ranger captain, Daniel Webster Roberts and the men who served under him battled Comanches and arrested outlaws. In the early 20th century he wrote a book on his experiences. (Author's collection)

Capt. Neal Coldwell spent eight years in the Frontier Battalion before taking up ranching and horse raising in the Texas Hill Country.
(Author's collection)

A trio of Frontier Battalion Rangers at Musquiz Canyon near Fort Davis, Texas in the 1880s. Apaches no longer posed a threat, but outlaws still ran roughshod in far West Texas.
(Author's collection)

The men of Ranger Co. E in 1892 posing for an unknown photographer. (Courtesy Former Texas Rangers Association Foundation)

Co. D Rangers rest their horses and themselves in camp near Ysleta, Texas in the mid-1890s. Capt. John R. Hughes reclines fourth from left. (Courtesy Former Texas Rangers Association Foundation)

Former Ranger Buck Barry sported a full white beard when serving in the Texas Legislature in 1883. After years in the saddle, he looked older than his 63 years.
(This and lower image, Author's collection)

Ranger Jim Gillett and fellow state lawmen tracked down three of four men suspected of the 1884 robbery-murder of German pioneer John Wolfgang Braeutigam. Shown here is a mid-20th century photo of the remodeled but then vacant Braeutigam family residence, now part of the Old Fort Martin Scott complex in Fredericksburg, Texas.

Good with a gun and popular with the ladies, Jeff Milton posed for a photographer while a young Ranger. (Author's collection)

From the early 1880s through the early 1900s, Rangers—sometimes called State Rangers—periodically camped in or near Colorado City. Early on, locals referred to the Mitchell County seat simply as Colorado. (Author's collection)

Six Mexican Revolution-era Rangers ready to ride. Of these half-dozen men, only the lawman on the left manages a smile. Note the Ranger third from the right is equipped with tinted goggles to protect his eyes from dust and extreme sunlight.
(Courtesy Former Texas Rangers Association Foundation)

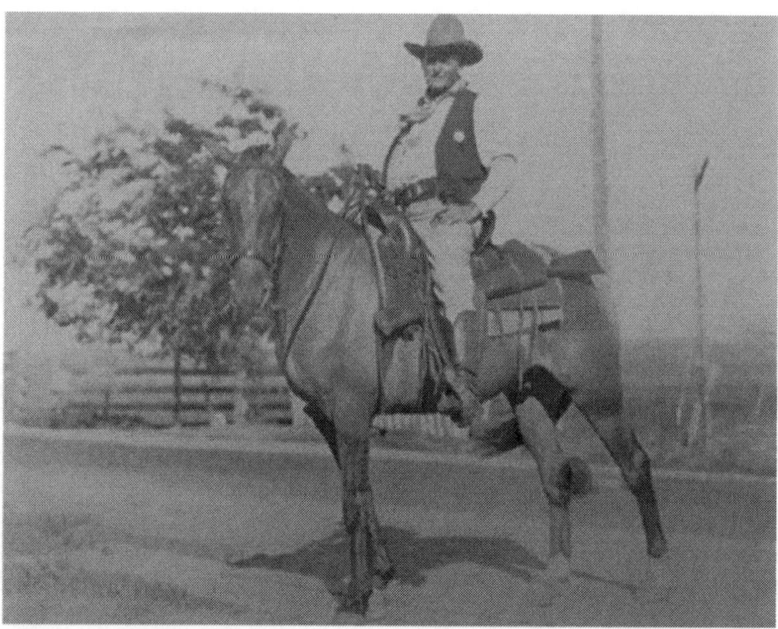

This unidentified West Texas Ranger—a cigar stump in hand and a Winchester within easy reach— looks like he's been around a while.
(Courtesy Former Texas Rangers Association Foundation)

Rangers Joe Brooks and Alonzo Taylor holding bandit skulls in South Texas. (Author's collection)

Soldier of fortune and journalist, Tex O'Reilly claimed to have been a Ranger. Not true, but he did once drink a group of Rangers under the table. (Author's collection)

Two newly enlisted border Rangers in 1915. Charles Wright, left, packs a Colt .45 revolver, while Jim Malone carries a Colt Model 1911 semiautomatic. Both hold Winchester Model 1895 lever-action rifles.
(Author's collection)

These three South Texas Rangers slept on the ground but did get to enjoy chuckwagon cooking.
(Author's collection)

Lonely grave of former Ranger Joe Sitter at Valentine, Texas. In 1915, he and a younger Ranger died hard when ambushed by Mexican bandits.
(Mike Cox photo)

After a bloody 1917 Christmas day raid, the L. D. Brite Ranch built this adobe fortification. For months following the attack Ranger Lee Trimble kept solitary watch from an elevation overlooking the ranch headquarters. The ranch installed a telephone for him to use if he saw suspicious riders approaching, but bandits never returned.
(Portal to Texas History)

Despite a report that Ranger Frank Patterson had been killed by Mexican bandits, he'd only gotten separated from his fellow lawman during a fight. He later served as Kimble County sheriff and lived a long life.
(Author's collection)

During Prohibition, Rangers stayed busy trailing "Tequileros," Mexican liquor smugglers. In this mid-1920s image, Rangers dispose of booze they confiscated somewhere near the border in South Texas.
(Author's collection)

Sometimes, armed liquor smugglers opened fire on lawmen catching them in the act. Here Rangers have taken cover and are shooting back. The image might have been staged, but these Rangers look dead serious as they bear down on their sights.
(Author's collection)

These two Flapper-era ladies weren't Rangers, but their boyfriends—Lee Trimble and a Special Ranger identified only as "Hoyt"—were. Taken in Smithville, Texas in 1922.
(Courtesy Former Texas Rangers Association Foundation)

From 1901 to the 1930s, Rangers helped pacify rowdy oil boom towns across the state. (Author's collection)

Former Frontier Battalion captain Dan Roberts as sketched by young artist Warren Hunter in 1927. That's the year his murdered son's widow received a mysterious caller in the middle of the night who had something bizarre to say. (Author's collection)

When they arrested a suspected criminal, the Rangers didn't want to hunt for them all over again if they escaped. This unidentified Ranger clearly has no intention of letting this prisoner get away. (Courtesy Former Texas Rangers Association Foundation)

In the 1920s Rangers still relied on horses that could get them where an automobile could not. Somewhere in South Texas these unidentified state lawmen have their saddled mounts in the modified bed of a 1928 Ford truck. (Author's collection)

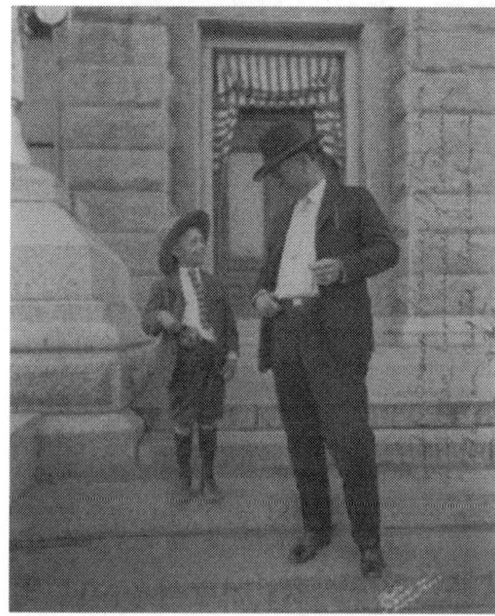

From private to sergeant to captain, Frank Hamer played a major role in building the 20th century Ranger reputation. In this image, taken on the steps of the state Capitol, surely the pistol tucked in the youngster's britches wasn't loaded. (Portal to Texas History)

Co. D Rangers enjoying coffee and conversation somewhere in South Texas during World War Two. (Courtesy Former Texas Rangers Association Foundation)

In 1950, Rangers disabused two visiting West Coast mobsters of plans to expand their operations to Texas. Rousting them from a Wichita Falls hotel room, they put the crooks on a plane back to California. From left, Sgt. Manuel T. "Lone Wolf " Gonzaullas; notorious Mafia boss Mickey Cohen, his unidentified bodyguard and Co. B Capt. Bob Crowder.
(Author's collection)

Noah Armstrong, 94 (left); W.H. Rischert, 94 (center) and C.M. Grady, 93 (right) attended the 1946 Ex-Rangers Association meeting in Santa Anna, Texas. If any attendees knew all of Armstrong's story, they didn't bring it up at the reunion.
(Courtesy J. Evetts Haley Library)

Since they first gained law enforcement authority in 1874, Rangers have been involved in catching cattle, goat and horse thieves and recovering stolen stock. (Author's collection)

Ranger W.E. "Dub" Taylor and Capt. Ernest Best enjoy a campfire breakfast on the Bill Kuykendall Ranch near Buda, Texas ca. 1945.
(Portal to Texas History)

Oil field theft kept West Texas Rangers busy. Here Ranger (and future Co. D captain) John M. Wood inspects a pump jack.
(Courtesy Former Texas Rangers Association Foundation)

Shortly before his retirement, Co. F Ranger Charlie Miller gave a younger, newly sworn Ranger a Mexican silver coin and made a startling offer.
(Author's collection)

Senior Ranger Capt. Clint Peoples holds a set of Daisy BB gun Colt .45 replicas produced to commemorate the Rangers' 150th anniversary in 1973. (L.A. Wilke photo)

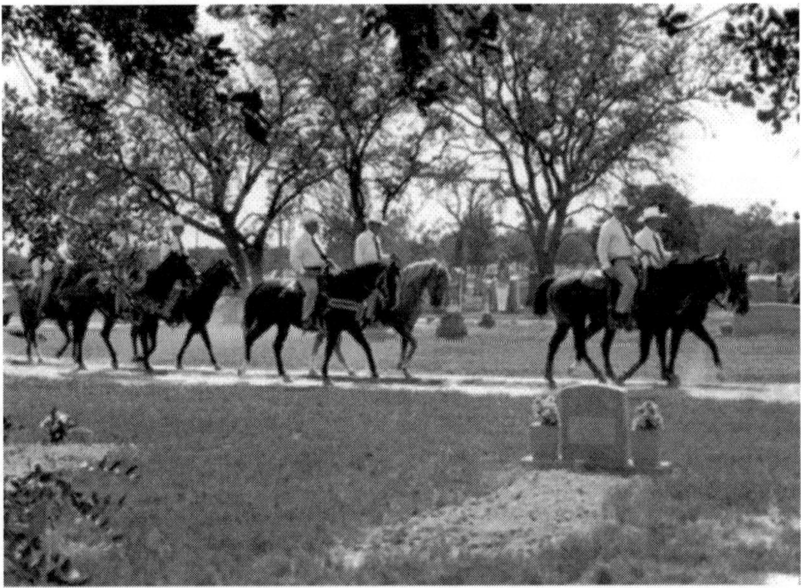

Mounted late 20th century Rangers on hand for the 1986 dedication of a state historical marker at the Center Point Cemetery, the Arlington of the Rangers.
(Mike Cox photo)

Dedicated in 1961, for decades this bronze Ranger statue greeted hundreds of thousands of travelers at Dallas' Love Field. But when Rangers got caught in the crossfire of a new cultural war, the City of Dallas removed it in 2020.
(Author's collection)

BORDER TROUBLES: 1902-1918

WHAT REVOLUTION?

The elderly President had been reelected—but his opponent believed the incumbent had stolen the election. The loser could have graciously accepted defeat or plotted to take the presidency by somehow changing the vote count. Instead, he chose revolution.

Eighty-year-old Porfirio Diaz began his seventh consecutive term as Mexico's president in October 1910. Though a ruthless authoritarian, during his reign he brought relative peace and prosperity to his country. Consequently, people living along the U.S-Mexico border enjoyed a level of tranquility they hadn't experienced for years. Given that, and with the Indian Wars more than two decades in the past, the U.S. military had abandoned most of its frontier-era garrisons in Texas and elsewhere in the Southwest.

But on Nov. 23, 1910, when forces loyal to defeated presidential candidate Francisco Madero attacked an element of the Mexican Army in northern Mexico, the U.S. military put its existing southwestern posts on alert in case bloodshed spread across the boundary. The Texas Rangers also girded for possible trouble.

Journalists descended on San Antonio and El Paso to cover what they supposed would be full-fledged warfare. They made the telegraph wires sing with speculative or over-hyped dis- patches on their way to eager newspaper readers from San Francisco to Washington. "If the alleged Mexican revolutionists were only half as active as the San Antonio war correspondents are, there would soon be something doing," the Laredo Weekly Times opined on Nov. 20, 1910.

Only a day after Madero made his move, page one newspaper articles across Texas and the nation proclaimed the revolt had already ended. "Mexican Revolution Short Lived; Diaz Is Now In Control," the Fort Worth Star-Telegram trumpeted on November 24.

It did seem as if Diaz' army had snuffed out the revolution like so many prayer candles at a Dia de los Muertos (Day of the Dead) celebration. Six days later, the Galveston Daily News observed, "The Mexican revolution is believed to have safely passed from the revolutionary to the reminiscent stage," the Galveston Daily News observed on November 26.

As it turned out, those who thought a Mexican civil war had been averted were merely whistling their way past the proverbial graveyard. Hostilities began in earnest in 1911 and would continue in Mexico and along the border for nearly a decade. The revolution would claim an estimated 1.5 million people. Some sources place the death toll even higher. Most of those deaths occurred on the Mexican side, but hundreds—both Mexican and Anglo—would perish on the U.S. side of the border, particularly in Texas.

In 1914, war broke out in Europe. In January 1915, the British government intercepted and decoded a secret cable from German Foreign Secretary Arthur Zimmermann to the German minister in Mexico. The message said that if the U.S. did not remain neutral in the conflict pitting Germany against France and England, Germany would offer to align itself with Mexico. Should the U.S. declare war on Germany, and if Mexico joined the fight against the U.S., the Kaiser's military strategists said Mexico could have the American Southwest back if they won.

Britain released the telegram to the U.S. and on March 1, American newspapers revealed its contents. In Texas, the Bryan Eagle called the plot a "diabolical perfidy" though many Texans thought it laughable that Mexico and Germany believed they could successfully take Texas. Still, for a while outright war between the U.S. and Mexico seemed likely. The idea set forth in the telegram was far-fetched, but German war planners clearly thought they could engineer such a scenario if necessary.

Behind the scenes, the border teemed with Mexican operatives from both sides of the revolution, German spies and propagandists, soldiers of fortune, regular soldiers, National Guardsmen, federal agents, bandits, con men, profiteers, prostitutes, gamblers, and draft dodgers (aka slackers). Ground zero was El Paso, the largest city on the American side of the border. And then, on April 17, 1917, the U.S. declared war on Germany.

The Texas Rangers got sucked into a towering tornado, their role during the revolution and World War I still a matter of controversy.

PARTNERS DON'T ALWAYS GET ALONG

Before the Rangers got involved in the Mexican Revolution their regular work continued apace. Less than a month after Madero's forces attacked Diaz' army, an incident in San Antonio showed that the Rangers and Texas' law enforcement agencies did not always get along. In fact, at times relations between the Rangers and local officers in places like Amarillo, El Paso, Galveston and San Antonio broke down almost entirely.

An Associated Press dispatch published in late November 1910 is an example of strained relations between the Rangers and San Antonio police:

Efforts of the police to serve warrants on Capt. Bill McDonald, state revenue agent [and noted former Ranger], *and Capt. Marvin E. Bailey, of the... Texas Rangers, charged with discharging firearm*[s] *within the city limits, proved futile. It is alleged they fired several shots during an automobile ride Thursday night.*

That would have been after dark on Nov. 24, 1910. In more harmonious times, while the San Antonio officer involved probably would have told the two to quit with the recreational gun play, he likely wouldn't have filed charges against brother officers.

On Dec. 9, 1910, Capt. Bailey traveled on official business from Austin to the Alamo City. As soon as he alighted from the train, he went to police headquarters.

There, rather than asking the captain what he could do for him, police Capt. Frank Newman asked the ranger if he had a gun on him. The captain allowed as how he did. He was a state ranger, after all. Hearing that, the San Antonio officer demanded that Bailey hand over his pistol and placed him under arrest. An officer then escorted Bailey to the county court, where he was charged with unlawfully carrying a weapon.

By that time word had spread that the local police had taken a Ranger into custody for merely doing his job. Legally, the state officer had as much authority to tote a pistol in San Antonio as the local officers did.

As soon as the Bexar County district attorney's office heard about it, an assistant DA hurried to a district judge and readily obtained a habeas corpus hearing. Thirty-seventh District Court Judge Edward Dwyer promptly ruled that a Texas Ranger was a peace officer and had a right to go armed. After that, the captain went about his business.

Ill feelings toward the Rangers on the part of some San Antonio residents would continue until the mid-1920s.

TEX O'REILLY

A colorful hard-drinking newspaperman and battle-hardened soldier of fortune, Edward Synotte "Tex" O'Reilly not only served as a war correspondent during the early days of the Mexican Revolution, he joined in the fighting.

Born in Denison in 1880, O'Reilly grew up in San Saba. His father, a Civil War veteran, made his living as an itinerant stone mason. He traveled the state plying his trade on various courthouse, jail and bridge construction projects. When county officials in San Saba approved funding for a new courthouse, the elder O'Reilly moved his family there for yet another job.

After the Spanish-American War began in 1898, young O'Reilly enlisted. The tall, thin Texan soon found that while he had a taste for fighting he did not much care for military discipline. After seeing combat in Cuba, the Philippines and in the Boxer Rebellion, O'Reilly left the military and hired on as an international policeman in Shanghai. He also spent time as a drill instructor for the Chinese army, worked again as a police officer in Japan, and even taught school there for a while.

Returning to the U.S. as a stowaway on a tramp steamer, he began a brief but successful-to-a-point career as a stunt cowboy in the Oklahoma-based 101 Ranch Wild West Show. He also performed in rodeos, at least until he tried to impress a crowd by roping a steer from an automobile. O'Reilly lassoed the steer successfully, but when he jumped from the moving car to tie the animal's legs, he broke one of his own.

That's when O'Reilly turned to journalism, working as a reporter on various papers in Chicago and St. Louis before returning to his home state to write for the San Antonio Light, one of two scrappy dailies serving what was then Texas' largest city.

In addition to covering the news, O'Reilly occasionally made news. He rode a horse 1,700 miles from the Alamo City to Chicago to meet with President William Howard Taft and invite him to Texas. When the Texas Legislature became annoyed at the Light's coverage of that body's proceedings, they barred the newspaper's representative from sitting at the press table in the Senate. O'Reilly showed up at the Capitol wearing a six shooter, marched past the sergeant-at-arms straight into the Senate chamber and announced that the Light would once again shine upon the lawmakers, beginning right then.

Beyond his flair for the flamboyant, the Irish Texan had wandering feet. In 1910, O'Reilly and his wife Dixie left San Antonio and acquired a ranch near Sanderson, then a thriving West Texas railroad town. Living with his family in a tent, he began publishing a humorous newspaper called the Rio Grande Coyote.

When the Mexican Revolution began that November, O'Reilly sent his family back to San Antonio and alternated between covering the fighting for the Associated Press and participating in it. He rode with Francisco Madero's rebels and later with Pancho Villa, who reportedly wanted the journalist-soldier of fortune to write his biography.

O'Reilly packed many amazing adventures and close calls into the first four decades of his life. Some of them actually happened. But his assertion that he served for seven months as a Texas Ranger private under Co. D Capt. John R. Hughes is as bogus as a deed to ocean-front property at the foot of El Paso's Franklin Mountains.

Even so, in Born to Raise Hell—an as-told-to autobiography written by noted 20th century news commentator Lowell Thomas—an entire chapter is devoted to O'Reilly's claimed Ranger career. While it has been documented that the journalist served for a time as an informant for Hughes, the Texas State Library and Archives in Austin has no records supporting the soldier of fortune's claim that he'd held a Ranger commission.

However, O'Reilly could certainly claim he'd associated with the Ranger force. That's because Rangers arrested him for violating federal neutrality laws after he recruited a group of pro-Madero muchachos in Texas and led them across the Rio Grande for one of the first battles of the revolution.

Wounded in the fight, O'Reilly managed to make it back to the Texas side of the river only to be taken into custody by the Rangers. He protested that he'd only been in Mexico as a war correspondent, not as a rebel leader. He finally persuaded the Rangers to wire the Associated Press representative in San Antonio, who confirmed the Irish Texan's media credentials. Though they released him from custody, the Rangers still wanted him to name names and reveal the location of Madero fighters along the border.

When the newspaperman refused to do that, the Rangers tried a different tact. Four Rangers working in the Comstock area, knowing O'Reilly had more than a wee taste for whiskey and beer, decided to loosen him up by getting him drunk. Then they'd pump him for information. Unfortunately for the state officers, O'Reilly had a much greater capacity for alcohol than they did. In a Comstock saloon he drank them under the table and disappeared. Of course, there's no contemporary paperwork to back up what O'Reilly told Thomas.

The Irish Texan didn't do all his fighting in Mexico. At various times while in his 20s and 30s O'Reilly hired out as a soldier of fortune in Venezuela, Honduras, Nicaragua and North Africa. In April 1917 the U.S. finally entered the war with Germany that had been raging in Europe since 1914. Too old to rejoin the Army, O'Reilly became a captain in the Texas National Guard, commanding a machine gun company. In all, he claimed to have taken part in 10 wars on four continents.

Having jammed more living into 38 years than most people manage in a lifetime, in 1918 O'Reilly sold an action-filled autobiography called Roving and Fighting. The book attracted a fair amount of attention and sold well enough, but it fell well short of making him independently wealthy.

Like many a newspaper reporter before and since, O'Reilly realized that while he might have a lot of fun working as a journalist or hired gun, he'd never get rich that way. He and his wife lived on a strict budget. As he wrote, tongue firmly in cheek, one fourth of their income was allocated for food, one fourth for rent, one fourth for whiskey, and one fourth for fines, court costs and incidentals.

Hoping to meet these expenses more adequately, he turned to full-time freelance writing. He even wrote scripts for two-reel silent Western movies. When the Pictorial Review, then a major national magazine, invited him to join its stable of writers, O'Reilly's many friends in San Antonio collected money to send him to New York.

Unfortunately, he spent the money on a huge going-away party, not transportation. When a police officer spotted O'Reilly hooting and singing on Commerce Street at 3 a.m., he placed him under arrest for public intoxication. Well, he tried. Seventeen officers later, O'Reilly finally went to jail. When a friend bailed him out the next morning, he found O'Reilly covering his face in shame. The friend assured O'Reilly being arrested for drunk and disorderly was not that disgraceful, especially for a newspaperman, to which O'Reilly said, "San Antonio's not a big city yet I let only one police force arrest me."

O'Reilly lived in New York for a time, but by 1923 he was back in San Antonio. That October Century Magazine, then a widely circulated national publication, published a fanciful Western tale of his that gave birth to one of the nation's enduring folk characters—Pecos Bill. As O'Reilly told the story, when someone had the audacity to settle only 50 miles from their cabin in East Texas, Bill's family pulled stakes for the wide-open far West. Unfortunately, when their wagon splashed across the Pecos River, Bill fell out. Being one of "16 or 17" kids, no one missed him for a good while. Meanwhile, a pack of coyotes adopted him. Running with them, he grew up thinking he was just another member of the pack. Eventually a passing cowboy, noting that Bill didn't have a tail, reintroduced him to human society.

By then a young man, Bill "got to enjoying all the pleasant vices of mankind." But after some years of dissipation, he mended his ways and became a cowboy known for performing all sorts of super-human feats. To get water for his ranch, for instance, Bill dug an irrigation ditch that became the Rio Grande. He invented all sorts of things connected to ranching and cowboying, including the bucking bronco.

That turned out to be something of an irony when the love of his life, Slew-Foot Sue, pestered Bill into letting her ride his horse Widow Maker. The spirited steed bucked Sue so high she barely missed the moon. Landing on her spring-steel bustle, she kept bouncing for three days and nights. Poor Bill finally had to shoot her to keep her from starving to death. After that, he was never the same. Some said he died from drinking too much nitro laced with fishhooks, others that he died laughing at a Yankee dressed up like a cowboy.

O'Reilly claimed that he'd first heard of Pecos Bill in his youth, listening to old cowboys swapping yarns around a campfire. But J. Frank Dobie, no slouch when it came to Texas folklore, believed O'Reilly created the story out of whole cloth. Indeed, O'Reilly had probably heard old Irish tales about giants from his father, knew of Paul Bunyan, and set about developing a mythical Texan merely to make a buck. Too, as a Spanish-American War veteran, he'd doubtless seen the rotund Gen. William "Pecos Bill" Shafter. A Civil War veteran, Shafter had served for a time in West Texas during the Indian wars. O'Reilly's awareness of Shafter's nickname may have been how he came up with the name for his cowboy character.

"It is highly probable that Paul Bunyan…and Pecos Bill, mythical cow-boy hero of the Southwest, were blood brothers," one compiler of folklore later wrote. "At all events, they can meet on one common ground: they were both fathered by a liar."

Unfortunately for O'Reilly and his heirs, written words can be copyrighted but not a character name or title. The writer quickly lost any control of Pecos Bill as a succession of authors added more and more wild details to O'Reilly's original version.

Still hoping to hit the big time, O'Reilly again left his native state for the Big Apple in the late 1920s. In 1937, he and a partner marketed a Pecos Bill comic strip, but it never caught on. Rich only in experience, he died in Syracuse, New York, in 1946 of a disease that had plagued him most of his life, tuberculosis. His son, John O'Reilly, who also went by "Tex," had been a noted war correspondent for the New York Herald-Tribune. John died in 1981, but Tex's other "son," Pecos Bill, lives on as an American folk hero.

CHICO AND JOE

When Willie Nelson popularized song writer Townes Van Zandt's classic ballad "Pancho and Lefty," he put his melodic magic into the song's chorus line:

Pancho met his match, you know
On the deserts down in Mexico
Nobody heard his dying words
...but that's the way it goes

The song speaks to me because I spent more than 25 years, off and on, tracking down the details of another story that happened in the desert not far from Mexico in the vastness of the Big Bend, Texas' last frontier.

In the Van Zandt song, "Pancho" is Mexican Revolution leader Pancho Villa, and "Lefty" a fictional representation of the unknown person paid to assassinate Villa in Chihuahua City in 1923. If I wrote songs instead of books, I'd do a ballad called "Chico and Joe." It would be the musical telling of a border saga every bit as dramatic as Pancho Villa's story. As with "Pancho and Lefty," it's a tale of lives lived large, and death come hard climaxed by two brutal killings in a particularly hard country. And just like the hit man in Pancho and Lefty, the killer in this story lived a long time before dying. When he did breathe his last, he did so with his boots off. Whether he ever came to regret what he did, we'll never know.

In March 2015, I finally found the spot where the story reached its dramatic peak...a lonesome canyon in the middle of nowhere in Presidio County. That's where a well-respected former Texas Ranger and a younger Ranger met their violent deaths in an ambush straight out of any number of B Western movies.

I first encountered the story early in my career as spokesman for the Texas Department of Public Safety, which includes the modern Texas Rangers. Though I'd been interested in the Rangers since the mid-1950s, I did not seriously begin collecting books about the Rangers until 1985, the year I started at the DPS. One day, perusing a newly acquired early edition of Zane Grey's Lone Star Ranger, a novel published in 1915 that went a long way toward furthering the Ranger legend, I was struck by the fact that the Ohio dentist turned Western writer had come to El Paso in 1913 to do research for his book.

Grey spent time with Ranger Capt. John R. Hughes, and when the book came out, the Western tale-spinner thanked Hughes and his men in his acknowledgements. I already knew Hughes' story pretty well, but I decided it would be interesting to track down information on the other real Rangers Grey mentioned. One of those men was Joseph Russell "Joe" Sitter.

Born in 1864, Joe Sitter grew up in Medina County near Castroville, Texas. Descended from the Alsace Lorraine immigrants who settled there in the mid to late 1840s, Sitter is an Americanization of his French family name.

Like many Texans, as a young man he took up cowboying and ended up in the Big Bend country. He stood only five feet eight and had light blue eyes and reddish-brown hair. He had a low forehead and big, bony eyebrows.

Eventually, he transitioned from range work to rangering. He joined Co. D, Frontier Battalion on Aug. 1, 1893, just before he turned 30 and served until Oct. 25, 1896. But a Ranger, just like a Marine is always a Marine, is always a Ranger. Sitter served as a special Ranger for the Texas and Southwestern Cattle Raisers Association and later as a mounted U.S. Customs Inspector.

Not overly burdened with formal education—one person who knew him said Sitter "could hardly spell his name"—he dang sure could read a cold trail like a book. Not only that, he knew how to fight if necessary.

Capt. Hughes considered Sitter one of the best men who'd ever pinned on a Ranger badge. As an example of the Ranger's abilities, Hughes cited the time he'd left Ysleta for El Paso in a buggy. When he got to town, with considerable embarrassment he noticed his six-shooter had fallen out of its holster. He quickly dispatched one of his men to find it, but that Ranger returned and reported failure.

Then he sent Joe Sitter. Trailing his boss' buggy upriver from Ysleta, the sharp-eyed Sitter soon located an indentation in the sand where the pistol had fallen. But the handgun was nowhere to be seen. Following a set of footprints he'd found near where the captain's gun had fallen led him to a Mexican resting in the shade. When Sitter asked if he'd found a gun, the man said no. Noticing the man's hat lay on the ground near him, Sitter put his hand on the butt of his pistol and told him to slowly pick up the sombrero. Beneath it lay Captain Hughes' pistol.

As a border peace officer, Sitter jailed a lot of men and recovered many a head of stolen stock, but as Van Zandt's ballad says, "he met his match" with an outlaw named Chico Cano. Cano, whose gang included his two brothers, was an accomplished bandit of the Mexican revolutionary war period and an ally of Pancho Villa.

Sitter and other officers tried hard to catch Cano, but the border bravo had friends on both sides of the river and always managed to elude arrest, not to mention a Ranger bullet.

Finally, Sitter got word that Cano and his dos hermanos would be on the Texas side of the river to attend the wake of a relative who'd died. Sitter and several other officers decided to drop by and pay their respects.

They surrounded the building with the mourners inside and ordered Cano and his cohorts to surrender. The bandit shouted back that there were ladies present and requested that they be allowed to leave. After that, he said, whether the officers took him prisoner would be left to gunpowder mediation, though he didn't exactly put it that way.

Sitter and the other officers chivalrously agreed that the women could leave. However, unknown to the lawmen, Cano had a plan. His men borrowed dresses from their women so they could sneak out with the other ladies. Unfortunately for Chico, he couldn't find a dress that fit him. So, despite his big talk, he wisely opted to give up while his comrades made it safely across the river.

The next day, Feb. 10, 1913, as Sitter, fellow Customs Inspector Jack Howard and a Texas and Southwestern Cattle Raisers Association brand inspector J.A. Havrick were escorting Cano to jail at Presidio, the rest of Cano's band—no longer wearing dresses—ambushed the party to rescue their leader. In the process, a bullet badly creased Sitters' head. Howard suffered a more serious wound and Harvick was killed. Now, for Sitter, it was personal. Cano's gang had murdered a friend of his and the bandit leader had escaped, but he and Sitter would meet again.

Sitter went to El Paso to recover from his wound, and that's when Zane Grey met him. With a bandage still wrapped around his head, Sitter had assured Grey that along the Rio Grande, Texas was "shore an' wild as ever."

Back in the saddle again, on May 21, 1915, Sitter, rookie Ranger Eugene Hulen, two other Rangers, and a U.S. Customs inspector (and former ranger) rode south toward the river based on information that Cano and his gang were stealing horses in that area.

Three days later, following a trail Sitter should have realized was too easy, the lawmen saw a bunch of horses tethered in a box canyon south of Valentine and north of the river village of Candelaria. Then they rode straight into another ambush.

Sitter and Hulen, for tactical reasons, moved up the canyon on the right side while the federal officer and other two Rangers rode up the left side. All five officers soon came under fire. The three officers on the left, with covering fire from Sitter and Hulen, escaped the canyon but minus their horses.

When the shooting stopped, as they later reported, they assumed their two colleagues were dead or had escaped. Walking back to where they'd left their pack mules, they removed their loads and rode them to a ranch where they used the rancher's telephone to call Marfa for help. Early the following day, a posse returned to the ambush site. There they found the mutilated bodies of Sitter and Hulen. Sitter had been shot 10 times, Hulen eight. Just for good measure, their heads had been smashed in with rocks. The bodies, stripped of their clothing and possessions, were in such bad shape that the mules used to carry them out got sick and retched.

A Presidio County grand jury indicted Cano for the murders of Sitter and Hulen, but he was never arrested for the crimes. In fact, he lived for another 28 years, dying of cancer on Aug. 28, 1943, at 56. He is buried in Cedillos, Mexico, only a few miles south of the Rio Grande, in a grave that is now unmarked.

Forty-seven years later, in 1990, I spoke at the annual conference of the Zane Grey West Society, held that year at the Prude Ranch in Fort Davis. I decided to tell Sitter's story, which had essentially been forgotten. Naturally, I wanted to see where he and Ranger Hulen had died.

First I called Hallie Stillwell, who I'd known since I was a young reporter at the San Angelo Standard Times in the late 1960s. One of the best-known Big Bend old-timers, she came to the region to teach school in Presidio during the border troubles.

Hallie had met Sitter and in fact for a time lived with the family of another former Ranger who was a close friend of his. She told me she had been to the site of the ambush but couldn't remember exactly where it was. Giving up for the time being on finding the location, while in Fort Davis for my presentation, I did visit Sitter's grave in Valentine. At the time, all he had was a crude, hand-made metal marker on which someone using a cutting torch had spelled out "Joe Gitters." (Since then, a much nicer monument has been put up. And his name's spelled right.)

The following year, still eager to find the ambush location, I reached out to Ranger Joaquin Jackson, then stationed at Alpine. He told me he'd heard that the box canyon in question was on the Coal Mine Ranch in Presidio County and readily agreed to take me there.

Meanwhile, he'd contacted Presidio County Sheriff Rick Thompson, who graciously offered to loan us a four-wheel-drive unmarked county vehicle. Not only that, he'd furnish us box lunches packed by a jail trustee.

Ranger Jackson and I left Alpine after breakfast on Feb. 18, 1991. We drove to Marfa, where we met with Sheriff Thompson, got our grub and changed vehicles. The county law- man seemed particularly interested in where we'd be going and the route we'd be taking.

From the sheriff's office in the 1886-vintage Presidio County Jail, it took us four hours to get to the ranch. With mountains surrounding the spread, the only way onto the property was an old railroad tunnel drilled through solid rock. The ranch and the country around it remain among the most isolated spots in the continental United States.

The unpaved road we had to take to reach the ranch, Jackson told me, was a rough route by most people's standards, but was considered a virtual freeway by northbound drug smugglers.

Before we'd left Marfa, Jackson had handed me his sawed-off .30-30, a weapon known among gun buffs as a "Mule's Leg."

"Keep this next to you," the Ranger said. "We're going where there ain't no 9-1-1."

Actually, for all practical purposes, we were traveling in time back to the 19th century. Not only was there no three-digit emergency number to call, there was no telephone service. We were on our own, even out of range of the sheriff department's two-way radio.

When we finally reached the Coal Mine Ranch, the young manager told us he'd be happy to lead us to the ambush site, but that it would take another four hours by horseback to get there. He said empty brass left over from the fight still lay among the rocks and showed us some spent cartridges he'd picked up there.

I may or may not have been able to hold up to an eight-hour round trip on the back of one of the ranch's horses, but I didn't have time to find out. I needed to be back in the office the next morning, so after a four-hour trip back to Marfa, I drove another seven hours plus back to Austin.

In retrospect, I should have developed a rapid onset spat of stomach trouble and called in sick, but I was dutiful and went back to work.

Six months later, the Drug Enforcement Administration busted Sheriff Thompson for smuggling cocaine into the U.S. in the Candelaria area, not far as the crow flies from the Sitter massacre scene. Convicted in federal court, he ended up in prison for life without the possibility of parole. Clearly, the sheriff's interest in where the Ranger and I would be going had not been out of a sense of history.

I expanded the Sitter story for my 1997 book, Texas Ranger Tales. Two years later, I signed a contract to do a modern history of the Rangers and included the Sitter story in what turned out to be a two-volume, quarter-million-word book. After the book's publication in 2008, as is often the case, I continued to learn more about the story.

In early 2015, a descendant of Sitter who'd read my books emailed to ask if I had any better fix on the canyon where Sitter and the Ranger died. That got me interested in making another attempt to visit the spot.

When I mentioned this to my old friend Joe Davis, a retired Ranger who serves as president of the Former Texas Rangers Association Foundation he said he'd also like to see the site. That led to the formation of what turned out to be a heavily armed expedition of retired Rangers and other interested parties to locate and visit the canyon where Sitter met his match. Our base of operations would be a friend's ranch at Candelaria. We gathered there on Sunday, March 29, 2015, and our search began the next day. We had 12 people, including three retired Texas Rangers, riding in four four-wheel drive mules. Wary of Mexican cartel members, everyone except two ranch hands carried handguns and rifles or assault rifles.

One member of the expedition was a retired airline pilot, who with topo maps and GPS believed he had located the box canyon where the bloody gunfight had taken place. But we still needed a guide to get from Candelaria to the Coal Mine Ranch.

That would be Candelaria denizen Boyd Chamberlain. He agreed to meet us at our host's ranch house on Monday morning. But when the time came for us to depart, he proved to be a no-show. When someone finally got him on his cell phone, he said he'd been across the river the night before and had been a bit overserved.

After our hungover guide showed up, he took us back to the ranch I'd visited 25 years before. The first place we stopped was the ranch headquarters. The ranch manager (not the one Jackson and I met in 1991) was not around, but a group of mule deer hunters were in the ranch bunkhouse. Napping after an early morning hunt, they heard us driving up. One of them looked outside and saw all the men with rifles. For all he knew, we could be modern-day bandits. He chose to be more optimistic.

"My God," he said when he walked outside, "the cavalry's here."

Having checked in, from there, with his cow dog pacing his four-wheeler, Chamberlain led us to the place of Sitter's demise. He said he'd visited it with his father when he was a kid.

The area turned out to be even more rugged than I'd suspected. A younger expedition member and I stepped out of our vehicles and climbed to the upper rim of the box canyon to look for old rifle casings. We didn't discover any artifacts, but based on contemporary descriptions of the ambush, we felt sure we'd found where the bandits had waited for the lawmen to ride into view.

It had taken a quarter century, but I'd finally gotten to see the lonely place where Sitter and Ranger Hulen died. Hopefully someday the state, the FTRA or descendants of the two slain officers will put up a monument in this desolate place so it will be easier for others to find.

The adventure left me with an even greater understanding of the challenges a frontier peace officer faced with no off-road vehicles, no GPS, no cell phones, no large-magazine assault rifles, no Yeti packed with bottled water. As Joaquin had said a quarter century earlier, down along this part of the Rio Grande even today, "there ain't no 9-1-1."

DAYBREAK ON THE BRITE RANCH

On Christmas Day 1917, some 45 horsemen approached the remote Lucas C. Brite Ranch, a 125,000-acre spread 30 miles southwest of Marfa in the Big Bend.

The ranch headquarters, 18 miles south of the town of Valentine, itself amounted to a small community. There was a store called the Busy Bee, an attached post office, the adobe residence of ranch foreman Van Neill's family and several other structures. Brite and his family had gone to Marfa for the holiday, but Neill and his wife planned to host a Christmas dinner and had invited numerous guests. Already on hand for the event was Neill's father, former ranger Sam H. Neill and his wife.

Up early drinking coffee, about 7:30 a.m. the elder Neill saw a mounted Mexican with rifle in hand riding hard toward the ranch enclave.

The rider, as Neill later recalled, "hollered to his men—that was the first I knew there were any others there—and jerked his horse up, and he hollered at his men to kill all the Americans ["Mueran los gringos!"]. And as he said it, I shot and he didn't, of course, holler no more."

Neill's son joined him in shooting. Running from window to window, father and son fired from all eight of the ranch house's windows hoping to give the attackers the false impression that there were more than just a couple of defenders. With their two wives reloading their rifles for them, the pair kept up their fire for 30 minutes.

The raiders seized a young Mexican ranch hand who had been attending to the morning milking and sent him to tell the Neills to surrender. Though Sam Neill had been wounded, the two men answered the order with more rifle fire. Next the bandits sent the boy scurrying to the house of the postmaster and store owner to demand that he relinquish his keys or die. The man chose to do as told, which stopped the shooting as the raiders concentrated on looting the Busy Bee and post office.

When the mail wagon arrived from downriver, the bandits stopped their work long enough to kill the two Mexican passengers. Driver Michael "Mickey" Welch also died, but not as quickly. Annoyed by his incessant cursing, the bandits strung him up from the ceiling of the store and cut his throat. As one of several guests who had begun to show up for Christmas lunch turned his automobile back toward Marfa to notify authorities, the bandits loaded their loot and rode off toward Mexico.

News reached the U.S. Cavalry post at Marfa (later designated as Fort D.A. Russell) just as the bugler sounded mess call for Christmas lunch. Col. George T. Langhorne immediately ordered a detachment to pursue the raiders, but rather than saddle up, the horse soldiers headed to the Brite Ranch in automobiles. Additional mounted troops would follow.

Meanwhile, the next day's edition of the El Paso Herald reported that the raiders had killed three people before escaping with $7,000 in inventory from the ranch store. Troops and several Rangers had caught up with the Mexicans before they made it to the Rio Grande and emptied nearly a dozen saddles.

THE DAY FRANK PATTERSON "DIED"

"I was killed on Christmas Day in 1918," a smiling 84-year-old Frank Patterson told a reporter for the San Angelo Standard-Times in the summer of 1963. "At least, that's the way the records read for a long time, and they're supposed to be official, aren't they?" (He told journalist Jerry Lackey he'd "died" in 1918, but he'd been off by a year.)

The Christmas he "died," the former West Texas lawman told Lackey, he and several members of his Ranger company, along with a detachment of U.S. Cavalry, had been riding hard after the Brite Ranch raiders. After they'd engaged some of the men they'd been chasing,

Patterson's comrades realized their fellow Ranger had gone missing and concluded he'd been killed.

What the other Rangers didn't know was that on his own, thinking the raiders might have split up, by himself Patterson took a different trail than the Rangers had been following. When bullets began whizzing past him, Patterson realized his assumption had been correct. Dismounting and taking cover, he began returning fire.

"There was a nice young fellow who kept shooting at me from a draw," he told Lackey. "He kept up the fire so I finally had to shoot him, after he barely missed me several times."

All those years later, Patterson still remembered that he'd expended 18 rounds during the fight. When he needed to reload, he had trouble getting the sharp-pointed rifle rounds out of his ammunition belt. When the shooting stopped, he was still alive, but his fingers had been bloodied in extracting more cartridges from the tight loops that held them.

The following day, Patterson having been reported missing and presumed dead, Ranger Capt. Monroe Fox and some of his men went looking for the body only to find him alive and well. If Fox was relieved, he didn't show it.

"He was mad as hell," Patterson said.

In telling the story to the San Angelo newsman, the Kimble County native embellished it a bit. Patterson said that Fox was so furious that he pulled his revolver, vowed "that was as far as he was going to pack that thing" and threw it on the desert floor.

Fox, in his anger, might have done that with his revolver but Patterson claimed the captain left the pistol where it lay. He told Lackey that he'd picked it up and still had it in his gun collection. But a six-gun was a vital piece of equipment, especially in such a remote area, and there's no way Fox would have allowed someone else to claim his gun.

While Patterson survived the aftermath of the Brite Ranch raid, contemporary newspaper accounts said at least 10 of the fleeing bandits died in the pursuit. Later research fixed the death toll at 18 Mexicans. In the spring of 1918, the Adjutant General forced Capt. Fox to resign because of his company's attack on the village of Porvenir. Five of the Rangers who'd taken part in the massacre were fired. Patterson and six other Rangers who had not been involved in the raid were transferred to another company.

Born in Kimble County in 1879, Patterson already had considerable law-enforcement experience under his gun belt before enlisting in the Rangers. In the early 1900s, he'd been a city marshal in an Arizona mining town and also rode for a time with the Arizona Rangers. While with that short-lived organization, he took a bullet in the leg that kept him down for a time. He'd been working on the border as a civilian packer for the U.S. Army when he joined the Rangers on Sept. 19, 1917. He reenlisted Sept. 10, 1918, but as his payroll records note, he "jumped his company" and was listed as "off-roll" effective October 1.

The former Ranger later worked as a state game warden. served as a special Ranger from Aug. 5-Dec. 1, 1922, and in 1928 voters elected him sheriff of Kimble County. Reelected two years later, he served until Jan. 1, 1933. Patterson died at 89 on Aug. 29, 1969, and is buried in Junction.

PORVENIR

Fittingly, the darkest incident in Ranger history occurred in the dead of night.

The small village of Porvenir lay on the Texas side of the river across from the Mexican village of Pilares, about 30 miles upriver from Candelaria in one of the most isolated parts of Presidio County. Porvenir's residents, fewer than 150, supported themselves by farming or herding goats. But area Anglo ranchers, believing that some in Porvenir augmented their income through banditry, talked Ranger Captain James Monroe Fox into "rounding up" the community.

In late January 1918, Fox dispatched eight men to meet with rancher John Pool and other cattlemen for a raid on Porvenir. Fox placed 43-year-old Ranger Bud Weaver in command of the squad. Striking late at night, the Rangers and their civilian guides rode into Porvenir looking for those responsible for the Brite Ranch raid. They rousted 31 women, children and old men from their beds and gathered them in the center of the small village. A search netted only one old 10-gauge shotgun and two rifles, but an assortment of new shoes, Crystal White soap, and Barlow pocketknives also turned up—property reported stolen from the Busy Bee store in the Brite Ranch raid. The Rangers arrested three men and took them back to their camp for questioning, releasing them two days later.

On January 28, Weaver's detachment—accompanied by Pool, his brother and two other men—rode into an Army sub-post at the Evetts Ranch. Weaver handed Capt. Henry H. Anderson of the 14th Cavalry a set of orders from Col. George T. Langhorne in Marfa instructing him to cooperate with the Rangers, who the captain noticed seemed to have been drinking. The captain phoned Langhorne to express his concerns, only to be told to abide by his orders. The main thing Weaver wanted, he explained, was for the soldiers to surround Porvenir while the Ranger and his men looked for more weapons and suspected raiders.

The state-federal contingent reached Porvenir about midnight. The soldiers set up a perimeter around the town while the Rangers and the four cattlemen searched each of the pole and adobe jacales that made up the village. Assembling all but the oldest male residents, the Rangers marched the men about a quarter mile from town. Weaver told Anderson he intended to question the men and no longer needed any assistance.

Robert Keil, one of the soldiers on hand that night, later recalled that he and his fellow troopers had just made it back to their horses, about three hundred yards away, when they heard the loud voices of men followed by a woman's voice and then a woman's scream.

"For perhaps ten seconds we couldn't hear anything," Keil recalled, "and then it seemed that every woman down there screamed at the same time. It was an awful thing to hear in the dead of night. We could also hear what sounded like praying, and, of course, the small children were screaming with fright. Then we heard shots, rapid shots, echoing and blending in the dark."

The cavalrymen rushed back and found what Keil called "a mass of bodies" at the foot of a bluff, "the most hellish sight that any of us had ever witnessed." He continued: "The bodies lay in every conceivable position, including one that seemed to be sitting against the rock wall....A hospital corpsman...went over the bodies, but not a breath of life was left in a single one. The professionals had done their work well."

Fifteen men and boys ranging in age from 72 to 16 had been

summarily executed by the Rangers. All the bodies bore multiple gunshot wounds, some of the victims nearly eviscerated. Not only had the Rangers slaughtered more than a dozen people, they killed the town. Following the massacre, the roughly 140 remaining residents abandoned Porvenir.

Though his monthly report failed to mention the incident, Fox later tried to write the massacre off as an unfortunate accident. He said the Mexican males had been "carried out to the edge of town" so the Rangers could identify them. As his men tried to get their names, the captain continued, "some of their comrades" began shooting at the Rangers from the darkness. That, he said, caused the Rangers' horses to scatter, leaving his men afoot. "They [the rangers] immediately lay down returning fire on all moving objects in front."

At first the military also tried to cover up what happened at Porvenir, even though it claimed that no soldiers had taken part in the killings. But slowly, like a spreading bloodstain, word of the atrocity made it beyond the Big Bend region, thanks largely to the efforts of Porvenir school-master Harry Warren and J.J. Kilpatrick, Candelaria farmer, store owner and justice of the peace.

The Mexican government conducted a court of inquiry in Ojinaga and forwarded its findings to Washington and Austin. The Army sent in a special inspector who succeeded in putting together the true story and the Adjutant General's Department ordered Ranger Capt. William Hanson to investigate. Grand jurors in Presidio County heard testimony concerning the incident but returned no indictments.

Adjutant Gen. James A. Harley ordered Fox to Austin on May 16 to discuss the incident. Less than two weeks later, as outrage in some quarters continued to build, the adjutant general summoned Fox to a second meeting. On May 31, Fox sent Harley a letter of resignation "as I don't feel that I am getting a fair deal." On June 4, 1918, the adjutant general ordered Co. B disbanded and fired five of its men. (Three other Rangers who had been involved in the massacre had already resigned.) Seven other Co. B Rangers (including Private Frank Patterson) got transferred to another company.

For the most part, the state and federal investigations into the Porvenir incident ran their course behind the scenes. Vigorously campaigning for election to a full term as governor, William P. Hobby did not make a public issue of the disciplinary steps he and his adjutant general had taken. And as the decades passed, the incident largely faded from memory—except for the families and descendants of those killed that literally dark night in 1918.

A century later, a historical marker was finally erected by the Texas Historical Commission. Given the remoteness of the Porvenir site, the marker was placed off U.S. 90, a quarter of a mile west of Marfa.

TIME OF TRANSITION:

1919 - 1935

CAPT. WRIGHT'S WHEELMAN

Bob Snow never wore a Ranger badge, but he definitely had the appearance, aptitude and attitude of a Ranger. He'd have fit right in as an old-school state lawman. Even so, he rubbed shoulders with some of the best-known early 20th century Rangers, including the legendary Capt. Will Wright.

However, Snow did have a long career as a state game warden. Born in Williamson County, he grew up in Willacy County where his older brother Luther served as sheriff for years. Both of the Snow boys were tough as a rawhide bottom chair, and while Luther stuck to sherrifin', Bob developed a reputation as a solid conservation officer and rose in rank. He also became nationally renowned as a hunter of mountain lions and jaguars in South Texas and Mexico.

After he retired as a Texas Parks and Wildlife Department game warden captain, Snow went on the payroll of the YO Ranch at Mountain Home. He worked for then owner Charlie Schreiner III as a hunting guide, tracker of wounded game and, perhaps his best role, as resident colorful character. In the YO's chuck wagon during and after meals, Capt. Bob held court, telling one great story after another.

Before signing on as a game warden in 1925, Snow had been on the Ranger payroll, but only as a non-commissioned driver for Capt.

Wright. An old-school lawman, the captain still preferred horses to Model T's.

One day while working for Wright, Snow drove the captain to a point on the Texas side of the Rio Grande where the Rangers hoped to catch a suspected killer while crossing the river. The critical information in the case came from a man who, as Snow put it, had gotten "scratched up a little while they were taking a voluntary statement according to his constitutional rights."

While the Rangers waited quietly along the river, Snow stayed with the car, guarding the gate to the ranch they were on.

"A young reporter from the Brownsville Herald dressed up all fancy came up," Snow said. "For some damn reason I thought he was a deputy sheriff. He...asked me if any new developments had occurred in the case."

Snow told him about the man who'd provided the Rangers the critical information, confiding that the Rangers had him hidden so he'd have time to heal up before a lawyer saw him. "He wanted to go down on the river," Snow continued, "but I told him he couldn't because they were trying not to make any noise while they were waiting for the other man. They'd been out there before dawn."

The reporter left and eventually so did the Rangers, the suspected killer not having shown.

The next day, the captain, several of the Rangers and Snow sat in a café drinking coffee when someone walked up and asked Wright about the murder.

"Cap said, 'We are still making the investigation,' and this fellow says, 'Well, it says here in the paper ya'll skint up somebody to get a statement and that you know who did the killing.'" Wright asked to look at the newspaper. He read it carefully if far from admiringly, slowly drawing out the pronunciation of a seven-letter word having to do with a matter of parentage.

"I just kept real quiet," Snow said.

The legend grew that the next time Snow ran into the reporter who'd written the story that had so inflamed his boss, he pulled the .45 he was allowed to carry and put a bullet through the journalist's Speed Graphic camera.

"That's a darn lie," Snow countered when asked about it. "That camera belonged to the newspaper, not that reporter."

Another story Snow told about Capt. Wright had to do with the Ranger's well-worn, sweat-stained hat. Late one night, someone awakened the captain with news that he was needed somewhere right away. So as not to disturb his still-sleeping wife, Wright quickly dressed in the dark. After pulling on his boots and buckling on his gun belt, he grabbed his hat and hurried out the door. Not until he reached the scene of whatever the emergency had been did he realize that he'd donned Mrs. Wright's fancy feather-plumed hat, not his Stetson.

Not every Ranger activity on the border centered on life-or-death situations.

Sunday cock fighting was a long-standing tradition in South Texas. During Wright's time on the border, one ranch—owned by someone with considerable political pull—hosted a rooster fight every Sunday.

"It was pretty well off the road and as long as they had the fights where the good folks going to church Sunday morning wouldn't have to see them, the fights were okay with the sheriff, mainly because he had the winningest rooster," Snow remembered.

But when a new sheriff got elected, the lawman soon learned of the regular blood sport going on in his county and asked assistance from the Rangers in putting a stop to it.

"They let it go on a couple of months and then one Sunday morning they surrounded the ranch," Snow said.

When Rangers and county officers rushed in to stop the fight, they arrested dozens of spectators and chicken owners. The Rangers ordered everyone to gather their roosters and get in their cars. Then they'd be escorted to the county seat where charges would be filed.

"The caravan started off down the highway about the time church let out," Snow recalled. "Every time a family of church folks came by, they pulled over...[and] the men...[removed] their hats respectfully, thinking there was a funeral in progress."

Suddenly, all the roosters started crowing. "You never saw such shaken-up folks," Snow continued. "When they figured out what...[was going on], they got back in their cars and drove off disgustedly."

The arrested miscreants paid their fines and likely several weeks passed before the local cockfights resumed.

PRUNING GLEN ROSE

Covering only 192 square miles, Somervell County is the second smallest of any of Texas' 254 counties.

In addition to its compact size, in the 1920s the county also ranked as the second poorest in Texas. But with the advent of national prohibition, Somervell County reigned as one of the state's top moonshining venues. A lot of folks of otherwise modest means suddenly had full pockets.

In his book on longtime Glen Rose lawyer Ernest T. Adams, author Jeffrey J. Pruitt said that by 1923 the illegal production and selling of alcoholic beverages ranked as Somervell County's top industry. (In addition to his prosecutorial work, as a lay archeologist Adams had a hand in discovering the county's famous dinosaur tracks.)

If the way the map had been drawn left the people who lived along the Paluxy River with a postage-stamp county compared with the state's other political subdivisions, its proximity to the Dallas-Fort Worth area provided a large and growing market for Somervell County's liquid "crop." The cedar-covered hills around Glen Rose hid scores of stills, and out-bound truck traffic crowded the roads.

Good deals don't last forever, of course.

Early in the morning of Aug. 25, 1923, on orders from Gov. Pat Neff, Texas Rangers under Capt. Rudolph D. Shumate descended on the county intending to put its residents out of the bootlegging business.

By sundown, 27 men languished in the county jail. Among them was T. Walker Davis, the sheriff. Joining him behind bars was E.L. Roark, the county attorney. Twenty-three stills had been destroyed and put on display outside the courthouse along with stacks of confiscated cases of whiskey and homebrew.

The cleanup continued for most of the week. On August 29, one fleeing bootlegger made the mistake of firing on the Rangers with a .38 revolver, a move that permanently got him out of the whiskey-making business or any other worldly endeavor.

While the Rangers had definitely disrupted the making and selling of moonshine, adjudicating the defendants proved more difficult. For one thing, shortly after the raids began, the district attorney had found it necessary to leave the county on some urgent business and had not been heard from since.

With the county attorney awaiting his trial, Adams had been appointed as his replacement. After the DA left town, the commissioners court asked Adams if he'd take on that job. Since it meant another $30 a month, he accepted.

Soon after Adams recited the oath of office, a Ranger approached him.

"Ernest, you know where every still in the county is," the lawman said. "Show me, and we will make a cleaning."

The new DA didn't need to mull that over before responding. He was not going to rat out friends who had just been trying to make a living, albeit not technically an honest one.

"That is your job," he told the Ranger. "You bring 'em in and I'll prosecute them."

That said, Adams' first order of business as DA was bringing the former county attorney to trial.

The proceeding began in Cleburne on Feb. 20, 1924. The state's first witness was one James Aaron "Dick" Watson. A 28-year-old World War I veteran, he had been collecting information as an undercover state prohibition agent. While not technically a Ranger, he had been working under the Rangers.

His testimony offered detailed insight into bootlegging in Somervell County and outlined how the defendant had been taking bribes to look the other way.

If Adams had any thought of putting Watson back on the stand the following day, Watson had told all he was going to tell.

That night, someone blew the married father of two away with a 12-gauge shotgun fired through the window of the Glen Rose boarding house where Rangers had stashed him—ostensibly for his safety.

Rangers quickly rounded up 15 suspects, including the person who likely pulled the trigger, but justice was not only blind, she couldn't hear or talk. Six men were charged with the undercover officer's murder, but no witnesses to the killing could be found and no convictions would be forthcoming.

Meanwhile, newspapers in Fort Worth and Dallas distilled their own brew of black ink and purple prose.

"The little town [of Glen Rose], nestling in the hills in which great rum stills have long been hidden, has been rocked these last two days as it never expects to be rocked again," reported the Fort Worth Record.

But by February 23, Glen Rose was quiet. Still, the newspaper noted, the "mountain village," scene of "Texas's great moonshine murder melodrama" crouched over a powder keg that could be touched off by "someone unable to contain the growing wrath within him."

Better judgment, or at least enhanced discretion, prevailed and Glen Rose returned to business as usual. And as soon as things settled down, that business again included moonshining and bootlegging.

The young DA who had at least succeeded in prosecuting some of the local distillers and marketers the Rangers had arrested did eventually feel some of the wrath the Fort Worth newspaper had written about. But no buckshot flew his way. When Adams ran for a full term in 1926, he lost the election. Somervell County voters clearly wanted in office someone a bit more in tune with the community's values.

THE DEMISE OF GRUBE

One of Texas' least-known ghost towns, Grube had a short, wild history capped by what some say was literally an explosive end.

A West Texas oil boom town, in the late 1920's it sprouted faster than a sage brush bloom after a good rain, no matter that it lay a hard, dusty drive from nowhere. Soon Grube became noted as a place where an off-duty oil patch worker could gamble his wages, swill bootleg booze and enjoy for-hire feminine companionship.

When the initial well of what would become one of the richest oil fields in the world blew in on Oct. 29, 1926, on Ira Yates' ranch in Pecos County, word quickly spread that the 67-year-old Yates was suddenly worth millions. That was back when folks having only a few thousand dollars in the bank were considered nicely well-to-do.

Soon, Model T's coming from McCamey, Rankin, Fort Stockton and San Angelo caravanned along unpaved roads toward the new field to see the amazingly prolific discovery well and hopefully cash in on the coming boom.

"In a little while," Yates later recalled, "you could see the clouds of dust set up by motor cars as the people came to the well to see what had really taken place. Excitement was pretty high."

A kind-hearted man even when he had been poor, Yates the millionaire extended hospitality to all comers. The rancher-turned-mogul converted his large barn into a makeshift guest house, partitioning it with fiberboard. He even threw on a new coat of red paint. Packed with oil scouts, camp followers and newspaper reporters, the barn soon became known as the Red Barn.

As the field began to develop other structures went up around the barn. The Red Barn soon grew into a new town, Red Barn, Texas.

Just across the Pecos River from Red Barn another town rapidly developed. They called it Grube (pronounced Groo-bee). As had been the case in other oil field boom towns, prostitutes, bootleggers and gamblers made up most of the community's new arrivals.

By November 1927 the owners of the Grube Townsite Company were placing large ads in newspapers operating in other oil towns, hoping to attract lot buyers and businessmen. "Grube, Texas/The New Oil Town/"In the Heart of the Yates Pool"/ was "The Seminole of West Texas," the ad shouted in substantial bold type. In Crockett County only three-quarters of a mile from the flourishing Yates Field and adjoining Red Barn, the new town lay on the Thompson Ranch, 32 miles south of Rankin and "92 miles due south of Midland." Grube was so new it didn't have a post office, but the ad said correspondence from prospective buyers could be addressed "Grubie [sic] Townsite Co., Rankin, Texas."

Earlier the following year, on the night of Jan. 15, 1928, rangers and U.S. Customs inspectors descended on the free-wheeling town. The lawmen arrested 32 residents described as gamblers or bootleggers. In addition, as the El Paso Evening Post reported on January 19, "Many women were run out [of town.]" In making the arrests and causing the soiled doves to flee, the Rangers seized 60 gallons of whiskey, 100 cases of beer and "a great number of slot machines."

While Grube had no shortage of bad types, its residents did suffer from lack of good water. Since Red Barn did have a rudimentary water system, thanks to a well on the Yates ranch, the working girls (who had returned to town when the Rangers left) and other denizens of Grube's dives went to Red Barn for baths. "We never had any trouble with them," recalled one old-timer who had run a business on the more proper Red Barn side of the river.

Well, there was the time a man armed with a shotgun showed up at one of Red Barn's accommodations, intent on murder.

"He said he was waiting for so-and-so who was inside taking a bath," Corky Huddleston remembered nearly 60 years later when a writer for the Marathon Oil Co. interviewed him for a forthcoming corporate history. "'You can't come in here and shoot people,' I says to him."

The man with the scattergun hastened to explain himself. He had no intention of entering the building and alarming anyone else.

"I'm going to shoot him out here," he said, seemingly a little offended that someone would think he'd kill a man in a place of business.

The proprietor went inside and warned the intended victim, who promptly left by a back door.

The extent of liveliness in Grube waxed and waned with the flow of money. Oil workers got paid twice a month, in cash. Accordingly, every two weeks things perked up considerably in Grube.

"On payday," Huddleston later recalled, "the girls from Grube would get into big cars and cruise [Red Barn and the nearby newer and larger oil town of Iraan] with megaphones calling, 'Come on over and see me tonight.'"

Most oil boom towns dried up or went into decline when a discovery field slowed down and new play erupted somewhere else. But Grube, the Sodom and Gomorrah of the Pecos, came to an end only a year after its founding. "Grube, Once Seen As Future City, Nearly Deserted," the San Angelo Standard-Times reported on Nov. 27, 1928.

Though no official paperwork has been found to document the claim, persistent West Texas legend has it that not only did the Rangers shut down the wide-open town, they dynamited all its corrugated metal buildings and any other structure capable of accommodating a bar or brothel.

STRANGER AT THE DOOR

As a boot-tough frontier Ranger captain, Daniel Webster Roberts survived Indian fights and captured dangerous criminals. But something that happened only three days after his 86th birthday ripped open an old wound that had nothing to do with his illustrious career.

Forty-two-year-old Mayme Byrd Hudson Roberts—the captain's daughter-in-law—ran a two-story boarding house at 2103 Nueces St. in Austin. She catered to male University of Texas students, providing her young renters room, board and often, a little mothering. In turn, most of her "boys" felt protective of her.

About 2 a.m. on October 13, 1927, someone began banging loudly on the boarding house's front door. Awakened by the racket, one of the student renters threw back his covers and went to the door. When he opened it, a well-dressed, middle-aged man stood before him.

The dark-suited stranger told the student that he needed to speak to the landlady.

"I must see her at once," he implored. "It is urgent. Let me talk to her in private for a few minutes."

The student told the man to wait while he went to check with Mrs. Roberts. Quickly dressing, she met the man in the parlor of the 1890s vintage house. Meanwhile, the student who'd answered the door and several other young men awakened by the commotion stood protectively outside the room.

"Mrs. Roberts, you do not know me, and must never discover my identity," the visitor said as he shook hands with the puzzled woman.

"What do you want?" she asked.

"I want to award you for years of faithful work," he replied. "It is a debt I must repay. You have cared for your fatherless children. It has been a herculean job, but you have come through. I must see that you are repaid."

He talked in staccato bursts, briefly pausing between sentences.

As the baffled Mrs. Roberts tried to make sense of the situation, the man stuck both hands into his pockets and started pulling out rolls of cash. Tossing the money—ten-, twenty- and hundred-dollar bills—into the woman's lap, he said, "There! That's part of it. But you'll get more. The debt is still unpaid."

Still foggy headed after being roused from sleep, Mrs. Roberts may have wondered if this was just a weird dream.

"Who are you? What is the money for? I've never seen you before. Take it back!" she yelled. Then, frantically, she called for her boys. Nearly two dozen young boarders rushed into the parlor to surround their landlady. At this, the strange visitor stooped, gathered all the bills and began stuffing the cash in his pockets.

"I'm sorry, Mrs. Roberts, that you saw fit not to accept this money," he said. "But you will! It will come to you through the mail from Oklahoma—not ten- or twenty-dollar bills, but thousands of dollars at a time. Goodbye."

Grabbing his coat and hat, the man wheeled and vanished out the front door. "Money, money, worlds of money," he muttered as he disappeared into the night.

At that, Mrs. Roberts' brave veneer broke down and she became hysterical. While some of the students remained to calm her, the others ran after the mysterious visitor. Without success, they spent three hours searching the city, checking the highways, train stations and any eating places that happened to be open.

Meanwhile, Mrs. Roberts phoned the police. Officers hurried to the scene and listened to the shaken woman's bizarre story. At first, they found it difficult to believe but then one of the policemen noticed a $10 bill on the floor. Based on that, and Mrs. Roberts' obvious angst, they began their own unsuccessful hunt for the nameless visitor.

Later that morning, making his rounds at police headquarters a reporter for the Austin Statesman learned of the weird incident and turned it into a front-page story complete with dialog furnished by Mrs. Roberts. The local Associated Press bureau condensed the article and distributed it statewide.

"Mrs. Roberts could advance no reason for the strange visit," the wire service reported.

Yet there was one thing. Ten years before, she'd told the reporter, someone shot her husband to death in New Mexico. Her late spouse had been a sheriff at the time, Mrs. Roberts added. In his article, the unnamed journalist noted that the murder had taken place in Alamogordo "one dark winter night" and that "all attempts through the intervening years to discover the murderer [had] failed."

As the AP dispatch concluded: "[The lawman's] widow thinks it possible that some relative of the unknown slayer may be trying to make amends to her."

The next day's Statesman did not follow up on the bizarre story. But there was much more to it. While it was true that Mrs. Roberts' husband had died violently at the hands of another, the widow left out all the salient and salacious details. Reputation is important, and clearly, even though she'd been an innocent victim of what had transpired, the truth would be embarrassing to her, her children, Capt. and Mrs. Roberts, their daughter Lillie and others in the family.

The story goes back to 1887, three years after Captain Roberts and his wife Lou left Texas and settled in the mining town of Nogal, New Mexico Territory. Then in his 40s, the former Ranger opened a store and worked in mining. Later he served two terms as sheriff of Lincoln County. When the wife of his brother George Travis Roberts died back in Texas in Gillespie County, the sudden widower realized he could not properly take care of his children. He asked the captain if he and Lou would be willing to raise them and the couple said yes. They soon adopted 12-year-old Lillie and 18-month-old Fred, two children the couple went on to cherish as if they were their natural offspring.

In 1892, Lillie married James Fielding Hinkle, a Missouri-born cowboy turned cattleman and businessman who went on to serve as New Mexico's governor from 1923 to 1925. Fred, who'd been working as a cowhand, married Mayme Hudson in the summer of 1907 in El Paso.

Capt. Roberts' father had served in an early Texas minuteman company, tantamount to being a Ranger. By 1917, Fred had become the third-generation Roberts to take up the family law-enforcement trade. He served as a constable (not sheriff) in Oscuro, New Mexico, a rough mining town.

While the 32-year-old did get shot to death on March 1, 1917, it had not been in the line of duty. That night, 44-year-old cattleman Columbus H. "Lum" Byfield came home to find his front door locked. Once he got inside the house, in their dimly lit living room he saw Constable Roberts sitting on the divan next to his attractive younger wife, Virginia.

The circumstances being obvious, neither Byfield nor Fred said anything. Instantly convinced Roberts was having an affair with his wife, the infuriated husband ran to their bedroom and grabbed his pistol. Meanwhile, the still-silent Roberts dashed for the back door. Byfield ran outside through the front door, circled the residence and confronted the constable. The cuckolded rancher then put three bullets in Roberts' head, killing him instantly.

Byfield left almost immediately to turn himself in to the sheriff in Carrizozo, the county seat. Appearing before a local magistrate the next day, Byfield waived a preliminary hearing and the judge bound the case over to the grand jury. Bond was set at $2,500.

Learning that her late husband had been cheating on her devastated the new widow, then nearing the final month of pregnancy with their fourth child.

At the coroner's inquest, Virginia Byfield testified that her husband had "good reason" to shoot the constable. Byfield claimed he only started shooting when the officer had made a play for his gun, but Roberts' revolver had not been fired.

Three years before, Capt. Roberts and Lou had moved back to Texas. However, the couple happened to be back in New Mexico for a visit when their son was killed. In what would be the old Ranger's last law-enforcement-related action, the day after the shooting he personally filed a murder complaint against Byfield. At his arraignment, the rancher entered a plea of not guilty. But after weighing the facts, the prosecutor did not proceed with the case.

Following Constable Roberts' March 5 funeral in Alamogordo, as soon as the new widow could pack her things Capt. Roberts and his wife took their grieving daughter-in-law and grandchildren back to

Texas by train. The couple were living in Dripping Springs, a small Hays County town west of Austin. Mayme's parents also lived there, and she and her children stayed with them until her father's death in 1923. Then she moved to Austin, joined by the captain and his wife.

Who was the remorseful mystery man who four years later offered Mayme money in the middle of the night?

Was it Byfield? At some point after the shooting, he'd moved to Arizona. Still kicking in 1927, he lived until 1936. But if it had been him who'd shown up at the widow's door, surely Mayme would've recognized him. If not Byfield, maybe a son or some other relative acting on his behalf. Or maybe it had been some kind-hearted person who knew of the killing and simply felt sorry for the widow. Finally, it could have been a crazy person who knew part of her sad story. Whoever it was, judging by the dialog Mrs. Roberts reported, the pre-dawn visitor seemed genuinely remorseful over what had happened in New Mexico.

Capt. Rogers lived another eight years, dying in Austin in 1935. Lou followed him in death in 1940. Mayme Roberts, who never remarried, spent her final years with a daughter in New Braunfels, Texas. She died there at 70 in 1959 and is buried in Comal Cemetery.

If the old Ranger's family ever solved the mystery of the man with the money, it was never publicly disclosed.

FOUR BITS TO WATCH MY BACK?

During the East Texas oil boom in 1931, Kilgore-based Ranger Manuel T. "Lone Wolf " Gonzaullas was not popular with the criminal element. While few would be willing to take him on face-to-face, Gonzaullas figured no shortage of local thugs wouldn't mind shooting him from behind.

Since he did not have eyes in the back of his head, the Ranger hired 18-year-old John Musgrove to discreetly follow him as he made his rounds in the afternoon and evenings. His job was simple: watching the state lawman's back. Lone Wolf paid the young man fifty cents or a dollar, depending on the amount of time the teenager spent on guard.

Born in Spain on July 4, 1891, to a Spanish father and Canadian mother, Gonzaullas lost his parents in the devastating 1900 Galveston hurricane. He got his first taste of gunfire as a major in the Mexican Army in 1911 during the Mexican Revolution and later spent five years as a U.S. Customs inspector. Gonzaullas joined the Rangers in 1920.

While serving as a ranger in the 1920s and early 1930s, Gonzaullas made a lot of cases and a lot of headlines but did not earn a lot of money. On top of that, the State of Texas was not lavish in its payment of per diem to state employees on official business. To save money, the Lone Wolf sometimes slept in a county jail rather than pay for a hotel room. Long-time Parker County lawyer Jack Borden once put the Ranger up at his house rather than have him spend the night in the county lockup.

Newly elected Gov. Miriam "Ma" Ferguson fired Gonzaullas and all the other Rangers in 1933.Two years later, following the organization of the Department of Public Safety, the director of the new agency hired Gonzaullas to set up the state's first crime lab.

After getting that done, in 1940 he opted to return to the Ranger service and soon became captain of Co. B in Dallas. Among many high-profile cases he handled, Gonzaullas spearheaded the investigation into Texarkana's infamous Phantom Killer murders in 1946. The captain usually prevailed in what he set out to do, but the Rangers never apprehended a suspect in the Texarkana slayings.

Not everyone used Gonzaullas' "Lone Wolf " nickname. Retired Ranger Lewis Rigler later recalled driving Public Safety Commission member (and former Ranger captain) Tom Hickman to Austin for a commission meeting. The two North Texas men met with Gonzaullas and former Ranger Frank Hamer at the Stephen F. Austin Hotel for a cup of coffee. "How's the solitary coyote?" Hamer asked as he and Gonzaullas shook hands.

Lone Wolf retired in 1951 and died at 85 in a Dallas hospital on Feb. 13, 1977.

"In my opinion," his old boss DPS director Col. Homer Garrison said in 1963, "Gonzaullas will go down in history as one of the great Rangers of all time."

READY FOR THE NAZIS

By 1941, the world had changed to an almost unbelievable extent from the early 1880s when W.H. Roberts—a cousin of noted Ranger Capt. Dan Roberts—had ridden as a Frontier Battalion Ranger.

Born Oct. 6, 1861, on Onion Creek in Travis County eight miles south of Austin, Roberts spent much of his teenage years as a cowboy. But as he told an interviewer in the spring of 1950 when he was 88, "I appreciate my Ranger days better than my cattle- or trail-driving days."

Roberts spent two years as a Ranger. He enlisted in 1880 at 19 and served until 1882. His first unit was Co. D, which his uncle Dan commanded. Later transferring to Fort Davis, he served in Co. E under Capt. Charles L. Nevill.

"My Ranger service was quite a schooling for me," Roberts later said. "I was associated with men of fine qualities." And some men of not so fine qualities.

As the tracks of what would soon be the nation's second transcontinental railroad moved west across Texas, a detachment of Rangers including Roberts arrived at the rough-and-tumble rail worker camp of Vinegarroon in sprawling Val Verde County. The Rangers were responding to a report that the soon-to-be-famous Judge Roy Bean and some of his pals had raided a camp of Canadian rail workers and riddled their "bean kettles and coffee pots" with bullets.

"[Ranger] Tom Carson and a couple others of us walked into Bean's saloon, and the judge was very courteous, mentioned that he was glad we were there and inviting us to have a drink and make his saloon our headquarters," Roberts told a correspondent for the Fort Worth Star-Telegram in July 1941.

Carson then said to Bean, "Judge, you're the cause of our being here, wrecking railroad construction camps and such."

"Just a little harmless fun," Bean said. "Warn't no one hurt was there?"

"Just scared to death," the Ranger replied. "But I'm here to tell you that one more outburst out of you and you'll go to [Fort] Stockton—in shackles. And we'll have our kind of a preliminary hearing for you—not yours."

After that, Roberts said, the Rangers had no further trouble with Bean.

While with Co. D, in far West Texas he took part in the last fight between Rangers and a small band of Mescalero Apache in January 1881. Asked by the reporter if he had accounted for any of the Indians, he said, "Oh, yes, I killed a couple of Indians—they got after me, and I ran them to death!"

Like most Rangers of his time, Roberts always had a Model 73 Winchester within easy reach. He kept the .30-30 for years, later passing it on to his grandson, Matt Roberts.

When World War II began, Matt Roberts enlisted in the Army. One day, before reporting for duty, he saw his 80-year-old grandfather walking up 9th Street toward the family residence at 9th and Highland Avenue in West Austin. The younger Roberts greeted his grandfather, and they went inside. After the usual preliminaries, what the old Ranger said next caught Matt off-guard.

Observing that since Llano was fewer than 40 miles from the still mostly German town of Fredericksburg, the elder Roberts said he'd like to have his .30-30 back. With a war coming on, he explained, those "damn Germans" in Gillespie County might cause trouble.

Matt said of course and went to get the vintage lever gun. The old man wrapped it in newspaper and walked back to where he could catch a streetcar. From downtown, he took a bus back to Llano, carrying his trusty Winchester.

In 1945, back home from the war after flying 59 missions as an enlisted man in a B-17, one day Matt saw his still-spry grandfather walking down 9th Street again.

"He had something wrapped in newspaper and I knew right away what it was," Matt recalled years later. "He climbed the steps to where

I sat on the porch. 'Now that the war's over, I thought I'd bring this back,' he said." Then Roberts handed his grandson two unopened boxes of cartridges he'd bought just in case.

The old Ranger spent most of his last years at the veterans hospital in Big Spring. (He was considered a veteran because of his Indian fighting as a Ranger.) Up until his death at 97 on Feb. 14, 1958, in the words of his grandson, he was "as bright as a new nickel."

THE TWO NOAH ARMSTRONGS

Shortly before noon on Feb. 8, 1952, white-haired "Mr. Noah" Armstrong—the oldest living former Texas Ranger—slowly emerged from his daughter's car in front of the recreation hall at Coleman's city park.

Using a cane and crutch, he made his way inside the low-slung stone structure where more than 250 relatives, friends and former Rangers waited to greet him on the occasion of his 100th birthday. Wearing what one reporter called a "natty gray suit" and tie, with a cigar clamped firmly in his mouth, the old Indian fighter and outlaw hunter shook hands with folks like a politician running for office.

After the attendees had enjoyed lunch and consumed two birthday cakes, master of ceremonies J.T. Padgitt took the floor. A prominent Coleman County rancher, he reviewed the locally revered former Frontier Battalion Ranger's long life.

But Padgitt didn't tell the whole story.

That's because two Noah Armstrongs shared one aging body—the personable early day lawman and retired stockman reporters loved to interview about the frontier days and the man who 60 years before faced trial for his alleged role in assassinating a popular Texas sheriff. And that hadn't been the only crime the old Ranger had been accused of committing.

Born in Lincoln County, Missouri, on Feb. 8, 1852, Armstrong came to Texas with his parents when he was a year old. His father William B. Armstrong raised horses. The family settled at Salado in Bell County, where for a time they lived in the stagecoach stop that would become known as Stagecoach Inn. When local leaders founded

Salado College in 1859, the elder Armstrong was one of the original stockholders. He eventually sold his shares in the college, as his son later explained, "for a bunch of horses when horses were going at $25 a head."

Noah attended the local college for a time, but as he later related, "I ran away from home at 15, [later] joined the Rangers, served from the Red River to the Rio Grande, was shot at several times, but never hit."

Armstrong's Ranger service began May 24, 1877, when the 25-year-old enlisted in Frontier Battalion Co. C under Capt. John C. Sparks. Later serving under Capt. George Washington Arrington, Armstrong left the Rangers on Feb. 28, 1878.

"We scouted much of [West Texas] with particular attention to the plains area where marauding Indians sought refuge," Armstrong later said of his time as a state lawman.

As a Ranger, he took part in several skirmishes with hostile Indians but had a much more serious shootout with a wanted killer. That was a horse thief named "Bones" Wilson, charged with murdering Erath County Sheriff James Martin on June 25, 1877. Armstrong and other Co. C Rangers under Capt. Sparks tracked the fugitive to a plum thicket near present-day Colorado City. When the cornered outlaw opened up on the Rangers with his buffalo rifle, Armstrong quickly shot the wanted man's horse. Using the dead animal as cover, Wilson continued to fire at the state lawmen. As Armstrong later put it, "Bones" had vowed that he'd never be taken alive "and he wasn't."

Capt. Sparks and his men, with Armstrong and another Ranger riding in the wagon bearing the outlaw's body arrived in Stephenville—the seat of Erath County—on September 18. The Rangers collected $1,500 in rewards that had been offered for the outlaw dead or alive.

"...All of the subscribers to the rewards offered for [Wilson's] arrest... paid up cheerfully," the Austin Daily Statesman reported on Sept. 27,1877. Arriving in Austin, Capt. Sparks showed a Statesman reporter a letter from Erath County Sheriff H.M. Henderson saying that Co. C had "the thanks of all our country, and many are the praises bestowed on your brave boys."

Leaving the Rangers in early 1878, Armstrong settled in the new county seat town of Coleman. He married Bettie Alice Fullerton on

Nov. 30, 1879 and the couple went on to have six children. In addition to getting hitched, he opened a saloon and gambling hall. He acquired the business at a bargain, the previous owner happy to sell out after being "literally tossed out of his own establishment by high-spirited patrons."

"[Coleman] was wide open then," Noah recalled in an interview with the San Angelo Standard Times published July 19, 1951, "and I made a bushel of money. Wish I had kept it."

After a dozen years as a saloon owner, Armstrong sold his bar around 1890 and, as he later put it, "engaged in the sheep business."

Armstrong had 14 siblings, eight of them brothers. And not all of the boys were law abiders. On Nov. 25, 1880, the Brenham Weekly Banner commented editorially on a news article it reprinted from the Georgetown Sun:

The...Sun has [an] *account of the killing of Nealy* [Cornelius] *and John* [Henry] *Armstrong by John T. Olive near Taylor last week. The Armstrongs were charged with horse stealing and one of them had just been released from jail. Both were drunk when the shooting occurred. They attacked Olive, who fired six shots and hit [with] five, either of which would have been fatal. The killing was clearly justifiable.*

At the time, Olive served as Taylor's city marshal. Duly tried for murder—then routine procedure when a lawman killed someone in the line of duty—the jury acquitted him. Not long after, Olive hired on as a Williamson County sheriff's deputy. In that capacity, in October 1884, he killed a fleeing armed robber. Again, the shooting was deemed justified. Less than a month later, he was elected sheriff. The following year, he killed a man in Taylor violently resisting arrest for burglary. That brought the number of figurative notches on his gun to four. Noah Armstrong and his surviving brothers must have read with more than casual interest news accounts of these shootings and other exploits on the part of what one newspaper called "the fearless young sheriff."

In addition to sheep, Armstrong raised horses and enjoyed exhibiting his best steeds at the annual Bell County Fair, an event that drew numerous visitors from across Central Texas. In 1892, Sheriff Olive and a friend, Austin-based U.S. Marshal John Rankin, traveled by train to Belton to take in the fair.

About 2 a.m. on Sept. 11, as the two tired officers waited at a Bell County switch station known as Echo to board a train back to Williamson County, someone concealed by darkness fired a load of buckshot at the sheriff. Hit in the mid-section, Olive nevertheless pulled his six-shooter and fired in the direction of his assailant. So did Marshal Rankin, who pursued on foot, but the gunman escaped into the night and disappeared.

When the south-bound train pulled into the station a short time later, Rankin and others loaded the gravely wounded Olive aboard and wired for a doctor to meet them at the Missouri, Kansas and Texas depot in Taylor. When the train arrived, the physician found Olive moribund but still lucid. He asked the dying lawman several times if he knew who'd shot him and he said no. Heavily sedated, his stomach and bowels perforated by buckshot, Olive died later that day.

While the sheriff hadn't recognized his assassin, others in law enforcement definitely had their suspicions. Within three weeks, Williamson County officers and other lawmen had six men in custody, including Theodore (Theo) Armstrong and his younger brother ex-Ranger Noah. The other suspects were either non-fraternal relatives or family friends.

By December, the number of alleged conspirators had been culled to three—the Armstrong brothers and one Lafayette Bryant. On Jan. 3, 1893, a grand jury indicted the trio in "the assassination of Sheriff John T. Olive."

Tried in Georgetown later that month, the former Ranger was acquitted after only an hour of jury deliberation. The panel had made its decision on the basis of testimony from more than a hundred witnesses. The charge against Bryant was dismissed while the district judge continued Theo Armstrong's case until the court's July term.

Meanwhile, the nation's economy had been sliding downhill with increasing velocity. By spring 1893, the U.S. found itself in the midst of the worst financial crisis the nation had ever experienced. Only the Great Depression of the 1930s would eclipse it.

The stagnant economy may have been a factor in a sudden upsurge in train robberies. As the Fort Worth Daily Gazette quipped on May 21, 1893: "Train robberies are becoming epidemic; the robbers should be vaccinated with lead to prevent the spread of the trouble."

Only two days later, around 2 a.m. on May 23, a pair of masked men robbed a Gulf, Colorado and Santa Fe passenger train west of Coleman and made off with $1,000 from the Wells Fargo express car. (The holdup men's take had the buying power of more than $33,000 today.) After the robbery, the engineer backed the train to the Coleman depot, where the crew reported the robbery to the night operator. But for whatever reason, the trainmen offered no details or descriptions of the perpetrators. Given that, as the word spread, at first area residents doubted there'd even been a robbery.

When the train reached San Angelo, however, the crew proved more forthcoming. They said the masked men had boarded in Coleman. Once the train had made it some distance from the station the robbers covered the brakeman, porter and conductor with six shooters and compelled the Wells Fargo messenger "to open the express door at the point of a gun." The passengers, the report continued, "were not molested."

After collecting everything of value from the express car safe, the robbers fired a couple of shots "in close [proximity] to the heads of the crew and bid them goodbye, saying they would like to see them in heaven." Then they jumped off the train, ran to horses they'd left tied near the tracks and disappeared.

Five days after the robbery, authorities in Coleman arrested a young man named Bill Teague for the crime. "Every effort is being made to catch the other party to the robbery," the San Saba County News reported June 9.

The following month, when the judge called Theo Armstrong's murder case at the beginning of the court's July term, the Williamson County prosecutor moved that the case be dismissed. As the Galveston News reported July 5, 1893, "Under the evidence [presented in Noah Armstrong's trial] if either of the brothers was guilty the other was, and conversely, if one was innocent the other was."

Though Noah and Theo had been exonerated, in the court of public opinion the feeling prevailed—especially in Williamson County—that they had conspired to kill Olive as payback for killing their brothers.

Back in West Texas, so many train robberies were happening at the time that the Coleman holdup did not get much attention from the press. But in addition to Teague, two other men had been arrested, including one who apparently gave officers the name of another participant. Finally, authorities arrested that fourth suspect in September. That led to a short article in the September 13 Austin Daily Statesman, "In Trouble Again":

Sheriff [Emmett] *White* [of Travis County] *informed a Statesman reporter that Noah Armstrong, who was charged with the assassination of Sheriff Olive of Williamson County, was under arrest in Coleman County on a charge of train robbery being jointly indicted with a man named Will Teague.*

Armed with a search warrant, a detective for the Gulf, Colorado and Santa Fe Railroad and a Coleman County deputy had searched Armstrong's Robinsons Peak ranch nine miles north of Coleman. They found recently disturbed ground in Armstrong's garden and dug up a portion of the proceeds from the robbery.

The case progressed rapidly. Only ten days after Armstrong's arrest, the Galveston Daily News reported that a Coleman County jury had convicted Noah of "being [an] accessory in the train robbery" near his hometown. The veniremen assessed his punishment as five years in the state penitentiary. As for Teague, identified as Armstrong's 24-year-old cousin, following the former Ranger's conviction he entered a not guilty plea. However, after being confronted with the amount of evidence against him he changed his plea to guilty.

When his attorney put him on the witness stand, even though his cousin had already been convicted, Teague made "a strong effort to exonerate Armstrong." Teague testified he'd been the one who buried part of the take from the robbery on his cousin Noah's property.

After the trial, which left Teague facing a 25-year prison sentence, Coleman County District Attorney Elisha Snodgrass made a startling comment to one of the reporters present at the preceding. The journalist wrote:

"These convictions will effectively break up what attorney Snodgrass termed 'the Robinsons Peak and Indian Territory horse stealing and train-robbing association.'" The reporter concluded his article by noting, "The verdict meets the approval of the best citizens of the county."

Even though Snodgrass had just claimed that Teague and his cousin Noah had been responsible for additional train robberies across a vast region, nothing more on this appeared in the News, then one of the preeminent newspapers in the state.

Twenty-three years after Sheriff Olive's assassination, in a figurative sense the murder case arose from the dead. There are two versions of what happened.

The first is that in the fall of 1914, then 65-year-old Theo Armstrong walked into the Williamson County Sheriff's Office in Georgetown to tell Sheriff Lee O. Allen that he'd been the one who'd let fly with the load of buckshot that killed Olive. The other version is that a Williamson County grand jury, after hearing from a witness who'd come forward to swear that Theo had admitted to him that he'd slain the sheriff, indicted him in Olive's murder.

A paucity of court records aggravated by sketchy newspaper reports make it hard to determine which is the true version. Whatever revived the case, Armstrong's trial was set for February and he was released on $10,000 bond. But when the case was called, a key witness did not show up and the prosecution asked for a continuance until May.

On May 20, after only 10 minutes of deliberation, the jury found Theo Armstrong not guilty. Soon, he filed a libel suit against a Fort Worth newspaper for reporting that he'd confessed to Olive's murder. He easily won a $1,000 judgment and an appeals court rejected the newspaper's petition seeking a reversal.

While the two Armstrong brothers had been found innocent in the killing of the Williamson County sheriff and Noah Armstrong's train robbery conviction reversed on appeal, during Prohibition in 1928 the old Ranger got in trouble with the law again. This time he'd been busted for bootlegging. That caper netted him a $250 fine.

After that, Armstrong's name disappeared from the public prints until the 1930s, when he began to be mentioned in newspaper articles about the annual reunions of the Ex-Texas Rangers Association. In 1936, he got some ink when he attended the state's centennial exposition in Dallas. By the 1940s Armstrong had become a popular old-timer interviewee, especially for reporters with the Abilene Reporter-News and the San Angelo Standard-Times.

Armstrong proved quite quotable and told some good stories—along with making exaggerated claims that he'd been friends with Sam Houston and famed Comanche war chief Quanah Parker. But none of the feature articles mentioned the older Ranger's earlier legal tribulations. Instead, the feature stories elevated him to Old West superstar status as the deaths of his older former Ranger colleagues pushed him ever nearer to being the oldest living Frontier Battalion veteran.

In May 1949 Laredo civic boosters, hoping to better promote their city's annual Streets of Laredo Fiesta, staged a nation-wide competition to determine the oldest Ranger. They identified a handful of surviving old-time state lawmen, but Armstrong was the oldest. As an honored all-expenses-paid guest at the mid-border event, he got bussed by movie stars Mona Freeman and Corrine Calvert and served as guest umpire for a pistol match with teams from the U.S., Mexico and Canada.

At the event, Armstrong demonstrated his skills with a six-shooter as well. "If I…can't break a bottle at 40 yards I'll forget I was ever a Texas Ranger," he told a reporter.

When he turned 100 in 1952, newspapers reported on his big birthday party and went on to publish stories on each of his subsequent birthdays.

Armstrong's reign as the oldest Ranger ended July 26, 1956, when he died at the Coleman home of his daughter. Outliving the notoriety of his alleged 1890s outlawry, he'd made it past 104—the last of the Frontier Battalion rangers.

PAIN NEVER DID BOTHER ME MUCH

Not long after being sworn in as a Ranger in 1967, H. R. "Lefty" Block got a call from longtime Ranger Charlie Miller. Did he have time for a cup of coffee?

They met at a café in Brownwood, Block's new duty station. After the waitress set down their steaming mugs, Miller reached into the pocket of his khaki pants and fished out a silver Mexican 10-peso piece.

"I want to give you this," Miller said, handing the coin to Block. Block started to thank him, but the old Ranger had more to say.

"I guess you want to know what that's for," he said of the coin. "I'm giving it to you to help you remember something. You're young, but I've been around a long time. If you ever get in a situation where you need to kill somebody, call me if you can. It won't bother me."

The same thing is said to have happened when Bill Wilson made Ranger in 1962. Neither Ranger ever called on Miller to follow through with his offer, but they never forgot what he'd told them. Both believed he meant what he'd said about killing someone for them if needed. After all, as a Ranger for the better part of a half-century, he'd killed before. Former Crockett County Sheriff Jim Wilson (of no relation to Ranger Wilson) recalled that Miller was said to have killed at least seven men. Each instance, in law-enforcement speak for justified homicide, had been "a good shoot."

Before he retired, Co. D Capt. A.Y. Allee told Ranger Joaquin Jackson that he'd first seen Miller when he was about 15 years old. Miller was already a Ranger. As Allee and others looked on, Miller and a couple of other Rangers rode into Carrizo Springs with two dead Mexicans on the back of their horses.

Miller first enlisted in the Rangers Oct. 10, 1917, and over the intervening years served variously as a Ranger or officer for other law-enforcement agencies. In his last Ranger stint, he'd been on the job since 1951. Before his retirement in 1968, he'd been stationed in the Hill Country town of Mason.

As a young reporter for the San Angelo Standard-Times in the late 1960s, any time I happened to be in Mason I'd phone Miller asking if I could interview him. The newspaper's state editor told me that Miller would make for a really good Sunday feature—IF I could persuade him to talk. But every time I called (peace officers back then seldom bothered to get an unlisted number) the old Ranger declined. At least he turned me down politely.

Looking back, I guess it wasn't a great tragedy that Miller never agreed to meet with me. Judging from what I later learned about him, he wouldn't have had much to say even if he'd been willing to talk. A decade earlier, however, another Standard-Times reporter did get him to talk—but only a little.

In late February 1957, Ann Bryan covered a meeting of the West Central Texas Peace Officers Association in Ballinger. The meeting featured the showing of a new training film produced by the

Department of Public Safety on the psychological and scientific aspects of questioning criminal suspects. At some point, Bryan buttonholed Miller, who she noted was "the oldest active member of the Ranger service." Miller told her he'd been a Ranger "off and on" since World War I.

He'd recently been transferred to Comanche, which Miller said was the first time he'd ever been based "inland." Most of his time had been spent along the border, where he told Bryan he'd graduated from "horse and pack to an automobile." In those early days, he continued, Rangers only worked felony cases, mostly "smugglers, cow thieves and murderers." That's the way he still saw as his duty. "I never fool with a misdemeanor," he told the reporter.

Fortunately, from various Rangers and others who knew him, I later learned some of the things I'm sure he wouldn't have told me about.

For one thing, no one knew for sure how old he was. Approaching mandatory retirement age of 65, he'd furnished DPS Director Col. Homer Garrison with a signed, notarized document showing he'd been mistaken his whole life about his date of birth. He was actually a couple of years younger than he thought. No one really believed it, but Garrison let Miller keep wearing his silver star until he reached retirement age the second time.

One day in the early 1960s, a Llano County sheriff's deputy went to arrest a well-known local troublemaker for some minor violation. When the officer got to the man's house, he found that he'd piled sandbags in the windows and turned the place into a fortress. Suddenly seeing a rifle barrel pointed in his direction, the deputy ran back to his car, ducked behind the vehicle and radioed for help. Soon other deputies had the place surrounded. The sheriff, using a bullhorn, repeatedly called on the man to surrender. His only reply was an occasional gunshot.

That's when Miller got there.

The Ranger got out of his car, surveyed the scene and walked straight toward the house and the barricaded gunman.

"State Ranger," he said as he kept walking, his .45 stuck inside the waist of his pants. Miller seldom wore a gun belt, and he always kept the hammer down with a leather string tied around the grip safety to keep it from functioning. (For those not familiar with firearms, that meant all he had to do to fire the weapon was pull the trigger.)

"I'll kill anybody who comes up here!" the man in the house yelled. Miller kept walking.

The officers crouched behind their cars expecting that any second the barricaded man would shoot the Ranger. But to everyone's amazement, Miller made it to the house. He grabbed the barrel of the rifle and jerked it away.

"Now get out here," Miller ordered.

As officers ran to handcuff the man slowly emerging from the house, Miller strolled back toward his car. He handed the man's rifle to a deputy and drove off.

At the jail, one of the deputies asked the prisoner why he hadn't shot the Ranger when he had the chance.

"Didn't you see his eyes?" the man asked. "I was scared I wouldn't kill him on the first shot!"

Retired Ranger Bob Favor, who'd been Miller's sergeant, told ranger Joaquin Jackson that Miller was one of the hardest-working and best Rangers he ever knew. Another story Favor told had to do with a health issue Miller experienced.

The bachelor Ranger lived in a small house outside Mason. He liked horses and owned a stud and several mares. One day the stud got in with the mares when he wasn't supposed to, and Miller went to get him out of the pen. The horse didn't like that idea and kicked the Ranger hard. One kick broke one of Miller's legs and another knocked the tops off three of his lower front teeth.

Miller didn't like doctors, so he prevailed on a local vet to set his leg for him. Later, when an MD did take a look at the leg, he said he could not have improved on the job.

When Favor went to check on Miller, he found him in his bedroom, lying in bed with his broken leg propped up. Miller asked him to go to his car and bring him a pair of pliers, which Favor did. Then, as Favor watched in disbelief, the Ranger grabbed an old mirror and held it up to his face so he could see to pull out those three teeth with the pliers Favor had brought him.

"Pain never bothered me much," Miller told his supervisor.

JUSTICE FOR JANE DOE

Early on the morning of June 4, 1981, a highway department crew found the mostly nude body of a young Hispanic woman just off I-35 about seven miles south of New Braunfels.

Contacted by the Comal County Sheriff's office, New Braunfels-based Co. D Ranger Ramiro Martinez headed to the scene to join deputies and other officers already there. When he arrived, the Ranger saw the body lying on its back in a grassy area just off the south-bound frontage road. She had a bullet entry wound above her right eye.

No weapon was found at the scene, leading Martinez and Comal County Sheriff Walter Fellers to believe the victim had been killed elsewhere overnight by someone who'd then dumped her body alongside the busy highway. Officers searched the area for the woman's purse or wallet but didn't find anything. Nor did a check with area law-enforcement agencies turn up a missing person report for anyone matching the woman's description.

After the body had been taken to Austin. Martinez drove to Brackenridge Hospital, where Travis County Medical Examiner Dr. Robert Bayardo would be performing an autopsy.

"She had several head wounds," Martinez later told an Austin American-Statesman reporter. "She has black hair, and stud earrings in each ear. She has a birthmark on the right buttock."

The Ranger released as much detail as he could hoping that news coverage would bring forward someone who could identify the victim. He said she was in her late teens or early 20s and when found had on only a size medium multi-colored blouse, a bra and white cotton socks.

After completing the autopsy, Dr. Bayardo reported that she'd been shot six times with a .25 caliber handgun. Even though the young woman had been practically nude, with her blouse and bra pulled backward over her head, the pathologist found no evidence of sexual assault.

"The doctor told us she was face down when she died," Comal County deputy Gilbert Villareal said. "Since she was found on her back... we are pretty sure she was shot somewhere else. There are hand marks on her neck, and it looks like [the killer] held her down and tried to strangle her, then shot her [once] and turned her over and [fired five more rounds]."

In Georgetown, 30 miles north of Austin on I-35, Williamson County Sheriff Jim Boutwell closely followed the Comal County case. A year-and-a-half earlier, the body of a young woman clad only in orange socks had been found in his jurisdiction off I-35 near Georgetown. His department had not been able to identify the victim, much less find her killer.

Meanwhile, Department of Public Safety crime analysts had noticed a disturbing pattern—an inordinate number of murder victims were being found along or near I-35. Since the summer of 1976, from the Red River on the north to the Rio Grande on the south, 22 cases had been reported. All were unsolved. The Rangers, Boutwell and other officers had begun to suspect that a serial killer might be preying on women he found hanging around truck stops or stranded on the highway. At minimum, if a serial killer was at work, he seemed to view the interstate as a convenient place to dispose of his victims.

"A lot of bad people go up and down that highway," Ranger Ed Gooding said at a conference organized by the Department of Public Safety to discuss the unsolved I-35 cases. Gooding officed in Temple, a city bisected by the superhighway.

Well aware of all those unsolved murders, Martinez immersed himself in this latest case. But he wouldn't have much to go on until the body could be identified and he'd be able to talk with her family and acquaintances. To that end, he hoped the murder victim could be identified from her fingerprints. Martinez also provided the news media with a DPS-produced composite drawing of the victim's face. In doing that, he hoped that someone who saw the image would recognize her and come forward. But neither technique brought any results. Eventually the victim went to a pauper's grave in New Braunfels as Jane Doe.

Unknown to Martinez, a father concerned about the sudden disappearance of one of his daughters had called the San Antonio Police Department to file a missing person's report. But an officer told him that since the woman in question was 18 and there was no evidence of foul play, the department wouldn't open a file on the matter.

Not knowing the name of the victim made Martinez' work

particularly daunting. Still, he doggedly continued searching for leads until his retirement in 1991 after nearly two decades of Ranger service. But he never forgot about the case, and neither would the Rangers.

In 2001 the 77th Texas Legislature appropriated funds to stand up a new Ranger unit, the Unsolved Crimes Investigation Program (UCIP). A Ranger from each of the six companies would be centralizing cold case files for the counties his company covered and taking a fresh look at those that might still be solvable. The process would take a while, but it had begun.

Twenty-six years after the discovery of the body in Comal County, in 2007 a San Antonio woman approached the University of North Texas Center for Unidentified Human Remains in Denton to see if they had any cases dating to 1981 that might fit her sister's description. If so, she'd give them a DNA sample. But the center said it could take no action because a missing person's case had never been filed. The frustrated sister, still desperate to find out what happened to her sibling, turned again to the San Antonio police. This time, the department opened a missing person's file on the case.

The following spring, Co. D Ranger Trampas Gooding (a second cousin of former Ranger Ed Gooding) began going through a file cabinet at the company headquarters in San Antonio looking for any unsolved cases that might be worthy of a fresh look. Checking a county-by-county index of old murder cases handled by his company, he found an entry marked "Jane Doe and Henry Lee Lucas."

That got the Ranger's attention. He knew that back in the mid-1980s a one-eyed drifter arrested for killing an elderly woman in Montague County had gone on to proclaim himself as "the world's most worse serial killer." Lucas had confessed to 80 homicides in Texas and several hundred more cases in other states, but the majority of those confessions had been disproven.

Pulling the relatively thin case file, Gooding found that Lucas had been questioned by Ranger Martinez about the 1981 Comal County case. He denied committing the murder, but when re-interviewed a year later, Lucas said his mentally deficient running buddy Ottis Toole had killed the woman and that he had only watched while he did it.

While that was interesting—and almost assuredly untrue—Gooding was surprised to see that the victim still had not been identified. That's when he decided to take a fresh look at the case. First he drove to the Comal County sheriff's office hoping to find a more detailed case file. Initially they said they'd never worked the case and had no file. But after continued prodding by the Ranger the department discovered that the case records had been misfiled. Gooding next checked for any missing person reports dating from 1981. He found only one, the newly filed San Antonio report. But while the year was right, the report said the person had vanished in February that year, not June. Still, the missing person was a young Hispanic woman, so he contacted the woman who'd made the report.

The Ranger arranged to meet with her at the San Antonio Police Department's missing persons unit. The description the missing person's sister provided matched the Comal County victim. The sister even knew about the victim's birthmark. Still needing to absolutely confirm Jane Doe's identity, Gooding showed the sister a pre-autopsy photo of the victim's face. As soon as she saw it, she burst into tears. It was her long-lost sibling, 18-year-old Carol Joyce Deleon.

The Ranger's next step was to check with the DPS crime lab in Austin to see if it still held the evidence collected in the case. They found the evidence but told Gooding that it had never been checked for DNA. He requested an analysis and the lab not only came up with the victim's DNA but a partial male DNA profile. When the lab compared a DNA sample provided by Carol's sister Sarah, they confirmed that Jane Doe was indeed Carol Deleon.

In interviewing Sarah and her father, Gooding learned that Deleon had graduated from Thomas Edison High School in San Antonio on May 28, 1981. A few days later, on June 3, she'd gone to a local night club. No one who knew her ever saw her again.

With DNA testing technology continuing to improve, in 2019 at Gooding's request the DPS lab reexamined the 1981 evidence and generated another DNA profile from a "waxy substance" that had been found on the victim's body. Testing this new profile, the lab found DNA from what their report termed a male "foreign contributor." The unknown DNA profile was entered into the DPS' Combined DNA Index System (CODIS), but the database did not find a match.

About this time, Gooding got promoted to staff lieutenant as program coordinator for the Rangers' federally funded Sexual Assault Kit Initiative (SAKI). The U.S. Department of Justice money enables the Rangers to collect legally required DNA samples from sex offenders and certain other felons. Gooding's replacement would be Ranger Joshua Ray, who was transferred from Bryan to New Braunfels. A DPS officer since 2000 and a Ranger since 2015, Ray took over the Deleon murder investigation. But he continued to turn to Gooding for DNA advice, even though he'd already become fairly familiar with the latest in DNA testing in solving a high-profile murder case while stationed in Bryan.

In late December 2020, relying on SAKI funding, Ray submitted the unknown male DNA profile found on Deleon's body for advanced testing by Virginia-based Bode Technologies. That company employs genetics and genealogy to identify DNA from unknown persons. Founded in 1995, Bode and its subcontractors have processed more than 30,000 forensic cases in the U.S. and more than 15 counties. In addition to the company's role in solving cold case murders, its scientists aided in identifying victims of the 2001 World Trade Center terrorist attack, unknown war dead and victims of natural disasters.

Ray received a report from the private sector lab in the summer of 2021. They'd determined that the DNA in question almost unquestionably came from one of only three persons, San Antonio resident Larry Allen West or two of his male cousins. The report concluded that the probability of the sample being from anyone else was one in 422.1 quintillion. Quickly ruling out the cousins, Ray focused on the 68-year-old West. One thing the Ranger learned about West early on was that at the time of Deleon's disappearance, he'd lived in the same part of the Alamo City that she did. Also, court records in the Bexar County District Clerk's Office showed that law enforcement had dealt with the suspect before on numerous occasions.

"I spent a lot of time surveilling the suspect to gather evidence, but without luck," Ray recalled. "Eventually, I made the decision to confront the suspect and conducted an interview with him."

That happened Nov. 8, 2021, at Wests' workplace, a heating and air-conditioning repair company in the Bexar County town of Converse. While West told the Ranger that in 1981 he had been in the habit of hanging out in local bars to pick up younger Hispanic women, he denied any role in Deleon's death. He did agree to provide Ray with a DNA sample.

"We tested it, and it was a match for the DNA collected at the crime scene," Ray said. In interviewing people who knew West, Ray talked with the suspect's two former wives. West's first wife told him the marriage had lasted only 30 days but during that time she said that her husband had repeatedly assaulted and raped her. The second ex also reported domestic violence and forced sex.

Ray retired from the Rangers Oct. 31, 2022 to join the Guadalupe County Sheriff's office in Seguin as chief deputy. Despite having changed badges, Ray continued to consult on the case with his replacement in New Braunfels, Ranger Raymond "Conde" Benoist, Jr.

By April 2023, the Bexar district attorney's office believed that the Rangers had enough evidence to arrest West. Ranger Benoist wrote a probable cause affidavit and a magistrate signed off on an arrest warrant on April 12. The following day, Ranger Benoist and other state and local officers, including Ray, arrested West at his San Antonio residence without incident. The suspect was released later that day on $125,000 bond. As of the summer of 2023 the Bexar County district clerk's website showed the status of the case as "AWTG [Awaiting] Indictment."

While the work of four different Rangers finally provided the Deleon family with some degree of closure after 42 years, their mental wounds remained raw.

"To know that she fought such a violent death at the end," Sandra Deleon said, "it's just heartbreaking. The potential of what she could have been...will never be known. We were robbed of that; she was robbed of that."

Since the Rangers' unsolved crimes unit began operation in 2001, by mid-2023 it had cleared 46 cases. Of those, the oldest dated to 1960. Two of the cleared cases had occurred in the early 1970s, including the murder of a police officer in Alice, Texas. The unit's website lists 137 cases—the oldest from 1953—still waiting to be solved.

"This puts the message out to those who think they've gotten away with it, that you're never safe," Ray said not long after West's arrest. "There are good men and women who do this job, who take it seriously and we will continue to uncover evidence and do everything that we have to get justice for victims."

LOOSE CARTRIDGES

THRILLING EPISODES THAT NEVER HAPPENED

A decade after the Alamo, one of the wildest, bloodiest Indian fights in Texas history took place on the Concho River east of present San Angelo. Or so the story goes.

Forty Texas Rangers led by the legendary Capt. John Coffee "Jack" Hays faced 600 Comanches at a place known as the Painted Rocks. (So named because it is covered with ancient American Indian pictographs.) The fight lasted two and a half days. When the gun smoke drifted away, 100 once proud warriors lay dead, but not a single Ranger. In fact, only one Ranger suffered a wound, and that was not serious. A different account says the Rangers were not quite that lucky, having two killed outright with two others mortally wounded.

The legendary Big Foot Wallace is said to have declared the Paint Rock fight the hardest scrape with Indians he ever had. And when it came to taking on Indians, Wallace was not easily impressed. One of the many stories told about him reflects that attitude. He once cordially offered a visitor a steaming cup of coffee—served in an Indian skull.

The only problem with the Paint Rock story, seemingly another glorious chapter in the colorful history of the Rangers, is that it most likely never happened. Or, if it did take place, it's highly unlikely that it could have been on the scale that has been told.

Here's why the tale is almost certainly fiction or at best a huge exaggeration:

• Despite the battle's purported magnitude, no contemporary newspaper accounts have been found.

• No official correspondence in regard to such a fight seems to exist.

• Other than the claim that the fight happened in 1846, the various tellers of the story have given it five different dates.

• The alleged principal participants never publicly mentioned it. Even the garrulous Wallace never went on record about it, and his remark that it was his closet call appears to be mere hearsay.

• Finally, no archeological evidence of the fight has been found.

BATTLE OF BANDERA PASS

The Battle of Bandera Pass, an oft-written-about fight between Rangers under Jack Hays and a much larger Comanche war party also probably never happened. A historical marker says it did, but historians have never found any official documentation.

Legend has it that in the spring of 1841, while scouting in the Guadalupe Valley, Hays and 30-plus Rangers made camp for the night near present-day Bandera. The next morning, the rangers rode into Bandera Pass, a geologic feature about 500 yards long and 125 feet across.

Unknown to the Texans, a large Comanche war party sat waiting for their approach. The ambush worked, catching the Rangers by surprise.

Hays rallied his men, ordered them off their pitching horses and began a defensive action that soon degenerated into hand-to-hand fighting. Ranger Kit Acklen shot the Comanche chief with his pistol, but the Indian still had enough fight in him to draw his knife and charge the Ranger. Acklen unsheathed his knife and, in a vicious struggle, prevailed. When the other warriors saw their leader fall, they withdrew.

Five Rangers supposedly died in the battle with six others wounded.

In the legend's defense, many official Republic of Texas documents were burned when the state adjutant general's department caught on fire in 1857. Other documents of Hays' day were likely lost in the 1881 Capitol fire.

A marker detailing the history of Bandera Pass itself stands ten miles north of Bandera on FM 689.

The Bandera Pass fight may or may not have occurred, but Rangers did operate in this area during the Republic of Texas era. The reason was the Pinta Trail, a wagon road extending from San Antonio northwest to the old Spanish mission on the San Saba River in present Menard County. A historical marker placed in 1968 is titled the "Old Texas Ranger Trail," but it refers to the Pinta Trail.

ENCHANTED ROCK

The best-known fight Hays and his men ever had supposedly took place at Enchanted Rock, a towering mound of granite in what is now Llano County.

The story has been told so many times that it is rich in variants. Here's the basic version:

In the fall of 1841, Hays and his men had camped at the base of the rock. As they sat around their cooking fire that night, Hays busily cleaned and oiled his two five-shot Paterson Colts.

"I may not need you, but if I do, I'll need you awful bad," he is said to have declared as if talking to the weapons.

Well, as fate—and good storytelling—would have it, the next morning he did indeed need those two pistols. While his men busied themselves breaking camp, the captain climbed to the top of the giant rock to scan the country around them.

Just then, a war party of Comanches closed in on the lone Ranger captain. Hays took cover in a depression in the granite and grimly awaited their charge.

As one cliché-invoking newspaper writer put it in 1929, "the savages, their hideous features distorted with rage and hate, howling madly [were] bent upon taking 'Devil Jack,' as they called him, at all hazards."

In this variant, Hays not only had his brace of revolvers, he carried a rifle. "As each [warrior] reached the summit, the intrepid Hays would rise and level his rifle, the warriors dropping back, fearful of his unerring aim. For nearly an hour he kept the snarling, wolfish braves at bay. Still he withheld his fire."

That emboldened the Indians, who "came with a rush." At that point, the storyteller continued, "Hays went to work in earnest."

"The long-barreled rifle spoke, and the first Indian pitched on his head. Dropping the gun and snatching up his five-shooter, Capt. Jack mowed them down, holding them off until he could reload. For three hours the unequal contest raged, this long, desperate Ranger against half the band of wild redskins."

With the young captain down to only three bullets, the rest of his men charged up the rock "stabbing, shooting, slashing, some whirling their rifles as bludgeons, they gained the summit at last with the redskins routed.

As with the Bandera Pass fight, no records have been found to document the Enchanted Rock story. One curious note: A decade later, after Hays and his wife Susan had moved to San Francisco in 1851 she commissioned artist W.S. Jewett to do an oil painting depicting her husband. While the mountaintop setting is fanciful (there are even sailing ships on water in the background), the image of a buckskin-clad, red-cheeked Hays with flintlock in hand is said to be a realistic rendering of the young Ranger captain. While many believe the painting portrays the Enchanted Rock incident, again, no hard evidence of that has been found.

"THE BELLE OF SAN ANTONIO"

In the early 1840s a Comanche raiding party swept into Bexar County and after killing her parents carried off the beautiful Mariel King, "the belle of San Antonio."

Fortunately for Miss King, intrepid Ranger and Battle of San Jacinto veteran Logan Van Deveer along with two other experienced Indian fighters (William H. Magill and Noah Smithwick) tracked the raiders as they made their way northwest with their hapless prisoner. The trail led to what is now known as Longhorn Cavern, about 10 miles west of the present Hill Country town of Burnet. With their prisoner, the warriors camped in a 183-foot-long limestone chamber inside the cave that would come to be called the Indian Council Room.

The rangers wanted to rush in through the main entrance of the cave. But not only did they realize they were outnumbered, they figured the Comanches would kill their prisoner if they attacked.

After some strategizing, the men decided to slip into the cave via a smaller, secondary entrance mostly concealed by mountain juniper. Once inside, they crept toward the smell of an oakwood fire and roasting venison. Soon the rangers saw the raiding party sitting around their fire, their captive tied and leaning against the smooth limestone wall.

Concealed in the dark beyond the glow of the cooking fire, each ranger picked a Comanche and "a bullet went crashing into his brain." Caught off guard and not knowing how many men they faced, the rest of the raiding party fled to smaller passages in the cave. That is, all but one. As the rangers looked on a warrior lifted his tomahawk clearly intending to kill the young woman.

That's when one of the rangers rushed the Comanche and, wresting his weapon from him, buried it in his skull "mid the feathers of his war bonnet."

Not long after returning Miss King to San Antonio, she and her rescuer are married. Though quite a feat, the rescue of Miss King and her marriage to a handsome young Ranger did not appear in any contemporary newspaper. In fact, the story did not make it into print until Feb. 24, 1918, when the Austin American—the Capital City's morning paper—carried the story under this five-line headline:

Terrific Indian Fight
With Knives in a Cave
Gave Logan Van Deveer,
Austin's First Owner,
His Beautiful Bride

The author of the article was identified as Mrs. Samuel Posey. Her full name was Mary Rives Johnson Posey.

The newspaper shamelessly touted the tale: "The story is historically authentic and is taken from historical records. . .It is written exclusively for publication in this morning's Austin American...The story has never been before told."

Compelling as this story is, it never happened. The truth is, though he had served as a Ranger, and did fight Indians, Van Deveer was already married when he supposedly got hitched to Miss King. In fact, Van Deveer had been married to Lucinda Mayes since the late 1830s. The couple had met in Bastrop, where she was from.

Mary Posey either had a wonderful imagination or had been hoodwinked by some anonymous storyteller. Even though the Austin newspaper claimed the story was based on records, no researcher has ever located any records of such a rescue.

Following Posey's article, two decades passed before another writer told the story in an article written for Frontier Times magazine in June 1938. The story makes no mention of the story Mrs. Posey had written two decades earlier but essentially plagiarizes it.

Just shy of 60 years went by before True West told the story, this time in an article by David F. Crosby: "When three Texas Rangers race to rescue Miss Mariel King from her Comanche kidnappers, a fierce battle awaits them in the darkness of...Longhorn Cavern."

EL MUERTO

The words "legendary" and "Texas Rangers" often are seen riding together across the printed page, but at some point, two former Rangers got roped into a South Texas legend—the story of El Muerto.

Of course, maybe El Muerto did exist. The two Rangers at the center of the tale—Creed Taylor and Bigfoot Wallace—certainly were real. Both men served under Capt. Jack Hays during the days of the Republic of Texas.

More likely is that someone who had read The Sketchbook of Geoffrey Crayon, Gent. took it upon himself to Texanize one of the short stories it contained. The Sketchbook, as it's generally called, came out in 1820, an anthology of pieces by Washington Irving. Of those, the one that became a timeless classic is The Headless Horseman.

The basic headless horseman story goes even further back, across many centuries and numerous cultures.

In Celtic culture there's the dulachan, "dark man," a headless fairy (hey, he's Irish) who rides around with his head in his hands, whipping his horse with a quirt made from a human spine. The legend is that when this fellow shows up and calls out a name, that person soon will be headed to the other side of the rainbow—no pot of gold forthcoming.

A Scottish variation features not only a headless rider, but a headless horse. How man and steed manage to get around so impaired is not explained, only that they came out on the losing end of a vicious clan fight and are eternally unhappy about it.

The headless horse and rider story swam across the channel to Germany, where the rider evolved as a hunter who blows his horn as a warning to other sportsmen that something bad's going to happen if they head afield the next day. How Herr Headless manages to blow a horn is left to the imagination.

When the American British colonies started acting uppity and the Empire dispatched ships and troops to put down the rebellion, the headless horseman must have been a stowaway because he soon appeared in New England, thanks to Washington Irving.

Ever ready to ride into new country, the headless horseman eventually showed up way down in South Texas.

The story of El Muerto begins in Kimble County, where former Ranger Taylor settled in the late 1860s. Back then, nearly a decade before the county's creation that area lay well beyond the western edge of the Texas frontier. Indians still posed a considerable threat, and there were more outlaws than respectable folks.

So, when someone made off with some of Taylor's horses, he and a ranch hand set out to find the thieves and recover their stolen stock. Following the trail, the two men happened to meet up with Bigfoot. He and Taylor being friends from their rangering days, he said he'd be pleased to throw in with them on their search.

Somewhere south of Uvalde, in the still lawless Nueces Strip, Taylor, Wallace and the hired hand caught up with the horses and the man who had taken them, a well-known Mexican bandit. In the fight that followed the two aging Rangers proved they still knew how to shoot. Soon, Texas had one less horse thief.

While Taylor and Wallace both were as hard and tough as their leather saddles, according to the El Muerto tale, they were not without a sense of humor. No one had coined the term "mind games" yet, but perhaps the two former Rangers decided to do something that would discourage others along the border from driving off property that was not theirs.

Whatever their thinking, the two Texans cut off the outlaw's head. Then they tied his body to his horse, affixing that portion of his anatomy which once fit under his sombrero onto his saddle horn. After that, one of them slapped the already terrified horse on its rump and off he galloped.

The blazing South Texas sun soon did its work on the corpse, which became increasingly fearsome until it was nothing but a skeleton.

The dead outlaw's unfortunate horse, having done nothing wrong—at least that it had any control over—wandered the landscape.

People of a superstitious nature saw the headless rider not as a macabre warning to others, but as a mounted ghost whose appearance did not presage good news. Before long, the dead rider became El Muerto, the Dead One.

The horse and the headless skeleton astride it continued to roam South Texas until the animal died of old age. But horses can live 20 years or more, so El Muerto and his caballero scared a lot of people before the sightings stopped. When someone found the hapless critter's carcass on the edge of a water hole near Alice, they removed what remained of the headless outlaw and buried him at Rancho La Trinidad near present-day Ben Bolt in Jim Wells County.

But the story didn't end there. Though the bandit and his horse no longer existed on an earthly plane, the ghostly duo are said to have kept riding, a timeless warning that stealing horses—or anything else—is not only illegal, in Texas it's mighty risky.

FORCED TO DIG THEIR OWN GRAVES

Standing beneath a clump of ancient oaks that once shaded a Ranger campsite in what is now downtown Seguin is a metal historical marker dedicated by the city's mayor in 2011.

After correctly explaining that the town was founded by a group of former Rangers who'd once protected the area, the marker's text matter-of-factly says that in 1840 Rangers carried out a mass execution near the site. The ranking Rangers involved were Capt. Hays and James Callahan. They forced a group of "renegades and Indians" to dig their own mass grave and then shot them to death.

Historians, however, believe such a thing never happened there.

WILD SHOOTOUT ON THE KING RANCH

In February 1958 Amarillo Globe-Times reporter Patricia Masterman interviewed a fixture in the Potter County courthouse, 81-year-old 47th District Court bailiff John W. Graves.

As of the previous month, she wrote, Graves had been a law-enforcement officer for 55 years. Though most of his time as a lawman had been as a Potter County deputy sheriff, he also had served in the Rangers "during [the] wild days on the border."

Grave's law enforcement career began at 18 when he went on the payroll of the Bell County Sheriff's Department in Central Texas. After that, he said, he became a Texas Ranger and served for eight years. Much of that time, which was prior to World War I, he worked on the sprawling King Ranch in South Texas.

Once, he told Masterman, he'd scouted the famed ranch for two days and two nights looking for Mexican tequila smugglers thought to be traversing the ranch.

Here's how the reporter summarized what happened:

As he guided his horse across the rough countryside, three mounted men suddenly appeared before him. One reached for a saddle gun and died in the act as Graves opened fire. The others came up with .38 caliber firearms. Graves had taken cover behind a scant pile of dirt left beside a badger's hole, no more than a foot high. He shot the horse from under one of the marauders. The man hugged the far side of the animal, sheltered from the bullets. The third rider died under the Ranger's gun. Meanwhile, the Mexican smuggler behind the horse had worked to a point allowing a shot at Graves. The smuggler's bullet tore through the fleshy part of Uncle John's right arm.

But that didn't end the battle.

"He got me in the shoulder," Graves said. "I kept quiet for a spell. Then he stood up."

And that concluded the criminal career of that unhorsed tequilero.

With three dead smugglers on the ground, Graves collected 20 bottles of tequila and several thousands of dollars' worth of morphine. He loaded the bodies on the surviving horses and took them and the confiscated booze and drugs to the Ranger camp.

There, his unnamed captain railed at him for killing the three smugglers until he saw blood on Graves' shoulders.

While Graves' account of this gunbattle seems authentic enough, no newspaper reports of such an incident have turned up. More problematic is that records at the Texas State Library and Archives in Austin show that Graves had only been a Special Ranger, not a regular Ranger. And that was in 1933 and he only served a short time, not eight years.

Regular Rangers and special Rangers did have numerous smoky encounters with bootleggers during Prohibition, but the fight Graves described appears to be yet another thrilling encounter the Rangers never had.

In fairness, however, there is documentation that he'd seen gun play on other occasions after the King Ranch incident supposedly occurred. Also, record-keeping was far more casual during the early days on the border than it would later become.

Born Dec. 22, 1876, in Belton, Graves came to Amarillo in 1922. He died at 85 on May 16, 1962 and lies in Amarillo's Llano Cemetery.

TARNISHING THE SILVER STAR

An attractive 20-year-old just graduated from Sul Ross Normal College in Alpine, Hallie Stillwell took a teaching job in the remote border town of Presidio during the Mexican Revolution.

Teaching "readin', 'riting and 'rithmetic" she doubtless found it necessary to swat the occasional unruly kid, but she had more than a ruler or paddle at her disposal. While it was not legal, neither the Presidio school's principal nor anyone in law enforcement seemed to find it alarming that Hallie wore a pistol over her dress in class or elsewhere in town.

Decades later, by then a revered Big Bend ranch woman and writer-historian, someone who'd heard that she'd once openly toted a gun asked if she had done so to protect herself from Mexican bandits.

"No," she said, "I wore a gun to protect me from U.S. soldiers and Rangers."

Along a border turned war zone, it had not taken Hallie long to understand that not every state lawman or cavalryman measured up as a paragon of manly virtue. Good guys always outnumbered bad guys in the Rangers, but a young woman still needed to be careful. So did other citizens, both in the Big Bend region and elsewhere, especially during the 19th and early 20th centuries.

BEST NOT MAKE HOUSTON MAD

Texas governor Sam Houston relied heavily on the Rangers to help protect the state's frontier from hostile Indians. And for the most part, he respected them, once famously saying, "Give me Rangers and I will get it done."

But Houston had no use for bad rangers.

The executive wrote Capt. John H. Conner on March 10, 1860, saying he'd had reports that rangers in Burnet County had been supplementing their income by charging $5 to $8 a head for the return to their rightful owners of stolen horses recaptured from Indians. Also, contrary to orders, liquor had been allowed into the Ranger camp.

Houston ordered the captain to "destroy every bottle...but one for medical purposes." He concluded: "You will report by return Express whether...such things have been done; whether or not it has been the custom to charge for reclamation of horses and you will see that every dollar thus obtained is immediately refunded or the men dismissed without honorable discharges."

NO COWBOYING ON STATE TIME

A Ranger named Andrew Gatluf Jones and several of his comrades decided to put their duties aside long enough to build a herd of 400 mavericks they found along the Nueces River. Driving the cattle to Bandera, the enterprising rangers sold them for $2 a head. But the entrepreneurially minded rangers were discharged for what they did. Jones had served June 2, 1872-June 20, 1873, under Capt. Robert Ballantyne's Co. K, based in Bandera County.

"UNGENTLEMANLY AND UNSOLDIERLY..."

On Oct. 7, 1877, the Dallas Daily Herald noted that the Austin Statesman had recently complained editorially of Capt. John C. Sparks. According to the newspaper, the ranger had exhibited "ungentlemanly and unsoldierly conduct, amusing himself shooting out the lights in restaurants and committing other offensive acts."

AN UGLY INCIDENT

Interviewed by a newspaper reporter more than 50 years after the fact, former Frontier Battalion ranger Noah Armstrong recalled an ugly example of racism in San Angelo when black Buffalo soldiers were stationed at nearby Fort Concho. Not that he considered it inappropriate.

This is how the newspaper described the late-1870s incident.

Finishing a round of [checking] *buffalo camps [for fugitives], the rangers rode into Fort Concho, ready for a little social life….*[They] *entered one of the saloons, took a turn at monte, and then enjoyed dancing with such girls as the settlement afforded.*

The dance music was interrupted when eight or 10 negro soldiers entered and attempted to dance with white girls. Mr. Armstrong says the rangers went into action and beat the negroes over the head with the butts of their guns. The post commander, hearing of the trouble, arrived and was rebuked by the ranger captain. Mr. Armstrong recalls, it being made known, without reservations, that the rangers would not permit negro soldiers to dance with white girls.

'WILLIAM TELL' JAILED

The drunken antics of one Frontier Battalion ranger could have ended badly. As the Dallas Daily Herald informed its readers in the late winter of 1880:

A detachment of Captain Arrington's company of rangers came in Fort Griffin recently for fresh horses.

They reported a wearisome and fruitless scout after the redskins.

A ranger named Jenkins, on a lark in Griffin, sought to try a William Tell shot at an ornamental flower on a woman's hat. He was restrained in time and put in the cooler to sober off.

HOW ONE JP VIEWED THE RANGERS

One of the most remote parts of Texas is Terlingua, an old quicksilver mining town in the Big Bend region. In the 1890s, when mining began in the area, Rangers periodically pitched camp near the town to keep the peace.

But not everyone was impressed with their work there. C.A. Hawley, a mining company bookkeeper who also served as justice of the peace, later reflected about the Rangers he saw at Terlingua during his seven years there:

These officers traveled horseback, three or four in a group, and once or twice a year some of them would show up in Terlingua. At that time members of this ranger force received the small salary of $35.00 per month. Out of this meager wage they had to live, as nothing was allowed them for living or traveling expenses.... Such a job at such a wage would not attract very capable men.

Those I met at Terlingua were a pretty cheap sort—men who loved to show their authority and swagger around with a gun on the hip, ready to shoot somebody. They would make camp near the store and usually remain a week or ten days. Out of consideration for their services, which were more imaginary than real, these men were allowed credit at the store. I regret to say their accounts were the only ones that ultimately had to be marked 'uncollectible.' We were always sorry to see them come into camp and always glad to see them depart.

On the upside, Hawley noted: "They usually rode good horses and were always well armed."

THE RANGER WHO INVESTIGATED HIMSELF

Flavius L. Hamer, a younger brother of Capt. Frank Hamer, reportedly once investigated himself while serving with the Rangers.

The Hamer family story is that somewhere in West Texas their kinsman happened to be in bed with a woman he thought unmarried. At least until her husband unexpectedly showed up. As Flavius climbed out a window the cuckolded spouse got off a shot that slightly nicked the lawman.

Thinking fast, the woman tearfully thanked her husband for saving her from being outraged by an intruder. Next, the husband did what any citizen would do—he contacted the authorities and reported the incident. Whether by happenstance or design, the lawman sent to look into the matter was Flavius Hamer, who promptly launched a search for the "attacker." When he asked the "victim" if she could describe the man, she sobbed that she hadn't been able to get a very good look at him. Promising to do everything he could to track down the perpetrator, the Ranger politely excused himself.

TREASURE TALES

STEINHEIMER'S MILLIONS

One of Texas' most colorful treasure tales is hitched to one of the more significant but least known Ranger engagements—the fight between a group of Texas Rangers and one Manuel Flores and his men in May 1839.

When Texas scouts cut a suspicious north-bound trail in South Central Texas, they surmised a party of Mexican or Indians raiders was moving through the young Republic and probably up to no good. They were right. Flores' party had killed at least four people on their way north and possibly others. He was clearly a Mexican operative intending to cause trouble. Rangers led by Lt. James Ogden Rice began following the riders. On a bluff on the South San Gabriel, in what is now Williamson County, the Rangers caught up with Flores. Gunfire quickly ensued. Flores died of a rifle ball through his heart. Two of his men also fell. The rest hit the brush like so many quail, leaving their remuda and supply-laden pack animals behind.

In dividing the spoils, the Rangers found documents in Flores' saddlebags that proved up a Mexican plot to regain its recently lost province by forming an alliance with Texas Indians, particularly the Cherokees. Flores, who had fought for Texas during the revolution, had switched allegiance to become an agent for the Mexican government.

Historians have discovered no conclusive evidence that the Cherokees were being anything more than polite in talking with the Mexicans. But the paperwork brought to light by the Rangers solidified the anti-Indian sentiments of President Mirabeau B. Lamar. Texas troops soon defeated the Cherokees and ran the survivors out of Texas.

Though what came to be known as the Flores fight involved Rangers and Mexican operatives, one member of Flores' party did not have an interest in fomenting trouble for the young Republic of Texas. That person was German-born Karl Steinheimer, a one-time pirate's colleague, an unsuccessful filibuster and highly successful miner who made a fortune in the Mexican interior.

Having received a promising letter from a woman in St. Louis who he had courted but not won, Steinheimer had been on his way to Missouri intent on rekindling the romance. With ten mule loads of silver and gold acquiring in his mining ventures, he felt the lady he fancied might be much more receptive to his advances than before. Steinheimer had thrown in with Flores only because in Indian country there was strength in numbers.

When the Texans advanced on Flores' men, Steinheimer realized that even though he did not have a dog in the fight, he would not be able to separate himself from the difficulties of the moment while trailing a team of 10 pack animals heavily laden with silver and gold. While it's hard to imagine him taking the time to do so, he buried the gold. He drove a brass spike into an oak tree to mark the spot and hastily escaped.

He managed to get away while the Rangers and Flores continued to fight, but hostile Indians soon waylaid him. Though suffering a severe wound, he somehow escaped. As soon as he reached a place of safety, he wrote a long letter to the lady in St. Louis, filling her in on his career since they had last visited. He also told her where he'd buried his fortune. Not long after penning this missive, Steinheimer died of his wounds.

The lady in St. Louis got his letter and some years later, the story goes, dispatched a party to recover her "inheritance." They didn't find it.

The best way to unravel a treasure tale is looking into the guy who told it first. In the Steinheimer story, that would be one Lee D. Bertillion, a Southerner who got to Texas as soon as he could and stayed here until his death in 1947. Bertillion was a pretty interesting character in his own right.

Born in a log cabin in the vicinity of Dalton, Georgia, as soon as he was old enough— which was still way too young by today's standards—he went to work in a cotton factory for 35 cents a day. At some point in the 1890s, a sickly teenager, dreaming of life as a cowboy, he set out on foot for Texas to, as he later put it, "get well or die."

Reaching the Mississippi, he found it cost 25 cents to cross the river. Being short that amount by two dimes and a nickel, he prevailed on a kind-hearted stranger to give him 10 cents. With that, he retained the owner of a small, leaky boat to row him across the big muddy. Once he got to Texas, Bertillion spent some time in West Texas and down in Mexico, working on ranches. Cowboy life on the wide-open spaces apparently suited him, and he soon recovered his health. In addition to punching cattle, he also tried his hand at prospecting for silver in the vastness of the Big Bend region.

Somewhere along the way, he had become particularly fascinated with longhorns. These tough descendants of Spanish stock had helped to build Texas after the Civil War, but by the time Bertillion came to Texas ranchers had turned to short-horn stock and the longhorns were on their way to join the buffalo in near extinction. Lacking the means to save the critters on the hoof, at some point it occurred to Bertillion that polished, nicely mounted horns made fine souvenirs.

That moment of inspiration appears to have come when Bertillion discovered in the Big Bend "a large number of old bones and long cattle horns where evidently some herd had perished in a canyon many years before."

In 1916, having made some money selling horns, he came to Mineola in East Texas and bought a farm. He had married a woman he met when she came up to him and admired a set of horns he was displaying, and they had at least one child, a son. In 1924, the San Antonio Express published a story in which Bertillion claimed to have invented a super variety of corn that would produce up to 14 ears per stalk. The same story noted that several years earlier, Bertillion had been "employed by San Antonio men to help install an irrigation system for the Martin ranch near Poteet."

Bertillion seems to have been a reasonably intelligent, self-educated, well-spoken dreamer with a Horatio Alger-style entrepreneurial bent.

From the mid-1920s through the mid-Depression, he ran short ads in a variety of magazines offering mounted polished longhorns for sale. The San Antonio Light carried a page-one story about him in 1931 along with a photograph of him holding up a set of horns considerably broader than he stood tall. The caption above the photo called him the "Texas 'Horn King.'"

In December that year, he sent a postcard showing him standing by a set of his mounted horns with this note: "Mr. Smith, Dear Sir, My Big horns are over 7 feet mounted like photo. Price $100. I have smaller horns for much less money. Very truly, L.D. Bertillion."

But while he made his living as a businessman, Bertillion appears to have shared the near-universal dream of getting rich the easy way by finding someone else's lost treasure.

And if we are to believe our eyes alone, he became a writer. That happened in 1924, when his byline appeared over two stories included in Legends of Texas, a publication of the Texas Folklore Society edited by J. Frank Dobie. One of those stories is called "The Steinheimer Millions," and it appears to be the first written telling of the tale.

Given that Bertillion claimed only seven months of education, most of that time being spent studying an old blueback speller, it's hard to believe that by middle age he had gotten to a level where he could write folktales suitable for publication. Bottom line, I think someone helped him. It could have been his wife, who may have been better educated, or it could have been a well-educated man with an interest in both folklore and writing—Dobie.

Of 27 pieces in that 132-page book, 10 carry Dobie's byline. It's easy to imagine that in compiling the book Dobie came to realize that the folklore collection would look a little more rounded with a few other taletellers listed in the table of contents.

Dobie, who was interested in longhorns and would go on to write a classic book about the breed, likely knew Bertillion through his horn business. At some point, Bertillion may have told Dobie the Steinheimer story—at least the essence of it—and Dobie took care of the rest. Just to be polite, he put Bertillion's name on the piece.

After pointing out that everyone in Bell, Falls and Williamson counties had heard a version of the treasure tale involving 10 jack loads of gold, Bertillion allows as how he first heard the story from one Frank Ellis.

There is a Frank Ellis buried in Live Oak Cemetery in Bell County. He was born in 1889 and died in 1963. Of course, there's nothing yet to prove that this Frank Ellis is the one who told Bertillion the Steinheimer story, but he's a strong suspect.

Bertillion went on to say in the story that a fellow named Nalley Jones had told the story to Ellis. Jones, he said, heard it from three unnamed Mexicans who'd spent three months hunting for the treasure.

So, assuming the Steinheimer story is merely a transcription of oral tales, the tellers to whom Bertillion lent an ear knew their Texas history surprisingly well. They knew of the Flores incident; they knew the exploits of Texas pirate Luis Aury and of Hayden Edwards' unrealized vision of a republic called Fredonia with Nacogdoches as its capital. And that casts doubt on Bertillion being the author of the story. A man with only seven months of schooling who made his living selling cow horns does not seem like the sort who would possess the kind of historical perspective evident in the first written version of the Steinheimer tale.

Since the story appears with no credit to Bertillion in Dobie's classic work, Coronado's Children, published only six years after it ran under Bertillion's name in the Texas Folklore Society book, there's a good possibility that Dobie was its real author. That certainly was his literary MO.

Also, most people when telling a story don't bother with when and where the principal character was born. On the other hand, a smart writer knows that "facts," even if created out of whole cloth, make a story more believable.

Despite the fact that the story says Steinheimer was born in 1793 in Speyer, Germany, no indication has been found that Karl Steinheimer ever existed anywhere but in someone's imagination. His name does not show up in any books, articles, or documents. Searching the vastness of the internet, the only way his name comes up is in connection with the treasure attributed to him. "Steinheimer" is a legitimate German surname, and there are some people by that name in Texas, but again, no one named Karl. That said, there is a city in Germany called Speyer. But anyone could have looked at a map or consulted an encyclopedia and come up with that name.

Another major problem with the Steinheimer story is that there is no mention in any account of the Flores fight that a European had been traveling with Flores prior to the encounter. All accounts, dating back to Yoakum's 1855 History of Texas and J.W. Wilbarger's classic 1889 work, Indian Depredations of Texas, say it was a group of about 30 Mexicans and Indians that Rice's Rangers tangled with.

To cover that, whoever cooked up the tale has Steinheimer pulling ahead of the Flores party with his 10 burro-loads of gold. Considering that Flores and his men were riding at a gallop in their effort to escape the equally hard-riding Texans, Steinheimer must have had some awful fast jacks in his team.

Whoever wrote the story used in Legends of Texas obviously was aware of the Flores flight and artfully added the fictional Heir Steinheimer and his long-lost love to the tale.

Here's another reason the story must be phony: There just wasn't all that much gold and silver lying around Texas in the 1830s. As one Texas newspaper astutely observed in 1888:

The idea seems to prevail that years ago Texas was overrun with rich Mexicans who deposited vast sums of money here and there and then kindly died or got scalped, leaving their lucre to whom it might concern. . .yet strange as it may seem, men can be found credulous enough to believe in such prodigy.

Burying something is hard work. Those five words explain why the Steinheimer story and most other Texas treasure tales—beguiling as they are—are mere folklore. Think about it. Digging a hole big enough to hide a treasure would take a lot of work. And back then, those needing to hide treasure had only picks and shovels at their disposal. In the case of Steinheimer, knowing a company of red-eyed Texas Rangers was hot on your trail would not make the effort any easier.

There is one treasure waiting to be found on or near the San Gabriel: The site of the long-ago fight. If the location could be established archeologists might be able to unearth some period artifacts.

And somewhere in the vicinity there must be three unmarked graves. The scant official paperwork connected to the fight makes no mention of what the Rangers did with Flores' body or the two men they killed. Maybe the Texans just left the corpses where they lay for the wolves to chew on, but assuming those Rangers were God-fearing men of normal sensibilities surely they took time to bury the men.

RANGER SILVER

When A. S. Lowery signed on with the Rangers in 1875, the state paid its frontier lawmen $30 a month.

At some point during the Ranger's half-year of service with famed Capt. Leander H. McNelly, an old Mexican man came to him seeking help—his son had been stabbed to death. If Lowery could catch the killer, the old man continued, he would make the lawman rich.

Back in those days, peace officers routinely supplemented their pay with rewards offered for the arrest of wanted criminals. But the grieving father offered the Ranger another sort of incentive: a map leading to a horde of lost silver.

The old man told the Ranger the treasure dated to 1825, when as a youth of 13 his family and a few others came from the border to what is now Caldwell County (the closest community back then was Gonzales) to mine for silver. He said the second shaft they dug revealed a vein of silver ore near the later community of Iron Mountain.

The miners had produced 43 bars of the precious metal when a rider informed them that hostile Indians had been seen in the area. Knowing they did not have enough manpower to defend themselves, the miners sealed the shaft with two large flat stones they covered with smaller rocks and brush and then started packing to leave the area the following morning.

Unfortunately for the miners and their families, the Indians attacked their camp that night. All the men died, and the women and children were taken captive. He had been one of the captives, the viejo continued in his account to the Ranger.

The 13-year-old eventually escaped from the Indians and settled near El Paso where he married and raised a crop of children, including the son who got murdered.

Just how seriously Lowery took the old man is not known, but the Ranger's descendants later claimed he caught the killer. Lowery made the arrest when the man identified as the murderer crossed the Rio Grande into Texas near Del Rio to attend a Diez y Seis celebration.

When he learned that the Ranger had apprehended his son's killer, who reportedly got life in prison for his crime, the old man looked up the lawman and handed him a crudely drawn map to the old mine.

Lowery (state records show he served from June 22 to Dec. 20, 1875) must not have put much stock in the document. His nephew, Harvey King, said in a 1937 newspaper interview that Lowery never made any effort to find the treasure. But in his dotage, the former Ranger got to thinking about the long-ago incident.

In the early 1930s, King told his uncle that if he would give him the map, he would try to find the treasure. If he succeeded, he said, he would split it with him 50-50.

"He refused," King told the reporter, "saying he would visit me in a few weeks and we would make the search [together]...but about the time he was to arrive I received a telegram he had died."

The wire came on Oct. 1, 1930.

King either got the map from someone else in the family or got an oral rundown on the vicinity of the supposed mine, because he visited the site in 1935.

He had no trouble finding a rock smelter and an old mine shaft that had been closed with dynamite. He saw signs that someone had been digging in the area but found nothing.

King died in 1951. Various people have tried to find the silver since then, but if anyone ever succeeded, it went unreported.

While the story of the supposed Caldwell County silver mine is probably just another folk tale, there is one major difference in this one. Most treasure stories lack any physical evidence, save for the holes dug in search of supposed caches, but in this case, there are traces of the mine. Or something old. I got permission to visit the site back in the mid-1970s and found a few pieces of slag, the waste product of a smelting operation.

A researcher who gained access to the site in 2002 documented what appeared to be a horizontal shaft called an adit and the remnants of an L-shaped smelter constructed of cut sandstone. Someone using a metal detector found a few pieces of metal in the area, but no silver bars.

The major problem with the site has to do with metallurgy. It would have taken tons of ore to produce 43 bars of silver. All the slag from that would have been near the smelter, but there is very little.

Even though it does not appear that any precious metal came out of the mine, no one has been able to determine the purpose of the smelter. Since some iron ore can be found in the area, it might have been an early-day iron work. But again, where's all the slag?

Unless someone stumbles on the silver, the real treasure of Caldwell County can be found in nearby Lockhart—the barbecued brisket and sausage at Kreuz Market.

ANECDOTES AND APOCRYPHA

Beyond anecdotes, stories that seem too good to be true usually are apocryphal. Here's a sampling of anecdotes and apocryphal tales involving the Rangers:

"HE'LL DO TO RIDE THE RIVER WITH"

Many a Texas Ranger has been characterized as someone who'd "do to ride the river with." Translation: "If I had to pick someone I'd like to scout the Rio Grande with, it would be Ranger [X]." Shorter translation: "I'd trust that feller to watch my back."

Since the Rangers have been riding the river (Rio Grande) for generations, it would seem logical that the expression had been in use for a long time. But that's not the case.

The first documented usage of the term dates from 1922, when British-born American Western novelist William MacLeod Raine (1872-1954) wrote this line: "You're a good little sport an' you'll do to ride the river with." It was published in "Tangled Trails: A Western Detective Story." The same year, Raine used the term again—this time as "He'll do to ride the river with" in "Gunsight Pass: How Oil Came to the Cattle Country and Brought a New West." Raine went on to invoke the saying more and more often, in 1936 using it as a book title: To Ride the River With.

When death claimed Raine, the expression he coined lived on. In 1974, New York-based publishing house Doubleday brought out a novel by Michael Hammons titled One to Ride the River With. Finally, in 1983 Bantam Books published yet another novel by the prolific Western writer Louis L'Amour: Ride the River.

In his book, however, L'Amour was not writing about a Ranger and the setting was not Texas. As the jacket copy put it:

No matter that Echo Sackett was young, and a woman, and had never been far from the valley, she was still a Sackett. Sharp and smart and a better hunter than most of the men she knew....A sure hand with a horse, a dead shot with a rifle, and fast with her wits, Echo traveled to the mountains of Tennessee, coming up against ruthless killers who'd stop at nothing to cheat her out of her inheritance. There she'd prove once and for all that she could ride the river with the best.

Despite its fictional origin, "He'll do to ride the river with" remains a high compliment.

RANGERS AND RATTLERS

Generations before biologists understood that killing a rattlesnake is not good wildlife management, Rangers on scout killed any rattlesnake they got a shot at. In thinning the population of this venomous reptile, Rangers considered it a service to the people of Texas.

One time, however, killing rattlers on state time nearly caused serious trouble.

In 1884, on a ranch near Green Lake in Edwards County, a detachment of four Rangers under Corp. P.C. Baird caught a group of barbed wire fence-cutters in the act. Rising from concealment, the corporal leveled his Winchester at the men and ordered them to surrender.

Since his men had used most of their ammunition on their ride to the ranch on shooting rattlesnakes, Baird hoped the wire-cutters would comply without resistance. However, assuming the "nippers" would fight, Baird ordered his men to give him the cartridges they had left so he could divide the ammunition equally among them.

But instead of raising their hands, the wire-cutters ran for cover and began shooting at the Rangers. Returning fire, the lawmen proved the better marksmen. When the black powder gun smoke drifted away, one fence-cutter lay dead and the other three were handcuffed.

The ongoing war between Rangers and rattlesnakes was not always one-sided. Attending an Ex-Rangers Association 1929 gathering in San Saba, 81-year-old former Frontier Battalion Ranger J.B. "Jack" Hawkins recalled a long scout he took while serving under Capt. Dan Roberts.

A party of Indians had made off with some horses in Mason County and ridden northwest in the direction of the Llano Estacado. The warriors had a two-day start on the Rangers, but Roberts and his men still took up their trail. Somewhere in present-day Tom Green County, the Rangers made camp for the night near the South Concho River.

Unknown to the lawmen, they staked their mounts and laid their bedrolls in close proximity to a rattlesnake den. Rattlesnakes being particularly prone to forage at night, the Rangers woke up to discover that two of their 14 horses had been snakebitten. One of the animals belonged to Roberts.

The captain detailed two Rangers to stay behind with the horses, hoping they would recover. Then he mounted up on their pack mule and his company resumed their pursuit. Catching up with the warriors on Aug. 15, 1875, at the head of the Devil's River in what is now Sutton County, the Rangers killed several Indians in a fight that lasted only two minutes.

Roughly 115 years later, a 20th century Ranger company gathered on the famed 6666 Ranch in northwest Texas for an overnight meeting. Their agenda included in-service training and required quarterly firearms qualification. In addition, the men of Co. C would be com-paring notes on cases, visiting, and enjoying the ranch's hospitality. Senior Capt. Lefty Block drove up from headquarters in Austin to join the gathering.

Following lunch, as Block and the other Rangers sat beneath a tent put up by ranch hands, the captain locked eyes on Gary Henderson and whispered sharply, "Don't move."

Sitting just across from Block, the younger Ranger figured the good-humored senior captain was up to some kind of prank, but he wasn't sure enough to ignore a direct command. With Block laser focused on something at ground level, Henderson subtly glanced down.

Practically between his boots, a large rattler lay coiled beneath his chair. Henderson, Block and the now-alerted other Rangers inside the tent remained frozen until the reptile finally slithered away. As soon as the snake made it outside the tent, a Ranger's .45 slug removed the rattler's diamond-shaped head.

COFFEE, PLEASE

In the late teens or early 1920s, a Ranger walks into a café in South Texas and orders a cup of coffee. Clearly no fan of the Rangers, the proprietor refuses to serve him.

Hearing that, the Ranger whips out his Colt Model 1911 and puts a neat .45 hole in the café's shiny, tall coffee urn. As a stream of hot coffee spews out, he fills his mug and sits down to enjoy it.

The incident is most often attributed to Ranger Charlie Miller but in some versions of the tale, it was Capt. A.Y. Allee who resorted to gunfire for a cup of Joe.

LET'S SETTLE THIS LIKE MEN

A Ranger and a Mexican tequila smuggler are engaged in a long gunfight, each shooting from behind a large rock.

"Let's settle this like men," the Ranger finally calls out. "When I count to three, let's both stand up and get this over with."

Later, in recalling the story, the Ranger says, "You know, that stupid SOB actually stood up."

PARDON ME, MA'AM

In 1917, the Texas House of Representatives voted to impeach Gov. James E. Ferguson. Rather than face trial in the Senate, he resigns.

Five years later, the former governor's wife Miriam "Ma" Ferguson runs for governor and wins. She gets beaten when she runs for a second term, but voters return her to office in 1933. During both of her terms, it is well known that "Ma" Ferguson—with advice and consent from her husband—sells pardons.

One day, the story goes, someone accidentally bumps into "Ma" inside the Capitol. "Pardon me," he says. "Oh, you'll have to talk to 'Pa' about that," she replies.

HOW THE RANGERS GOT A NEW MAN

When Lewis Rigler became a Ranger in 1947, the service had 51 men. The next increase in full time employees (FTEs) brought the service to 52 men.

The story behind that, Rigler later recalled, was that DPS Director Col. Homer Garrison received a call from an East Texas lawmaker saying he knew a local officer who'd make a good Ranger. But Garrison did not have any vacancies.

The next legislative session, miraculously, the new DPS budget increased the size of the Rangers force by one position. Even more wondrously, the man the East Texas legislator had suggested got the job. Rigler said that despite being a political appointee, the man turned out to be a good Ranger.

Former Crockett County Sheriff Jim Wilson got to know Rigler while working as a police officer in Denton in the 1960s and '70s. He said Rigler wouldn't wear traditional Ranger garb (cowboy hat, starched white shirt, khaki pants, boots and fancy gun belt) unless he had to. "I'm just a short, fat farm boy," he told Wilson. "I'm not a cowboy."

In Texarkana trying to break up a prostitution operation, a succession of Rangers had failed to get inside to make a case. The captain was really insisting on an arrest, so Rigler volunteered himself and another Ranger. Going to the door, he put his arm around the guy and said, "My father and I wanna [crude term for sexual intercourse]." The madam said, "Come on in, boys," and they made the case.

Late in his career, Rigler had 20 feet of colon removed and had to wear a catheter for 31 days. "I coulda used one of those things when I was a Ranger," he laughed, "I would have got a lot more confessions."

Until he had surgery, Rigler walked around the courthouse square in Gainesville six days a week, dropping in at virtually every business.

Rigler retired from the Rangers in 1977 and died at 94 in 2009. But as his obituary noted, "He never stopped being a ranger."

CAPITOL RIOT

The war in Vietnam was a controversial subject in the late 1960s and early 1970s, especially among college students.

Anti-war protestors, many of them University of Texas students, forced their way into the Capitol in the spring of 1969 after National Guard soldiers shot and killed four war- protesting students at Kent State University in Ohio. When a U.S. District judge reversed the Austin City Council's refusal to grant a parade permit for a second protest, numerous DPS officers—including a large Ranger force—were positioned at the state house to keep protestors on the outside this time.

Senior Ranger Capt. Clint Peoples offered his men a little pep talk as the marchers neared the Capitol grounds:

"If those long-haired hippies get inside the Capitol, it better be over dead men. 'Cause if they get inside, I'll kill you."

This time, no one got in the Capitol.

On another occasion, Peoples was driving DPS Director Col. Wilson E. Speir and Lt. Col. Leo Gossett somewhere when the driver of a passing car shot them the finger. Peoples curbed the car and got out of his state vehicle to talk with the young man. Neither Speir nor Gossett could hear exactly what was said. But they did note that the bird flipper just kept nodding his head while repeatedly saying, "Yes, sir, yes, sir."

Not without his detractors in the Rangers, Peoples retired in 1974 to become U.S. Marshal for the Western District of Texas. Ranger Capt. Bill Wilson succeeded Peoples as senior captain. But Wilson and his predecessor had not gotten along well. Supposedly, before Wilson died on New Year's Day 1990, he'd given Co. F. Capt. Bob Mitchell a whiskey bottle containing a pale yellowish fluid. "If I die before Peoples," Wilson said, "I want you to pour this on his grave for me."

A year and a half later, on June 22, 1992, Peoples died in a traffic accident in Waco. What happened to the whiskey bottle and its contents is a mystery.

TAKING THE PROMOTIONAL EXAM

Whenever there's a vacancy in the Rangers, it's not unusual for a hundred DPS officers to apply. If they do well on the promotional exam, they're called before an interview board that will make the final decision on whether to promote them.

According to Ranger lore, the board told one applicant that they'd only be asking him three questions. First, they asked him to name the days of the week starting with T. He correctly answers Tuesday and Thursday. Question number two was, "Name two things you can't eat for breakfast." Again, he nails it: lunch and supper.

The third question was tougher: Who shot Abraham Lincoln? He asked for some time to think about it, which the board granted. That night when his wife asked how his interview went, he said, "Great, they've already got me working on a murder case!"

WHAT OLDER RANGERS TALK ABOUT

Alpine-based Ranger Sgt. Dave Duncan commented in 2002 on a common topic of conversation he'd observed among older Rangers. All they do," Duncan smiled, "is talk about retirement or their prostates." He retired as a staff lieutenant in 2015.

CAMP CHOW

CAPTAIN TOBIN'S LEGACY

By most accounts, William Gerald Tobin's career as a Texas Ranger left a lot to be desired. But he had an idea that left Texas, and the Southwest, an enduring gastronomical legacy.

Born in South Carolina in 1833, Tobin came to Texas 20 years later with his brother Dan, settling in San Antonio. He soon married well, hitching up with Josephine Smith, daughter of former city mayor John William Smith. He first rode as a Ranger in 1855, a year later serving as city marshal of the Alamo City.

In 1859, hearing that rancher-bandit-Mexican patriot Juan Napoleon Cortina had raided Brownsville, Tobin decided to raise his own company of volunteers and march to the aid of the terrified Valley community. On his way south, he sent a letter to Gov. E.M. Pease offering his services as a Ranger captain. The governor took him up on his offer and gave him an official commission

Not long after Tobin and his Rangers rode into Brownsville, the situation got even worse.

A party of vigilantes—historians today suspect Tobin's men—lynched a Cortina officer who had been captured before the arrival of the Rangers. That made Cortina so mad he threatened to burn the whole town down. Brownsville survived, but it took another company of Rangers under the celebrated John "Rip" Ford plus elements of the U.S. Army to squelch Cortina's mini war on South Texas.

Despite his lackluster duty in the Valley, Tobin got swept up in the martial spirit at the outset of the Civil War and gained a commission as a captain of the Confederate Army. He survived the war and returned to San Antonio.

In the 1870s, he turned his attention to what may have been his strongest suit: Business. He leased a structure known as the Vance Building and opened a hotel he called the Vance House.

Somewhere along the way, he acquired a taste for a particular dish favored in San Antonio and South Texas. That appetite on Tobin's part would play a part in this food's Americanization—and Texas iconization.

By the early 1880s, he had hit his entrepreneurial stride in the Alamo City. And then he had his grand idea: Canning chili. In 1881, Tobin negotiated a contract with the federal government to sell canned chili con carne to the Army and Navy.

Carne, of course, is Spanish for meat. One would assume that beef would have been the meat that Tobin used in his product, but he opted for goat meat.

Having figured out a way to make money off the government, Tobin opened a chili con carne processing plant and canning operation. But just as his venture had begun to take off, he died on July 28, 1884. (No truth to the rumor that he died of chronic indigestion.) Soon after his death, the business went bust.

In fairness to history, it must not be intimated that this former Texas Ranger invented chili. All he did was think to can it.

Some say chili came from the Spanish, who supposedly found that antelope meat tasted better when cooked with onions, tomatoes and chili peppers. Others claim that chili originated over the campfires of California-bound Texans during the 1849 gold rush. More likely, Tejanos (Mexicans of Texas origin) developed chili as a way to get a lot out of a little meat.

No matter how chili came to be, long before Texas became a state in 1845, Mexican women sold chili and tortillas on the streets of San Antonio. Eventually these street vendors came to be known as "Chili Queens," and they lasted until health regulations forced them out of business.

The next evolutionary development was the invention of chili powder, which came about 1890. Three years later, Texas introduced the rest of the nation to chili at the Columbian Exposition in Chicago.

Not until 1921 did someone finally get around to following up on Tobin's idea of canning chili. That was Lyman T. Davis of Corsicana, who started peddling canned chili from the back of a wagon. He named his product after Kaiser Bill, his pet wolf.

Wolf Brand Chili, of course, remains on the grocery shelf today. But nowhere on the label is any credit given to former Ranger William Tobin for his Texas-sized idea—putting chili in a can.

STOUT ENOUGH TO FLOAT A HORSESHOE

That 19th century Texas Rangers required a good horse, a good six-shooter, and a good rifle should go without saying. But before they saddled up in pursuit of hostile Indians or outlaws, they by golly needed a good cup of coffee.

They preferred what baristas now refer to as "robust" coffee. What Samuel Colt did for frontier weaponry, John and Charles Arbuckle did for coffee drinkers in the West, including the Rangers. Indeed, their product came to be known as "The Coffee that Won the West."

Coffee had been around a long time before Arbuckle's, but with one grande latte of a difference: Merchants sold green coffee beans only. A few urban coffee sellers did do their own roasting, but fresh-roasted coffee had to be used right away. Most consumers had to do their own roasting. After a long, hard day in the saddle, a cowboy or lawman wanting a cup or two or three of Joe had to roast coffee beans in a skillet over the campfire (or, if such convenience was available, over a wood-burning stove). Of course, before brewing a pot, the roasted beans had to be ground.

Meanwhile, back east, about the time the Civil War ended Pittsburgh grocers John and Charles Arbuckle came up with an idea, doubtless after a strong cup of coffee, which changed everything for coffee sellers and coffee consumers. In 1868, the brothers Arbuckle patented a process for covering roasted beans with a glaze made of egg and sugar. That, they had discovered, kept the beans fresh and aromatic. Now their product could be shipped anywhere.

They began selling their new product in air-tight, one-pound paper packages under the brand name of Arbuckles' Ariosa Coffee. Each package had a yellow label with the word "Arbuckles'" in large red type. Below that was their trademark, a flying angel (who better to deliver coffee to a caffeine-needing populace?). Beneath the trademark, in a red- bordered box were the words "Ariosa Coffee" in black type.

("Ariosa" is a created name with "A" standing for Arbuckles' while "rio" and "sa" refer to the company's South American coffee bean sources.)

The new product proved an immediate success. It smelled good, it tasted good and it was strong. The old joke is that when brewing a pot of cowboy coffee made with Arbuckles', the only way to tell when it was ready was to toss in a horseshoe. If the horseshoe sank to the bottom, the coffee wasn't fit to drink yet. "The cook firmly believed there is no such thing as strong coffee but only weak people," writer-historian Edward Everett Dale wrote of one chuck wagon boss.

Especially in the West, Arbuckles' became a synonym for coffee. Shipped in strong wooden crates, Arbuckle's' spread nation-wide, particularly across the wild West.

The crates, made of Maine fir and holding 100 packages each, became almost as popular as the coffee they contained. Seldom simply discarded, the crates usually ended up being taken apart for use as interior paneling, shelves, storage boxes, baby cradles, coffins, wagon seats and more. If nothing else, they made good firewood. Accordingly, today vintage Arbuckles' boxes are pretty rare and costly when they do show up on the market.

Beyond knowing how to make good coffee, the Arbuckle brothers had a genius for marketing. The backside of their coffee bags featured a coupon redeemable for assorted products then categorized as "notions." A cowboy who went to the effort of cutting and saving coupons could redeem them for handkerchiefs, razors, guns and even wedding rings. Each coupon was worth one cent.

Not only that, each package of Arbuckles' included a stick of peppermint candy. Chuck wagon bosses learned to use the candy as an inducement to get some cowpoke to grind the coffee. The candy was tasty enough to trigger competition for the "right" to take on the extra work of turning the crank on the coffee grinder, truly a sweet deal for a cook who had no shortage of other chores needing his attention.

In the 1880s, the Arbuckle brothers moved their company to Brooklyn, where at the high point of their business they operated 85 roasting ovens in a large warehouse that still stands.

Despite its huge popularity, Arbuckles' did not survive the Great Depression. But in the late 1970s, Pennsylvanian Denney Willis acquired the Arbuckles' brand and began roasting and selling coffee marketed under the famous name. He and his wife eventually relocated to Tucson, where the couple and their son kept the brand alive.

In 1994, El Paso professor and writer Francis L. Fugate wrote a book on the history of Arbuckle's'. Published by Texas Western Press, the now out-of-print 233-page book was Fu-gate's final work. In fact, he died sitting in front of his desktop computer, putting the finishing touches on his manuscript.

One of the last things he must have typed was this refrain from an old cowboy song, which does a good job of summing up Arbuckles' mystique:

Under the star-studded canopy vast
Arbuckle's' Coffee and comfort at last,
Bacon that sizzles and crisps in the pan,
After the roundup smells good to a man.
Tales of the ranchman and rustlers retold,
Over the pipes as embers grow cold;
These are the tunes that memories play;
So make me a cowboy again for a day.

RANGER COOKIES

Here's an unsolved mystery: How did a popular sweet, crunchy cookie come to be named for the Texas Rangers?

Long ago, did some dust-covered frontier Ranger captain say to his weary fellow lawmen: "Boys, we've had a hard time of it lately what with all them Indians we've been a-fighting. How's about some milk and cookies? Holster yer guns, salt yer scalps, wipe the blood off your Bowie knives, and I'll cook us up a batch of Ranger cookies so good you'd slap your mama just for one."

In other words, Texas Rangers and baking cookies seem about as likely a pairing as say, roadrunners and rattlesnakes, ministers and bartenders or doctors and undertakers. This is not to imply that Rangers can't be handy in the kitchen, or that the men and women who wear the distinctive silver cinco peso badge don't have a taste for sweets. Few folks can resist a homemade cookie or two or three or more, but that a horseback-era Ranger would have time or inclination to come up with a distinctive cookie recipe seems unlikely.

So how did the name originate?

One answer comes from Boston, a city where you'd think no one knows baked beans about the Rangers, much less Ranger cookies. But a student at Harvard has rhapsodized in a blog about the Ranger cookies served in the cafeteria at that venerable Ivy League school.

Curious as to how the cookies became so named, the blogger checked with the university's head of food services and received an email saying: "Some claim that the cookie originated in Texas and was originally called the 'Texas Ranger Cookie' or 'The Lone Ranger Cookie.' The recipe is similar to the Cowboy cookie which has oats, chocolate chips and pecans."

OK, fine. But that still begs the question: If the Ranger cookie indeed hails from the Lone Star State, which by all rights it should (it would be humiliating to learn that Ranger cookies trace to, say, Alaska, or worse yet, Oklahoma), who DID create the recipe?

The smoking gun has yet to be found, but the prime suspect is the Lone Ranger. Well, not the masked rider himself, but the sponsor that made it possible for millions of Baby Boomers to grow up enjoying the adventures of Kemosabe and Tonto—General Mills. That venerable corporation, of course, manufactures cereal products, including corn flakes. It seems likely that at some point between 1941, when it began sponsoring the radio show and 1961, when the Lone Ranger TV show ended, the company developed a cookie recipe with corn flakes as an ingredient. Hence, Ranger cookies.

Etymology aside, one certainty is that no matter who named the cookies, as the old Ranger expression goes in regard to a trusted partner, "they'll do to ride the river with."

Ranger cookie recipe:

1 stick margarine
1/2 cup shortening
1 cup sugar
1 cup brown sugar
2 eggs
2 cups flour
2 teaspoons soda
1 teaspoon baking powder
1/2 teaspoon salt

1 teaspoon vanilla
2 cups oats
2 cups corn flakes
1 cup crushed pecans
1/2 cup coconut

Cream the margarine, shortening, sugars and eggs, then sift the flour, soda, baking powder and salt. Next slowly mix that with the creamed ingredients. Then add the vanilla, followed by folding in the oats, corn flakes, pecans and coconut. Roll a tablespoon of dough at a time into a ball and then flatten on a cookie sheet. Bake for eight minutes at 375 degrees.

THE RANGERS' "ARLINGTON"

When the family and friends of George W. Moore stood at his grave side that day in 1886, they doubtless pondered the fundamental question that always comes to mind when a young person dies: Why did it have to happen?

Moore was only 28 when he died. But he packed a lot of living in that short life, serving as a private in Frontier Battalion Co. D under one of the most illustrious of the Ranger captains, Dan W. Roberts. (Moore's funeral took place Dec. 11, 1886.)

Not much is known about Moore—when he enlisted on March 1, 1877, it was noted that he was 5 feet, 8 inches tall and had black hair—but under Roberts, his Ranger service would not have been boring. Death did bring him one lasting distinction: He was the first of 32 one-time Texas Rangers to be buried in the Center Point Cemetery in eastern Kerr County.

Actually, there are probably 35 Ranger graves in the small cemetery, but Bobbie J. Powell— whose great-grandfather Robert J. Lange is one of the former Texas lawmen buried there— could only document 32 of the burials as the graves of former Rangers.

"I think there are at least three more who were Rangers, I just haven't been able to prove it," she said.

The Center Point Cemetery has 1,450-plus graves, but by one measure it is unequaled anywhere else in Texas. No other cemetery in the state, not even the sprawling State Cemetery in Austin, has more Ranger graves.

"There's no reason for it that we know of other than the men buried there were all from this area," Powell said. "When I started my research, I knew the families of most of the Rangers." Ranger Moore's kinfolks certainly did their part to give the cemetery its unusual distinction. He was the first of nine Moores buried there. Five of them had served in the Rangers. The history of the cemetery goes back to the first half of the 1850s, when Elizabeth Denton and her children settled in what is now Center Point in 1852. Six years later Dr. Charles Ganahl and his family moved to the area.

A native Austrian, Ganahl named the community Zanzenburg after his hometown in Eu- rope. By 1872 enough people lived in and around Zanzenburg to justify calling it a town, though someone decided Zanzenburg did not roll off the tongue all that well. What they came up with instead sounded much less exotic but proved a lot easier to pronounce: Center Point.

Soon a small tract of land was set aside for a church (it later was moved to a different location) and cemetery. In 1875, Lydia McCain Burney, having died at 80, became the cemetery's first occupant. As the number of burials grew, in 1883 two more acres were added to the cemetery. A final land acquisition in 1901 enlarged the cemetery to its present size of 5.3 acres.

The second ex-Ranger buried in the cemetery was George Moore's older brother, Marshall Francis Moore. Born in Weakley, Tennessee, in 1854, he served in the Frontier Battalion June 25, 1875-May 31, 1877.

For reasons unknown today, Marshall died the same year as his younger brother.

The number of Ranger graves increased to three with the burial of James Hampton Lane in 1887. The fourth burial occurred in 1893, followed five years later, in 1898, with the final burial of the 19th century.

During the first decade of the 20th century, six new graves were added, bringing the number of ex-Rangers to 11. In the teens, another five burials occurred.

With two deaths in 1920, the tombstone count for ex-Rangers in the cemetery had grown to 18. From 1921 to 1929, another eight Rangers were interred there—the largest number of burials in any decade. That put the Ranger grave count at 26. Only three former Ranger burials occurred in the 1930s, followed by three more former Rangers, the last one buried in 1947. (Four later burials occurred.)

Despite the extraordinary number of ex-Rangers buried in such a small cemetery, no one noticed until the 1980s when Powell began doing research on her great-grandfather. Based on what Powell was able to learn about the cemetery and its unusual number of Ranger burials, the Kerr County Historical Commission applied to the Texas Historical Commission for a historical marker.

When Kerr County historians began planning for the marker dedication, someone approached Senior Ranger Captain H.R. (Lefty) Block and asked him to speak at the ceremonies.

Those who attended the Aug. 22, 1987, event got to see something not many had witnessed before—almost an entire company of modern Texas Rangers on horseback. At the beginning of the ceremony, the mounted Rangers rode through the cemetery in an equestrian salute to their ranger predecessors. Counting the riders, nearly 100 Rangers or retired Rangers had shown up for the dedication.

"The thirty-two one-time Texas Rangers who lie here don't have much in common," Block told the visitors. "They didn't look alike, they went on to do different things after they left the Rangers, and they had different joys and different sorrows in life. But they were Texas Rangers and that did give them something in common, then and now."

Though each of the former Rangers buried there had been an individual in his own right, as a group, the Center Point Rangers represent two distinct periods in the history of the Rangers. From their tombstones and extant governmental records, some interesting patterns emerge.

The first group are men who rode as Rangers in function if not in name during the Civil War as members of the state's frontier forces. For whatever reason, these men preferred protecting their homes from Indians and scouting for draft dodgers rather than marching off to join the fratricidal slaughter as gray fought blue.

The second category of burials are those who served either during Reconstruction or in the Frontier Battalion, the organization that contributed so much to the Rangers' reputation. All the Rangers in the cemetery had ridden to protect Texas, but only three were born within its borders. Seventeen, just over half, came from Tennessee. One each came from Alabama, Mississippi, Missouri, North Carolina and Pennsylvania. Two came from Kentucky. One of the Rangers hailed from England. Where the other seven Rangers were born remains to be determined.

Rangers buried in the Center Point Cemetery include:

• William DeWitt Clinton Burney (1828-1920). Became Kerr County's first sheriff in April 1856 and served one two-year term. Later served as a Ranger during the Civil War.

• Neal Coldwell, (1844-1925). Took command of Frontier Battalion Co. F at Silver Creek June 4, 1874. In 1880, promoted to Quartermaster and served until 1882.

• James Alexander Gibbens (1857-1945). Served in Frontier Battalion Co. F, Sept. 1, 1875-Aug. 31, 1876, and in Co. D, Sept. 1, 1875-Nov. 30, 1876; reenlisted March 1, 1877, serving to Feb. 28, 1878.

• Rev. Henry Truman Hill (1836-1922). Served two years as a Ranger.

• Felix L. Holloway (1837-1903). Served in Frontier Force, Co. C, March 1871-May 31, 1871.

• Richard Jones Irving, Sr. (1824-1910). Served in Gillespie County, Texas State Troops, 3rd Frontier District, under Capt. William A. Hudson in 1864.

• Robert J. Lange (1860-1936). Served in Frontier Battalion, Co. C under, at various times, Captains G.W. Arrington, John Hoffar and Neal Coldwell, March 1, 1881-Aug. 31, 1883.

• James Hampton Lane (1834-1887). Served in Frontier Battalion, Co. F , June 4, 1874- June 6, 1875.

• John Tarleton Lane (1847-1912). Served in Frontier Forces Aug. 25, 1870-May 31, 1871, and in the Frontier Battalion, variously under Co. D and Co. F, Sept. 1, 1875-May 31, 1877.

• Samuel Ramon "Sam" Lane (1836-1907). Served in Frontier Battalion, Co. F, under Capt. Joseph Shelly, Jan. 10, 1884-Aug. 31, 1884.

• Miles Abernathy Lowrance (1827-1900). Served as Ranger in

Texas Mounted Volunteer Regiment during Civil War.

• James LaFayette McElroy (1856-1929). Served in Frontier Battalion Co. C, under Captain A.W. Arrington, Sept. 1, 1879-Aug. 31, 1880.

• Stephen Goldsby McElroy (1846-1938). Served in Frontier Battalion Co. F, June 4, 1874-June 4, 1875.

• Francis M. Moore (1833-1909). Served in Frontier Battalion Companies D and F, variously, June 4, 1874-Sept. 23, 1877.

• Gabriel Rogers "Gabe" Moore (1861-1946). Served in Frontier Battalion Co. A, Sept. 1, 1878-Feb. 28, 1879.

• George Kendrick Moore (1827-1893). Served in Frontier Battalion Co. E, under Capt. W. J. Maltby, June 6, 1874-Dec.12, 1874.

• George W. Moore (1858-1886). Served in Frontier Battalion Co. D under Capt. Dan Roberts, 1877-1878.

• Hughes Cleon Moore (1848-1915). Served in Frontier Battalion Co. F, June 29, 1875-Aug. 31, 1875.

• Daniel C. "Dan" Nowlin (1857-1925). Served in Frontier Battalion, Co. A, Sept. 1, 1875-Nov. 30, 1877.

• Dr. James Crispin Nowlin (1817-1898). Served in Frontier Battalion, Co. F, May 31, 1876-March 8, 1877.

• Richard Wade Nowlin (1841-1900). Served in Frontier Regiment Co. B during the Civil War.

• Peter Osbourne Alonzo Rees (1837-1919). Served in Kerr County Minute Man company prior to Civil War.

• Nelson Orselus "N.O." Reynolds (1846-1922). Enlisted May 25, 1874 in Frontier Battalion Co. D under Capt. Cicero Rufus Perry. Served variously under other captains, having reached the rank of lieutenant of Co. E when he resigned in 1879. Served two terms as Lampasas County Sheriff, 1886-1890.

• William Henry Rishworth (1852-1947). Born in Leeds, England, he came to Texas in 1870 and joined Frontier Battalion Co. D in 1874. His end date as a Ranger has not been determined, but he told a newspaper reporter a few months before his death that "an attack of fever" forced him to leave the Rangers while the company was at San Saba.

• James L. Sellers (1848-1920). Served in Frontier Battalion Co.

F, June 4, 1874-Dec. 9, 1874.

• William Henry Witt (1853-1925). Served in Frontier Battalion Co. F under Capt. Neal Coldwell, June 4, 1874-June 4, 1875, and in Co. D, Sept. 1, 1876 -Aug. 31, 1877.

• Stephen Goldsby Wray (1839-1917). Served in 36th Texas Cavalry 1862-1865. During the first part of the Civil War, his unit provided frontier protection in Texas.

The Former Texas Rangers Association unveiled rust-colored steel Ranger crosses at each of the Rangers' graves on Oct. 23, 1999. The keynote speaker at the event was Senior Ranger Capt. Bruce Casteel who succeeded Block when he retired. FTRA President Joe Davis also spoke.

Four 20th century Rangers also lie in the cemetery: Sgt. Henry F. Manning (1928-2002); Capt. John M. Wood (1913-2013); Sgt. James "Jim" Peters (1927-2014). and Capt. Grady Sessums (1937-2017).

ANOTHER CONFLICT

The Texas Rangers have been contending with one foe or another for two centuries. Now they—and their iconic historical forebears—are caught in the crossfire between the mainstream and a revisionist camp asserting that anyone who looks close enough will see that the Rangers as an institution have boot-covered feet of clay.

And as this cultural war continues, there's already one Ranger down.

The City of Dallas in June 2020 removed the iconic, 12-foot bronze "One Riot, One Ranger" statue at Love Field, a fixture of the busy North Texas airport since 1963. The reason: Jay Banks, the Ranger who stood as the model for sculptor Waldine Tauch, did not try to force school integration in Mansfield, Texas on Sept. 3, 1956. That's the day the parents of five black children tried to enroll their offspring in two white-only local elementary schools in the Tarrant County community.

While it is correct that Sgt. Banks and the other five Rangers with him that day did not attempt to override the local school board's decision not to accept black children on white-only campuses, they had zero authority to do so. Banks' assignment that day was to prevent anyone—black or white—from getting hurt, not to single-handedly end generations of school desegregation in Texas. The nationally publicized incident saw ugly name calling, hateful signs (one white man clutched a pet monkey holding a sign that said "I want to play football at Mansfield High") and even two hanged effigies of blacks. But despite the ugly crowd, no one got hurt.

It did get dicey for a time. When the white crowd began jostling a white Fort Worth Episcopal minister for suggesting there could be a Christian solution to racial issues, Sgt. Banks had to escort him off campus to assure his safety.

Arguably, the Ranger presence that late-summer day prevented the situation from getting out of hand. A widely distributed news photo taken in front of Mansfield High School shows Banks nonchalantly leaning against a tree during the protest, one booted foot cocked against it for support. Wearing a white straw Western-style hat, a starched white shirt and khaki pants—his six-shooter secure in a leather holster on his right side—the Ranger's body language did his talking for him.

In recent years, a revisionist school of historians have labeled the 19th and early 20th century Rangers as bloodthirsty practitioners of genocide against American Indians and Mexicans. They view the Rangers of old as gun-toting tools of a greedy, land-grabbing, racist Anglo establishment. While there's no question that rangers riding in the name of frontier or border protection killed some people who, as the old Texas expression goes, might not have "needed killin'," those instances were rare compared with their successes in preventing violence and enforcing the law.

To compare the Rangers as an institution to regimes whose troops have systematically killed thousands and even millions of innocent people—as in Nazi Germany or Cambodia—is not accurate and certainly not fair.

"Where I find the most fault with many of today's revisionist writers," best-selling Western novelist Elmer Kelton has written, "is in their penchant for seeing our forebears' pioneering experience only in the darkest terms. Surely it must be possible to exalt the minority view-points of the Western experience without automatically condemning the white male pioneers to perdition."

Kelton believed that the actions of 19th or early 20th frontier figures—including the Rangers—can't be realistically judged on the basis of 21st century values.

No question, the Rangers did not all wear white hats. Bad men sometimes did saddle up for Texas. However, more often than not, those rangers either were disciplined, discharged or left of their own volition. Some Rangers, though neither dishonest nor holding themselves above the law, merely proved inept or mediocre. Fortunately, other rangers excelled at their duties and helped build their legend.

Concerning that legend, the author of one recent book on the Rangers sought to make the case that over the years, the Rangers have carefully cultivated their heroic image. The Rangers certainly have had their show boaters—men like Capt. Bill McDonald, Capt. W.W. "Bill" Sterling and Senior Capt. Clint Peoples—who never minded being quoted or photographed and definitely contributed to Ranger mythology. But many more Rangers simply chose to do their job as best they could, keeping a low profile and disdaining publicity.

The Ranger myth of near invincibility, as much a part of the Lone Star State as bluebonnets and barbecue, is more the cumulative result of popular culture and news media coverage than any kind of deliberate Ranger strategy. Not that Rangers, much like Marines, aren't well aware of their reputation. None of them want to be the one to bring embarrassment to the force.

The term "the truth lies somewhere in the middle" is a familiar cliché, but it fits when it comes to the history of the Rangers. The 19th century Rangers and their early 20th century counterparts can neither be classified as all bad nor all good. And since the founding of the Texas Department of Public Safety in 1935, only a comparatively small number of Rangers have been disciplined and even fewer have been cashiered for not measuring up.

Indeed, it's hard to sustain an argument that the Rangers do not fall in the middle of what philosophers term the dichotomously variable continuum. With most issues, that bell curve has a small set—a group, belief, characteristic, whatever—on one end as well as a small set on the other end. But most of the set falls in the middle, whether the continuum is good versus evil, or truth opposed to falsehood. Or, as the adage holds, "There is your truth, there is my truth and there is the truth."

In 1966, Sergio Leone directed a movie starring Clint Eastwood called "The Good, the Bad and the Ugly." Though this Italian-filmed Western would become something of a classic, following its release the film got some criticism for being too sanguinary. Leone answered that with a line that works for the Rangers as well: "The west was made by violent, uncomplicated men." Of course, he forgot to mention some pretty feisty women, like the wife of Ranger Capt. Dan Roberts, who traveled with him on his company's scouts along the frontier during the 1870s.

It's well-documented that Roberts and other 19th century Rangers did much toward the betterment of Texas. By scouting for hostile Indians, and in some pointed fights with the Comanche, Kiowa and Apache peoples they doubtless saved lives. Rangers escorted surveying parties and blazed new trails, including the route through Texas to the California gold fields in the late 1840s. In the 1880s, Rangers protected transcontinental railroad construction crews and worked to keep their track-laying camps law-abiding.

In rounding up outlaws, Rangers helped tame a rowdy frontier. They caught or killed livestock thieves, barbed wire fence cutters, bank robbers, train robbers and other felons, identified and tracked down murderers, hunted escaped prisoners and more.

Rangers in the 20th century rode to protect the border during the Mexican Revolution— excluding the 1918 Porvenir massacre in the Big Bend and other death-dealing rogue actions. Rangers also suppressed riots, prevented lynchings (Rangers under Capt. Frank Hamer alone have been credited with averting 17 extrajudicial hangings), pacified wide-open oilfield towns, trailed bootleggers during Prohibition, and dealt with Depression-era bandits.

During the last half of the previous century and into the 21st century, as an arm of the DPS, Rangers have used state-of-the-art forensics and investigative techniques to identify unknown murder victims and bring killers and other criminals to justice. They've also arrested corrupt public officials, investigated white collar crime, child sex trafficking and more. Since the 1990s Rangers have used DNA testing and other cutting-edge technologies to solve decades-old cold cases and track down serial killers. While they're at it, they handle SWAT situations, arrest drug runners and as they have for generations, patrol the Rio Grande.

Revisionists will continue to duke it out with the mainstream over the amount of culpability the Rangers have for their past behavior, but the reality is that the Rangers have always existed for only one purpose: To protect the people of Texas. At a governor's direction, they may have aided in strike-breaking or become enforcers of the majority's idea of racial justice or social mores, but most of the time, rangers just worked to make Texas a safer place to live and raise a family.

Rangers had a part in civilizing what in the 19th century and for more than half of the 20th century was the nation's largest state, a huge hunk of land bigger than France. In the process, they forged the words "Texas Ranger" into an internationally recognized icon that will endure as long as stories are told.

TEXAS RANGERS: DEVELOPMENTAL TIMELINE

Author's Note: The following timeline covers major Ranger organizational events from 1823 to 2023. But it would take a book to chronicle all developments in Ranger history. Some developmental aspects had to be left out. Also, this timeline does not include Indian-fighting or law enforcement activities.

January 1823

Jose Felix Trespalcios, governor of the Mexican province of Coahuila y Tejas, receives letters written January 7 by John Jackson Tumlinson and Robert Kuykendall. Tumlinson is alcalde of the Colorado District of Stephen F. Austin's colony and Kuykendall is commander of militia. The two seek permission to raise a Ranger-like company of men separate from the colonial militia.

May 5, 1823

Led by militia lieutenant Moses Morrison, a 10-man volunteer company—some mounted, some not—is authorized by Trespalcios to protect the colony from hostile Indians. The men also are charged with building blockhouses and boats for use in fighting coastal Indians.

Aug. 5, 1823

On the back of another document, Austin scratches out a proposal to augment Morrison's force with another 10 men to be paid the equivalent of $15 a month in land to "act as rangers for the common defense."

August 1826

With Indian hostilities a growing problem, Austin favors a permanent mounted force to patrol the frontier. He suggests a ranger company of up to 30 men to be composed of landowners who would serve for a month (or furnish a substitute) for every half-league of land he held.

While there is no concrete evidence that either of the companies Austin envisioned were ever formed, volunteer ranger-like companies, raised when needed, continue to periodically engage hostile tribes for the rest of the decade and into the early 1830s.

Oct. 17, 1835

The Permanent Council of Texas's newly organized provisional (and independence-minded) government votes to approve a motion by member Daniel Parker authorizing creation of a force of "twenty-five rangers whose business shall be to range and guard the frontiers between the Brazos and Trinity rivers." The measure also authorizes 10 rangers to operate on the east side of the Trinity and 25 rangers "to range" between the Brazos and Colorado rivers. The men would be paid $1.25 a day.

Nov. 24, 1835

With a war for Texas independence from Mexico looming, the legislative body of Texas's provisional government—styling itself as a Consultation—passes an ordinance creating a corps of 150 Rangers. These men not only rode to protect settlers from hostile Indians, when Mexico sent troops into the province of Coahuila and Tejas and the revolution began, they participated in the war.

March 6, 1836

Thirty-two men of the Gonzales Ranging Company who'd ridden to help defend the besieged Alamo died along with all the other defenders. The Gonzales men, who came to be called the Immortal 32, amounted to 20 percent of the slain defenders.

April 21, 1836

Thirty-six Rangers participate in the Battle of San Jacinto, an event that assured Texas independence.

Dec. 5, 1836

The new Republic of Texas Congress passes "An Act, To protect the frontier." The measure requires President Sam Houston "to raise, with as little delay as possible, a battalion of mounted riflemen, to consist of [280] men, for the protection of the frontier..." The nine-section act sets the term of enlistment as 12 months "or upwards," with the men having to furnish "a suitable, serviceable horse, a good rifle, and one brace [a pair] of pistols..." Further, the measure authorizes the President "to cause to be erected such block houses, forts, and trading houses, as in his judgment may be necessary to prevent Indian depredations."

Dec. 10, 1836

Congress passes an act setting the pay for "Mounted Riflemen, now and hereafter in the ranging service on the Frontier" at $25 a month. Officers would be paid more, but all Rangers would be entitled to a land grant for their service.

June 12, 1837

The Congress of the new Republic of Texas approves an act "For the better protection of the northern Frontier" authorizing a 600-man "corps of mounted gun men." The act also allows the Rangers to hire friendly Indians to assist them as spies and scouts. One of those Indians, a Lipan Apache chief named Flacco would ride with Capt. John Coffee Hays in 1841-1842. Hays later said Flacco had saved his life while fighting Comanches.

1838-1845

The Texas Congress passes 13 measures—10 acts and 3 joint resolutions—related to frontier protection. During this time Rangers are variously referred to as "the ranging service," "mounted volunteers," "spy companies," "volunteer companies," "mounted men to act as rangers," "mounted men," "mounted gunmen," and "troops for the protection of the frontier."

Feb. 1, 1845

In its final Ranger related act, "For the Protection of the Frontier," the Congress appoints Jack Hays to organize and command "a detachment of troops for the protection of the frontier." This marks the second time Congress specifically names Hays as a Ranger captain, the first on Jan. 23, 1844.

Dec. 29, 1845

The near decade of Texas' status as an independent republic ends with Texas's admission to the union as the 28th state.

May 1846-February 1848

Federalized Texas Rangers fight in the Mexican American War while a force of state- funded Rangers contends with hostile Indians north of the Rio Grande.

Feb. 2, 1848

A treaty between the U.S. and Mexico formally ends the war. The document is signed at Villa de Guadalupe Hidalgo, a community on the north side of Mexico City. Handing over 525,000 square miles, the pact puts most of North America (excluding Canada) under the U.S. flag.

Aug. 11, 1849

Under the Treaty of Guadalupe Hidalgo, the Federal government assumes responsibility for preventing incursions by hostile Indians in Texas and much of the rest of the West. But doing so in Texas proves more than the military can handle. San Antonio-based Bvt. Maj. Gen. George M. Brooke, commander of the Army's Department of Texas, asks Gov. George T. Wood to raise three companies of Rangers "78 strong in the aggregate" for federal service.

Jan. 7. 1850

The Legislature passes a joint resolution authorizing eight companies of Rangers to protect the frontier. Lawmakers also approve retroactive payment of men who had served as "mounted volunteers on our border country" at the same rate that U.S. soldiers were paid.

July 5, 1855

In response to a flurry of complaints from frontier county officials, particularly Bexar County, Gov. Elisha M. Pease writes Texas Revolution veteran James H. Callahan authorizing him to organize a Ranger company. Callahan enlists 111 men, telling them the governor had promised they would be paid by the Legislature.

Nov. 27, 1857

Legislators approve a joint resolution authorizing the governor to "order out mounted volunteers, not to exceed [100] in number...divided into two or more companies" to protect the frontier. The Rangers would be enlisted for three months' service "and as much longer as the Governor may think necessary." The measure provided $20,000 to fund the force.

Jan. 27, 1858

The Legislature authorizes the governor to raise a 100-man Ranger force "in addition to the force now in service..." Those enlisted would serve for six months or be continued in service "if the safety of the frontier require it." For the first time, state lawmakers created the rank of Senior Captain for someone "experienced in such service." That position would be held by Senior Capt. John S. "Rip" Ford. With a $70,000 appropriation (the equivalent of $2.6 million today), Rangers under Ford fight several pitched battles with hostile Indians.

Nov. 18. 1859

Lawmakers approve a one-paragraph joint resolution authorizing the governor to "call out such a number of volunteers to quell the insurrection or invasion of [Juan] Cortinas [sic] and followers on the Rio Grande as may be necessary..." Volunteers (most of whom already headed for the border) would be paid the same as U.S. soldiers and officers.

Jan. 3, 1860

"An Act for the Protection of the Frontier" declares that "a state of hostilities exists between the people [of Texas] and various Indian tribes who inhabit the unsettled portions of the State and adjacent territory" and authorizes the governor to raise a 10-company regiment of mounted men to protect the frontier. Each company would consist of no more than 83 men. Led by a captain appointed by Gov. Sam Houston, the Rangers would elect their own officers and furnish their own horses, weapons and equipment. Privates would be paid $25 a month with tiered pay for officers based on rank. The colonel in command of the regiment would be paid $180 monthly.

Jan. 28, 1861

Against the urging of Gov. Houston the Texas Legislature adjourns and turns the House chamber over to a body of delegates from across the state assembled as a Secession Convention.

Feb. 1, 1861

After voting to secede from the Union, the Convention appoints a Committee of Public Safety. That committee divides the state's frontier into three districts, each commanded by a colonel. The job of this Ranger-like force was to take possession of federal military posts in the state and protect the frontier from hostile Indians. Chosen to lead the districts are former Ranger Capt. "Rip" Ford and former Ranger captains Benjamin and Henry McCulloch.

Feb. 7, 1861

Lawmakers pass an act "to provide for the protection of the Frontier..." allowing the chief justice (county judge) of each of 37 frontier counties to organize a company of minute men "not to exceed [40] in number rank and file." Each member of the company would have to provide "a suitable horse, gun, navy revolver, at least [100] rounds of ammunition, [10] days provisions, and all necessary equipments [sic]..." Privates would be paid $1.25 a day when in service. In addition, the minute men would be exempt from poll tax, militia, compulsory road work, and jury duty. Ten privates and one officer were to be kept on scout at all times.

Feb. 23, 1861

Texas voters ratify secession, 44,317 to 13,020.

March 5, 1861

Gov. Houston resigns and Texas formally joins the Confederate States of America the day after Abraham Lincoln is inaugurated as the 16th President.

Dec. 21, 1861

Legislators pass an act creating a state-funded and controlled Ranger-like force designated as the Frontier Regiment. The measure provides for nine companies raised from counties along the frontier with a tenth company raised by the governor from anywhere in Texas. Occupying forts abandoned by the U.S. military and establishing 18 new camps, more than 1,000 Frontier Regiment rangers regularly patrol a 500-mile line from the Red River to the Rio Grande. But hostile Indians soon figure out the Rangers' routine and begin raiding where they knew rangers would not be. During this time the western frontier contracts to the east by a hundred miles.

Jan. 29, 1862

Gov. Francis R. Lubbock appoints James M. Norris commander of the Frontier Regiment.

February 1863

A change of leadership—replacing Col. Norris with Col. James E. McCord—improves Frontier Regiment effectiveness. Regular patrolling soon ends and the Rangers begin operating tactically.

Dec. 15, 1863

A new legislative act replaces the Frontier Regiment with the Frontier Organization of Texas State Troops and hands control (and the cost) of the existing Frontier Regiment companies to the Confederate Army. The measure also provides for Ranger-like local militia forces in each of 24 frontier counties.

March 1864

It takes nearly three months to stand up the new frontier defense organization and transfer the Frontier Regiment to the regular Confederate Army. Though not as well armed as their predecessors, and mostly made up of older men or teenagers, the Frontier Organization continues to do what it could to protect the state's western counties until the war ended in April 1865.

July 1865

Legislators pass an act to "organize a company to defend the northern and western borders." Designated as the Frontier Force, it consists of 20 companies of 25 men each.

March 30, 1870

Texas is readmitted to the Union.

June 13, 1870

Legislators authorize Gov. Edmund J. Davis to raise 20 companies of 62 rangers each for frontier protection. Rangers would be enlisted for 12 months' service. The state would provide each ranger a breech-loading carbine (though the cost of the weapon would be deducted from each ranger's pay), ammunition and food for man and horse. As usual, Rangers had to furnish their own mounts, revolvers and other gear.

July 1, 1870

Given that the Rangers were charged with guarding against hostile Indian incursions, to provide law enforcement at a particularly violent time the Legislature creates an organization to be known as the Texas State Police. Made up of 225 privates, and led by four captains, eight lieutenants and 24 sergeants, the new force would have broad law enforcement authority. Unlike the Rangers, they would wear uniforms, badges and be furnished with weapons.

Nov. 25, 1871

Legislature passes an act providing for the creation of 24 companies of minute men for 23 frontier counties. The companies would be "at all times...in readiness to meet and repel an Indian raid, or depredations on the frontier counties..." When in service, volunteers would earn $2 a day. But that service could not exceed 10 days a month. For the first and only time, Rangers recruited under this act were funded through the sale of state-issued Frontier Defense bonds. An amendment to this law passed the same day removes any reference to specific counties and makes the measure applicable to "any frontier county in this State..."

April 19, 1873

The state Senate votes 58-7 to override Gov. Davis's veto of a bill abolishing the State Police force. The now-defunct force had been relatively effective in bringing law and order to Reconstruction Texas, but it had never been popular with the citizenry.

April 10, 1874

Legislators pass an act "to Provide for the Protection of the Frontier of the State of Texas against the invasion of hostile Indians, Mexicans, or other marauding or thieving parties." The measure, containing 32 sections, basically does two things:

First, as had previous legislation, it authorizes the governor to raise companies of 25 to 75 men for any county experiencing depredation "upon ...lives or property..." Previous legislation (repealed by this bill) had authorized Ranger-like companies only for frontier counties.

Second, sections 19-28 authorize creation of a six-company battalion of "mounted men." Led by a captain, each company would consist of 75 men. Appointed as adjutant general by Gov. Richard Coke, Confederate veteran William Steel would have overall command of this force as well as the state militia.

John B. Jones, another Confederate veteran, is appointed to lead the battalion, having the rank of major. While the men of this new battalion were not referred to as Rangers, they would be Rangers in function. The force quickly came to be called the Frontier Battalion, but this designation is not mentioned in the new law.

Section 28 of the law broke new ground: "Each officer of the battalion and of the companies of minute men...shall have all the powers of a peace officer, and it shall be his duty to execute all criminal process directed to him, and make arrests under capias properly issued, of any and all parties charged with offense against the laws of this State."

July 14, 1874

With a vicious outbreak of violence that came to be known as the Taylor-Sutton Feud raging in and around DeWitt County, Gov. Coke appoints Leander H. McNelly (a State Police veteran) as "Captain of Militia" to lead the just-created Washington County Volunteer Militia. McNelly's charge is to restore peace and order in DeWitt County, but he soon expands his work to include the Nueces Strip, the sparsely populated part of the state between the Nueces River and the Rio Grande. Coke is able to do this without legislative approval, since the law creating the Frontier Battalion had given him authority to raise additional companies separate from the battalion. Though McNelly's command is technically a militia company, he and his men were generally referred to as Rangers. In function if not name, they were.

July 22, 1876

"An Act to Suppress Lawlessness and Crime in Certain Parts of the State" is passed by the Legislature. The bill gives McNelly's Ranger company its own statutory authority, transforming the Washington County Volunteer Militia into a 53-man force known as Special State Troops.

March 20, 1877

Maj. John B. Jones issues Special Order No. 15 instructing his captains to focus on "sup-pression of lawlessness and crime" From then on, he said, the Frontier Battalion would dis-continue routine scouting for Indian sign and only pursue actual raiding parties.

Jan. 25, 1879

Gov. Oran M. Roberts names Jones adjutant general after Gen. William Steele steps down.

July 19, 1881

Gen. Jones dies at 47 in Austin from complications related to a pair of surgical procedures for liver cysts. He is replaced as adjutant general by Wilburn H. King.

Jan. 7, 1884

Gen. King issues General Order No. 13 to remind Rangers of an earlier order still in effect: Rangers could not go around armed when off duty. Nor could they wear a gun in saloons, circuses, or other amusement places unless on duty. King's order also admonished Rangers they could not visit or "stay about" saloons, gambling houses, or places of prostitution "unless in the performance of public duty."

May 26, 1900

Attorney General Thomas S. Smith rules that only the Frontier Battalion's commissioned officers possess full police powers. That means that out of four Ranger companies then in the field, only four men, the captains of each company, could make arrests. Adjutant General Thomas Scurry promptly reorganizes the Rangers to make almost all the men either first or second lieutenants.

Jan. 10, 1901

The oil age in Texas begins near Beaumont with the spectacular blowout of the first well in the Spindletop field.

March 29, 1901

Legislature passes House Bill 52, "An Act to provide for the organization of a 'Ranger Force' for the protection of the frontier against marauding and thieving parties, and for the suppression of lawlessness and crime throughout the state..."

The measure abolishes the Frontier Battalion and replaces it in function with a Ranger force of four companies of no more than 20 men each. Men saddling up to enforce the law had been referred to as rangers for years, but this legislation marks their first formal designation as rangers.

July 9, 1901

House Bill 52 takes effect. The Frontier Battalion is no more.

Feb. 7, 1904

A new oil field in Hardin County northwest of Beaumont turns the small community of Batson into a wide-open, crime-ridden boom town. Capt. J.A. Brooks and three ranger privates are sent to calm things down. This marks the first use of the Rangers as boom town tamers.

Nov. 20, 1910

The Mexican Revolution begins when Francisco I. Madero takes up arms to overthrow ruler-dictator Porfirio Diaz Mori. At first, Texas, which shares 1,254 miles of border with Mexico, did not take the event that seriously. Neither, early on, did the Rangers.

The force already had a lot on their figurative tin plate. For one thing, both citizens and some legislators had begun to question if the law enforcement agency was even necessary in the 20th century. Among those were local figures in certain cities—particularly San Antonio—who thought the Rangers were intruding on their territory.

Oct. 1, 1911

A legislative act sets the Ranger force's size at no more than four companies "of mounted men." Each 20-man company would be commanded by a captain and a first sergeant.

1913

Ford Motor Co. begins mass production of its Model T as the public's transition from the horse-and-buggy era to the age of the automobile is off to a gallop.

April 4, 1917

The Legislature creates the Texas Highway Department to develop a network of driver-friendly roadways across the state.

April 6, 1917

The U.S. declares war on Germany and enters the European war.

May 25, 1917

Gov. James Ferguson signs Senate Bill 28, a Ranger act passed by the Senate May 9, followed by House approval on May 14. The measure authorizes the governor to organize a force styled as the Ranger Home Guard. The act caps the maximum size of the force at 1,000, the men to serve for three years "unless sooner removed by the governor." As standard for previous incarnations of the Rangers, the state would furnish each enlistee a rifle and handgun, the cost of which to be deducted from their pay. Legislators earmark $250,000 to fund the force. Part of that money would go toward increasing Ranger salaries. Historians have portrayed this act as a simple expansion of the existing Ranger force, and that was the net effect. But when Sen. Claude Hudspeth introduced the bill on May 4, 1917 he told the San Angelo Evening Standard that the measure would make possible a "reserve protective force" to be brought into service only when needed. No matter the intention of its author, after September 27, the term Ranger Home Guard disappeared from Texas newspapers.

Sept. 24, 1917

One day prior to being removed from office through the impeachment process, Gov. Ferguson resigns and Lt. Gov. William P. Hobby becomes governor.

October 1917

The small Eastland County town of Ranger, so named because it had been settled near the site of an old frontier-era Ranger camp, boomed with the discovery of oil in the area. Many of its residents, drawn by the prospect of easy money, were not particularly keen on abiding by the law. Texas Rangers sent to Ranger, Texas raided gaming halls, smashed drinking establishments, and corralled a wide assortment of miscreants and felons.

The same story would be repeated throughout the '20s and '30s. Only the names of the towns changed. From Borger to Mexia, Rangers preserved what peace and dignity they could in the wild oil field boomtowns.

March 11, 1918

Hobby signs House Bill 15, known as the "Hobby Loyalty Act." The measure empowers the adjutant general to organize a Loyalty Ranger Force of "three picked men from each county." Those commissioned as unpaid special rangers under the new law would "act as a secret service department for the State" and report to newly commissioned Ranger Capt. William M. Hanson.

A loyalty ranger's commission had validity only in the ranger's county of residence to ferret out "disloyal occurrences" and forward statements of witnesses to Austin. "You are not expected to make arrests but are supposed to work under cover as much as possible, and in a secret capacity," Adjutant Gen. James A. Harley concluded in his general order outlining their duties.

Nov. 11, 1918

The global conflict soon known as the "Great War" and later as World War I ends.

Jan. 30, 1919

Concerned about instances of Ranger brutality, State Rep. J.T. Canales of Brownsville begins conducting hearings on the force and its actions along the border.

February 1919

Three months after the end of the war, the Adjutant General nullifies all Loyalty Ranger commissions.

Feb. 13, 1919

Members of the committee having heard testimony from 80 witnesses, Canales concludes the hearings. Five days later the committee submits its findings to the full House. The 2,000-page report, published in three volumes, documents ranger abuses and recommends a reorganization of the Rangers.

March 17, 1919

Governor Hobby signs a watered-down version of Canales' House Bill 5 into law. The measure reduces the size of the Ranger Force to four companies made up of 15 privates, a sergeant and a captain. An additional headquarters company of six men would work out of Austin. For the first time since 1858, the body would be commanded by a senior captain. On the theory that higher pay would attract higher quality men to enlist in the Rangers, the salary for privates was raised to $90 a month; sergeants would get $100 monthly and captains $150. Each man also received a $30 monthly allowance for subsistence.

Jan. 17, 1920

National prohibition begins. In addition to their other law enforcement duties, Rangers begin arresting liquor smugglers and shutting down saloons trying to skirt the law. Many a burro train of bootleg liquor from Mexico is intercepted, and shoot-outs between Rangers and smugglers were not infrequent.

Aug. 1, 1924

John E. Elgin of San Antonio files suit against Gov. Pat Neff and other state officials seeking an injunction to stop all Ranger operations on the basis that the law creating the force violated six sections of the state's Bill of Rights and five articles of the state constitution. Elgin, an aging frontiersman, is the front for a cabal of Alamo City gamblers.

Jan. 15, 1924

State District Judge R.B. Minor of San Antonio rules that the Ranger statute violates three articles of the state constitution and enjoins the state from expending any state funds for Ranger salaries and operation.

Feb. 25, 1925

The Fourth Court of Civil Appeals in San Antonio reverses the lower court and upholds the constitutionality of the Rangers. The Texas Supreme Court upholds the Fourth Court on May 13.

Dec. 23, 1927

As Rangers and local officers comb Eastland County for suspects in the deadly robbery of the First National Bank in Cisco, Capt. Tom Hickman asks for an airplane to assist in the search. This marks the first-ever use of an aircraft by the Rangers.

1929

Texas Highway Department, seeing an increase in roadway crashes due to motorists ignoring speed limit signs and engaging in other unsafe driving practices, establishes the Texas Highway Patrol. This is the first uniformed state force with police power since Reconstruction.

Jan. 18, 1933

On her first full day in office, Gov. Miriam "Ma" Ferguson (wife of impeached former Gov. James Ferguson) fires all 44 Rangers in retaliation for Ranger political support for her opponent, Ross Sterling.

Sept. 25, 1934

The state Senate forms a committee to investigate crime and law enforcement in the state.

Jan. 16, 1935

A day after his inauguration, Gov. James V. Allred fires every Ranger appointed by his predecessor.

The committee appointed during the Ferguson administration produces a report in early 1935 singularly critical of Texas law enforcement. However, the document also proposes a solution: the creation of a state law enforcement agency to be known as the Department of Public Safety.

The Legislature begins consideration of Senate Bill 146, a measure authorizing such an agency, a department which would operate under a gubernatorially appointed three-member Public Safety Commission. The Rangers would be transferred from the Adjutant General's Department and the Highway Patrol would be moved from the Highway Department to form the new agency.

Aug. 10, 1935

A joint House-Senate conference committee makes some changes to the DPS law, but on Aug. 10, 1935, Senate Bill 146 becomes effective.

Under the new DPS, the Ranger force will consist of 36 men. Though smaller than it had been in years, the Rangers would finally have the benefits of a state-of-the-art crime laboratory, improved communications, and political stability.

The force is organized into five companies, each headed by a captain. Tom Hickman, a well-known former Ranger captain, is named senior captain of the Rangers.

Sept. 1, 1935

Homer T. Garrison is appointed director of the DPS. In their first year under the DPS, the Rangers took part in an estimated 255 cases.

1936

Within a year of their incorporation into the DPS, the Rangers receive national publicity with the opening of the Texas Centennial Exposition in 1936 at the State Fair in Dallas. The headquarters for Co. B was set up in a specially built log building on the fairgrounds. Rangers and visiting retired Rangers were seen in news reel footage in movie houses around the nation.

May 19, 1937

State lawmakers approve House Bill 77, an act tweaking the organizational structure of the DPS.

1941-1945

During World War II, among their other duties, Rangers provided internal security in Texas. Ranger war-time duties varied from showing air raid warning training films to tracking down escaped German POWs later in the war. When U.S. Army Rangers landed in France, the German press thought those commandos were Texas Rangers. This causes considerable anxiety among the German people. The Reich's minister of propaganda eventually has to clarify matters to avoid further panic.

1945-1947

By 1945, the authorized strength of the Rangers had been increased to 45 men. Two years later, the force grew again to 51 men.

1949

Legislators authorize construction of a $1.3 million DPS headquarters in North Austin. The same year, the DPS buys its first airplane and names a Ranger as the agency's first pilot-investigator.

1953

The DPS moves from its original headquarters at Camp Mabry, the home of the Texas National Guard, to a new building at 5805 North Lamar Blvd. in North Austin.

Sept. 1, 1957

Based on a Texas Research League report submitted to the Legislature, the DPS undergoes the most extensive reorganization to that point in its history. The Public Safety Commission divided the state into six regions, each under the command of a Highway Patrol major who would answer to the assistant director, and ultimately to the director. This new structure placed the captains of the six Ranger companies under a uniformed officer, which the Rangers did not like.

Jan. 1, 1958

Reacting to considerable behind-the-scenes politicking on the part of Co. F Capt. Clint Peoples, the Public Safety Commission reverses its mandate that the Rangers should report to the Highway Patrol. On this day, DPS Director Garrison sends a teletype to all DPS offices: "Ranger Captains and those under their command will be responsible to the director."

May 7, 1968

After running the DPS for nearly three decades, Col. Garrison dies. Lt. Col. Wilson E. Speir is named as his replacement.

Jan. 1, 1980

Following the retirement of Col. Speir, James B. Adams—then assistant director of the FBI—takes over as DPS director. Adams goes on to institute numerous changes in the department, including ending the long tradition of the director being able to appoint someone from another law enforcement agency as a Ranger.

May 31, 1987

Col. Adams retires and is replaced by Lt. Col. Leo E. Gossett.

Sept. 1, 1987

When internal consideration is given to folding the Ranger Division into the DPS' Criminal Law Enforcement Division, the Legislature amends the statue pertaining to the Rangers with the addition of these 11 words: "The division related to the Texas Rangers may not be abolished."

Sept. 1, 1988

The DPS promotes Lee Roy Young Jr. to the Rangers. He is the first black ranger in mod-ern times.

Aug. 3, 1993

For the first time in Ranger history, the DPS names two women as rangers—Marrie Reynolds Garcia and Cheryl Campbell Steadman. Also sworn in is Richard Lindsley Shing, the first Asian-American ranger.

May 2004

Earl R. Pearson appointed Chief of the Texas Rangers, becoming the first African American to hold command of the Rangers.

December 2008

Antonio "Tony" Leal replaces Pearson when he retires. He is the first Hispanic Ranger commander of the modern era.

August 2009

Retired FBI agent Steven McCraw, who has been serving as Texas Homeland Security di- rector, is appointed to head the DPS.

2010

The DPS observes its 75th anniversary.

2020

Ranger Lts. Wende Wakeman and Melba Saenz become the first two female captains in Ranger history.

2023

With events held across the state, Texas celebrates the 200th birthday of the Rangers.

SELECTED RANGER NUMBERS

Frontier Battalion's first 15 years

Beginning when the first Frontier Battalion Rangers took to the field in May 1874 and through Nov. 30, 1889, they took part in 56 engagements with criminals or Indians. In dealing with criminals, Rangers killed 69 men and wounded 27.

Indian war statistics

From May 1874 through the last Ranger engagement with hostile Indians in January 1881, Rangers only killed 35 Indians, wounded 12 and captured 4.

Bad people didn't do all the killing

Of 34 Frontier Battalion Rangers who died violently between 1874 and 1900, four were killed by a fellow Ranger or Special Ranger. Two others died in firearm accidents.

Use of force incidents

In his extensively researched book The Texas Rangers: A Registry and History (Jefferson, NC: McFarland and Co., Inc., 2010), author Darren L. Ivey—in a section labeled "Battle Record"—lists 482 use-of-force events from 1835 through 1998. These incidents range from skirmishes to true battles with hostile Indians or Mexicans to gunfights with criminals to riots, kidnappings, hostage situations and other major incidents. Ivey's list does not include major events or criminal cases not involving use of force.

How many men and women have served as Texas Rangers?

From 1835 to 1935, records in the Texas State Library and Archives at Austin show the number as 12,557. But there may have been more Rangers. Many of the state's earliest Ranger-related records were lost in a fire in 1857. The 1881 Capitol fire destroyed a collection of relics (aka Indian War trophies) gathered by the Rangers and possibly other pertinent paper records.

Since 1935, the year the Legislature merged the Rangers with the state's nascent Highway Patrol to create a new law-enforcement agency called the Texas Department of Public Safety, an estimated 2,000-plus additional men and women have worn the silver star.

The authorized strength of the Rangers in 2023 was 172. These men and women are organized into seven companies, A-F, plus a headquarters detachment in Austin. The Rangers are led by a chief, assistant chief, majors (for each company), captains and lieutenants. For more detail on the present-day Rangers, see dps.texas.gov/section/texas-rangers

In addition to the active Rangers as of July 2023, there were 218 living DPS-era Ranger retirees.

Medal of Valor winners

Four 20th century Rangers have received the DPS' Medal of Valor, Sgt. William R. Gerth, 1983; Sgt. Stanley K. Guffey, 1987 (posthumously); Sgt. John Aycock, 1987, 1995; Sgt. Danny V. Rhea, 1998.

Newspaper mentions

A search of www.newspapers.com, a subscription site that makes available more than 11,000 digitized U.S. newspapers, brought up 347,951 matches. Of course, the term "Texas Ranger" or "Ranger" can be used multiple times in one article, but the number shows that the Rangers have received a lot of publicity—good and bad—over the last two centuries. Incidentally, this number is only from Texas newspapers. In all U.S. newspapers, the number of matches is 1,755,064.

Ranger crosses

In 1999, the Former Texas Rangers Association began placing steel crosses at the gravesite of former Rangers. The marker is three feet high and 18 inches wide. At the apex is a circle-in-a-star Ranger badge. The crosses are free to any FTRA member who is a descendant of the Ranger to be honored. By 2023, more than 800 of these crosses had been placed across the state.

Books about the Rangers: 3,000-plus

Movies featuring Texas Rangers: 235

Television series featuring Texas Rangers: 7

Saddling Up

Two Centuries of Ranger History

Cox, Mike, Wearing the Cinco Peso: The Texas Rangers, 1823-1900, New York: Forge Books, 2008, passim.

Six Bullets

Cox, Wearing the Cinco Peso, passim.

Shaping Their Legend

Cox, Mike, "Texas Rangers: 10 Who Never Stood Down," True West (June 2023), pp. 26- 31.

Fighting Men: 1823-1859

They Rode From Gonzales

Author's presentation, Immortal 32 Descendants and Family Association, Gonzales, Texas, Feb. 25, 2023.

Donavan, James. The Blood of Heroes, New York: Little, Brown and Co., 2012, pp. 228-233, 235-236.

Huddleston, Scott. "Remember Alamo's Immortal 32," Gonzales Inquirer, May 11, 2017.

Sowell, A. J. "Frontier Days of Texas: Pathetic Incidents of the Battle of the Alamo—The Losing of the Little Cannon That Brought on the Texas Revolution," El Paso Times, Aug. 25, 1912, p. 28.

In Grateful Memory

"Leaves from the Unwritten History of Texas," (Austin) Tri-Weekly State Gazette, April 26, 1871.

Wilbarger, J.W. Indian Depredations of Texas. Austin: State House Press, 1999 (reprint of 1889 first ed.), pp. 146-150.

Makemson, Kate Holland. "Old Spanish Spur Revives Memories/Found on Brushy Creek Battle Site," Austin American, Nov. 28, 1926.

In the fall of 1926 someone found at the battle site a rusty, hand-forged spur with a 4.5- inch shank and a rowel 4 inches in diameter. Locals speculated that it was a right-foot spur lost during the fight by a Comanche, but Plains Indians did not use spurs. Given the size of the rowel, the spur likely was Mexican made. By the time the spur was found, the site had been in cultivation for many years. What happened to the artifact has not been determined. Thompson, Karen R. "Battle of Brushy Creek"

https://williamsoncountytexashistory.org/ battle-of-brushy-creek-taylor-williamson-county-texas/ accessed Aug. 6, 2023.

Cox, Mike. "Texas Ranger Tales," Former Texas Rangers Association Straight Talk (July 2005).

Rowdy Rangers

Cox, Mike. "Texas Tales," Nov. 30, 2016.

Findagrave.com, Rev John Wesley DeVilbiss, Memorial ID 8530887, accessed Aug. 6, 2023. Spellmann, Norman W., "DeVilbiss, John Wesley," Handbook of Texas Online, accessed June 06, 2023, https://www.tshaonline.org/handbook/entries/devilbiss-john-wesley.

Battle of Walker's Creek

Author's presentation, Sisterdale, Texas, June 8, 2014.

Weiser, Mark B. The Fight Along Walker's Creek: Introducing the Pistol That Won the West, Fredericksburg, Texas: Privately published, 2021, passim.

Two Uses for Lead

Cox, Mike. "Texas Tales," March 21, 2012.

Lawhon Family Papers, 1832-1959, Dolph Briscoe Center for American History, The University of Texas at Austin.

'A Wild, Rough Looking Set of Men'

Freeman, Elder John A., "Recollections of Early Days in Texas," Texas Historical and Biographical Magazine, Vol. II, No. 2 (February 1892) p. 94.

Remembering Mr. Hobbs

Elgin Historical Society. Elgin, Etc: stories of Elgin, Texas. Elgin: Elgin Historical Society, 2008, pp. 6-7.

Cox, Mike. "Texas Tales," Nov. 30, 2011.

Letters from Sesom

Corpus Christi Weekly Caller, April 28, 1893, p. 4.

Moses, J. Williamson. Murphy Givens, ed. Texas In Other Days. Corpus Christi: Friends of the Corpus Christi Public Library, 2005, pp. 37-38; 41-45.

Findagrave.com, John Williamson Moses, Memorial ID 202490141, accessed Feb. 9, 2023. Wagner, Frank. "Moses, John Williamson," Handbook of Texas Online, accessed Feb. 8, 2023.

A Ranger Hero Dies Hard

McMillin, N.D. to John Williams, Jan. 3, 1859.

White, James C. The Promised Land: A History of Brown County, Texas. Brownwood: Brownwood Banner, 1941, pp. 13-14.

Michno, Gregory and Susan Michno, A Fate Worse than Death: Indian Captivities in the West, 1830-1885, Caldwell: Caxton Press, 2007, pp. 174-177.

Findagrave.com, Moses Joshua Jackson, Memorial ID 100358907, accessed April 27, 2023.

Cox, Mike. "Texas Tales," Feb. 19, 2003.

Civil War and Reconstruction: 1860-1873

The Bear Hunt Didn't Work Out

Cox, Mike. "Texas Tales," Aug. 20, 2003.

Vollie's Ride

"Camp McMillin Still Has Interest of San Saba," Fort Worth

Star-Telegram, March 17, 1957, p. 38.

"Ceremony set to honor Capt. N.D. McMillan," Goldthwaite Eagle, Oct. 24, 2012.

San Saba County History 1856-2001, San Saba: San Saba County Historical Commission, 2002, pp. 104-106.

Cox, Mike. "Texas Tales," June 23, 2016.

______. "Texas Ranger Tales," Former Texas Rangers Association Straight Talk, (August 2016).

F.M. Peveler's Keepsake

Carlson, Paul H. and Tom Crum. Myth Memory and Massacre: The Pease River Capture of Cynthia Ann Parker. Lubbock: Texas Tech University Press, 2010, pp. 24, 48-50, 56,

175. Richardson, T.C. "One of Sam Houston's Minute Men/Grandbury [sic] Pioneer Was a Ranger Under Old Sam and Played a Part in Taming the Frontier." Farm and Ranch, Aug. 20, 1927, pp. 4, 7.

Selden, Jack K. Return: The Parker Story. Palestine, Texas: Clacton Press, p. 179, 181.

Voices in the Dark

Cox, "Texas Ranger Tales," Former Texas Rangers Association Straight Talk, (July 2011).

As Rance Moore Lay Dying

Fisher, O.C. It Occurred in Kimble, Houston: The Anson Jones Press, 1937, pp. 47-52.

Cox, Mike. "Texas Tales," June 6, 2018.

Writin' Ranger

Cox, Mike. Introduction to Sowell, A.J., Life of "Big Foot" Wallace. Austin: State House Press, 1989. pp. vii-x.

Hunter, J. Marvin. "A.J. Sowell, Ranger and Author." Frontier Times (September 1943), pp. 251-252.

Sowell, Andrew Jackson. "Around the Camp Fire." Unpublished manuscript, c.1907, Seguin-Guadalupe County Library, Seguin, Texas.

"Early Days in Texas." Unpublished manuscript, c.1917, Seguin-

Guadalupe County Library, Seguin, Texas.

______. "Half a Century Ago Texas Rangers Unfurled Lone-Star Flag on Plains." San Antonio Light, April 18, 1917.

______. "Texas Frontiersman Camps in the Wildest Part of Big Bend Country." San Antonio Express, Jan. 13, 1918.

Sowell, Russell Lee. From Three Years to Three Hours. np, nd. Typescript photocopy, Seguin-Guadalupe County Library, Seguin, Texas.

No Meat and Not Much Bread

Cox, Mike Cox. "Texana," June 25, 2003.

Sowell, A.J., Rangers and Pioneers of Texas, with a Concise Account of the Early Settlements, Hardships, Massacres, Battles, and Wars. Austin: State House Press, 1991. Reprint of 1884 ed., new introduction by Mike Cox, passim.

'The… Minute Men Do Their Business'

Barrett, Neal Jr. Long Days and Short Nights: A Century of Texas Ranching on the YO 1880-1980. Mountain Home, Texas: Y-O Press, 1980, pp. 19-26.

Carlson, Paul, "Charles Schreiner, One of Texas' greatest ranchmen and promoter of the 'Tex-as range livestock triumvirate," Ranch Magazine, October 1984, p. 14.

Schreiner, Charles III; Schreiner, Audrey; Berryman, Robert; and Matheny, Hal F., compilers, A Pictorial History of the Texas Rangers, Mountain Home, Texas: Y-O Press, 1969, pp. 10-13

Cox, Mike, Historic Kerrville: The Story of Kerrville & Kerr County, San Antonio: HPN Books, 2016, passim.

______. "Texas Tales," Oct. 12, 2016.

Prairie Policemen: 1874-1901

Ranger Bride

Roberts, Luvenia Conway, A Woman's Reminiscences of Six Years in Camp with the Texas Rangers, Austin: Von Boeckmann-Jones Co., 1928, passim.

Cox, Mike. "Texas Tales," May 14, 2014.

'I Had Good Luck This Morning'

Cox, Mike. "Texas Tales," July 24, 2002.

Love Letters from an Outlaw

"A Western Warrior Desperate," Daily Fort Worth Standard, March 20, 1877, p. 3.

Cox, Mike. "Ranger Tales," Former Texas Rangers Association Straight Talk (March 2008).

'Often Distressing Things to be Done'

Author's presentation, Texas Ranger Round-Up Bicentennial Celebration, Center Point, Tex- as, May 6, 2023.

Bennet, Joseph E. Sixguns and Masons: Profiles of Selected Texas Rangers and Prominent Westerners. Highland Springs, VA: Anchor Communications, 1991, pp. 50-55.

Hunter, J. Marvin. "Neal Coldwell, a Gallant Texas Ranger," Frontier Times (January 1926). Grinstead, J.E. "Conquering the Early Texas Outlaw," Fort Worth Star-Telegram, July 10, 1921, pp. 37-38.

Marshall Tri-Weekly Herald, March 4, 1876, p. 4.

Earning Some Extra Cash

Cox, Mike. "Texas Tales," May 10, 2017.

"Quail Shooting Brought $15 a Day When Ranger Wasn't Killing Thieves," El Paso Herald-Post, Nov. 19, 1938.

Buck Barry Writes His Grandson

Barry, James Buckner to John Buckner Barry, ca. February 1883, author's collection. John Buckner, born Jan. 15, 1871, to Kossuth "Koss" Barry and Martha America Snider Barry, died April 30, 1960. The old ranger's grandson is buried in the Barry Cemetery, Walnut Springs, Texas not far from his grandfather.

Cox, Mike. "Texas Tales," Oct. 7, 2015.

Greer, James K., ed. Buck Barry Texas Ranger and Frontiersman. Waco: Friends of the Moody Texas Ranger Library, 1978, p. 220.

The Disappearance of Ranger Woods

Cox, Mike. "Ranger Tales," Former Texas Rangers Association Straight Talk (July 2007)

Case Closed...Maybe

Cox, Mike. "Ranger Tales," Former Texas Rangers Association Straight Talk (November 2007).

Justified Homicide or Just Plain Murder?

Cox, Mike. "Texas Tales," March 12, 2003; Cox, "Ranger Tales," Former Texas Rangers Association Straight Talk (October 2007).

'Don't shoot no more. I'm dead!'

Galveston Daily News, Sept. 12, 1884, p. 1.

"Foul Murder," San Antonio Light, Sept. 27, 1884, p. 1.

"Arrest of Two of the Murderers of Mrs. Brautigan [sic]," San Antonio Light, Sept. 27, 1884, p. 1.

"Held For Murder," Fort Worth Daily Gazette, Sept. 28, 1884, p. 5. San Marcos Free Press, Oct. 2, 1884, p. 2.

"A Ranger's Story/Three Men Arrested in Travis County Charged With the Murder of a German at Fredericksburg," Austin Daily Statesman, Oct. 8, 1884.

"Safely Jailed," San Antonio Light, Oct. 10, 1884.

"'Occasionals' Valued Letter," Austin Daily Statesman, Nov. 13, 1884.

"Four Murderers," San Antonio Light, Nov. 24, 1884, p. 1.

"Fredericksburg Jail Destroyed," Galveston Daily News, Jan. 8, 1885, p. 1.

Alexander, Bob, Rawhide Ranger, Ira Aten, Denton: University of North Texas Press, 2011, pp. 53-55, 67, 91-102.

"A Prisoner Cremated," Galveston Daily News, Jan. 8, 1885. Austin Daily Statesman, Jan. 9, 1885, p. 3.

"Adjutant General's Office," Austin Daily Statesman, May 6, 1886.

"Adjutant General's Office," Austin Daily Statesman, May 26, 1886, p. 2.

Austin Weekly Statesman, June 3, 1886.
"Lawbreakers Met by Officers," Fort Worth Daily Gazette, Dec. 19, 1888, p. 6.
Galveston Daily News, Feb. 10, 1894, p. 6.
Fredericksburg, Texas. . .The First Fifty Years. Fredericksburg, 1896, reprint ed., Fredericksburg Publishing Co., 1971, p. 55, 79.

He Wasn't a Coward After All

Finch, O.H. The Lives and Times of A Family Named Finch, 1806-1954, Amarillo: Russell Stationery Co., 1954, pp. 51-52.
Cox, Mike. "Texas Tales," Jan. 4, 2012.

At Least He Got a Nice Funeral

"Killed by a Ranger," El Paso Times, Aug. 27, 1893, p. 7.
Austin Weekly Statesman, Aug. 31, 1893.
El Paso Times, Sept. 10, 1893, p. 7.
El Paso Times, Nov. 5, 1893, p. 7.
"Is Civil or Military Law Paramount in Texas?" Austin Weekly Statesman, Feb. 7, 1895, p. 2.
Alexander, Bob, Winchester Warriors: Texas Rangers of Company D, 1874-1901. Denton: University of North Texas Press, 2009, pp. 269-270.

Mistletoe for the Lady

Kelly, Herman, "Texas Lawman," Texas Highways (September 1973), pp. 4-6.

The Poisoning Parson

"Captain Sullivan Is Dead," Austin Statesman, May 22, 1911.
Sullivan, W. John L. Twelve Years in the Saddle For Law and Order on the Frontiers of Texas. Austin: Von Boeckmann-Jones Co., 1909.
Author's interview with Joe Warren, Round Rock, Texas, Dec. 7, 1998.
Lanehart, Chuck. Tragedy and Triumph on the Texas Plains: Curious Historic Chronicles from Murders to Movies. Charleston, SC: The History Press, 2021, pp. 42-47.

Foully Assassinated

"Death of Ranger Jim King," in Now and Then in Zavala County: A History of Zavala County, Texas Written by the people of Zavala County. Crystal City: Zavala County Historical Commission, 1986, p. 28.

Stephens, Robert W., "A Ranger's Grave: The Murder of Jim King," Quarterly of the National Association for Outlaw and Lawman History, V. XXIX, No. 4 (Oct.-Dec. 2005), pp. 14-15.

Happy Trails, Sunday

Cox, Mike. "Ranger Tales" Former Texas Rangers Association Straight Talk (Spring 2010).

Ex-Rangers Ready to Fight Over a Grave

"The Old Texas Rangers," Austin Daily Statesman, Oct. 10, 1897, p. 1.

"Sam Houston's Remains Belong in Texas," Austin Daily Statesman, Oct. 12, 1897.

Border Troubles: 1902-1918

What Revolution?

Harris, Charles H. and Louis R. Sadler, The Texas Rangers and the Mexican Revolution, Albuquerque: University of New Mexico Press, 2004, passim.

Cox, Mike, Time of the Rangers, New York: Forge Books, 2009, pp. 62-85.

Partners Don't Always Get Along

"Police Seek McDonald and Bailey," Abilene Daily Reporter, Nov. 27, 1910.

"A Galveston Echo. Ranger Arrested for Carrying a Gun and Was Released," Galveston Daily News, Dec. 11, 1910, p. 4.

"Tex" O'Reilly

Author's presentation, Pecos Chamber of Commerce annual banquet, Jan. 30, 2009. O'Reilly, Edward S. "Tex," Roving and Fighting: Adventures Under Four Flags, New York: Century Press, 1918, passim.

______. and Lowell Thomas, Born to Raise Hell: The Unbelievable but True Life Story of an Infamous Soldier of Fortune, pp. 168-204.

Harris and Sadler, The Texas Rangers and the Mexican Revolution, p. 101.

Chico and Joe

Author's presentation, Texas Ranger Day, Fredericksburg, Texas, Aug. 4, 2018.

Author's interview with retired Ranger Lt. Dave Duncan, Fort Davis, Texas, Jan. 18, 2023. Duncan said that following the raid, for a time the Rangers maintained a lookout on a high point overlooking the store and ranch house. The last time he visited the spot, he said, an old cookstove dating from the time of the border wars was still there.

Cox, Time of the Rangers, pp. 72-85.

The Day Frank Patterson "Died"

Harris and Sadler, The Texas Rangers and the Mexican Revolution, p. 355.

Lackey, Jerry, "Killed In 1918, Lawman Frank Patterson Spry at 84," San Angelo Standard- Times, Aug. 18, 1963.

Porvenir

Harris and Sadler, The Texas Rangers and the Mexican Revolution, pp. 352-354, 392, 450, 478.

MacCormack, John, "Findings shed new light on 1918 Porvenir massacre," Associated Press, April 4, 2016.

Taylor, Lonn, "Uncovering the truth of the Porvenir Massacre," www.bigbendnow, Jan. 21, 2016.

______. "The Worst Thing That Ever Happened on the River" in Marfa For the Perplexed, Marfa, Texas: Marfa Book Co., 2018, pp. 225-228.

The author visited Porvenir March 22, 2011, with two former Texas sheriffs. Glenn Willeford and Jim Wilson picked me up at Alpine's Holland Hotel at 8 a.m. Willeford is a former sheriff of Upton County, Wilson former sheriff of Crockett County. Both men had also taken up writing.

From Alpine we drove to Marfa and from there, we traveled on U.S. 90 until we reached FM 2017 in an area called Lobo Flats. We passed Needle Peak and continued until we turned left on Chispa Road, an unpaved county road that decreased in quality the farther south we went. Porvenir, or what is left of it, is about 20 miles down this road.

Once off pavement, we stopped and loaded our guns. This was even before we encountered two friendly Border Patrol agents. When Wilson told them where we were headed, one of them asked if we were armed. When Wilson said we were, the agent said, "Good." He said "they" (as in lookouts for drug smugglers) would probably be watching us from the other side of the river.

The first evidence of previous occupation is the long-abandoned Porvenir store, which appeared to have later been used as a house. About a mile farther down the road is the foundation of the old Porvenir gin. Before salt cedars choked off most of the moisture, farmers grew cotton in the Rio Grande flood plain between the gin site and the river. In looking around this area, I found a pretty good archaic tool of some sort and an old .45 auto shell with a rim. Wilson, a firearms expert, said the round dated to around the time of the massacre.

With Willeford standing guard, Wilson and I walked from the old gin to the river. The river was narrow at this point, but it was flowing well. We could see where someone had recently crossed but if anyone was watching us, we never saw them.

Returning to the gin site we "saddled up" and drove a short distance to the point where the massacre occurred. (By our reading, North 30.31.458, West 104 52.618). Willeford said he'd first visited the spot three years earlier and found a couple of spent shells about where the rangers would have been firing from. But on this foray, the only firearm-related artifacts I found were a .45 ACP shell used in the six-shot M1917 revolver adopted by the U.S. Army in 1917 (found near the foundation of the old gin), a .45 slug and a .32 shell.

Later archeological work at the site turned up numerous pistol and rifle slugs. One consultant reported that most of the spent cartridges they found were military issue and inferred that U.S. soldiers may have participated in the event. Other sources indicate the Rangers had carried rifles supplied by the military.

Time of Transition: 1919-1934

Captain Wright's Wheelman

Author's interviews with Bob Snow, assorted dates, 1967-1987.

The author met Bob Snow in 1965 near the end of his state service, shortly before he retired as captain in charge of the Texas Parks and Wildlife Department law enforcement district headquartered in Kerrville. Snow was an old friend of my late grandfather, L.A. Wilke.

From 1957 to his retirement in 1962, Wilke edited the monthly magazine produced by the old Texas Game and Fish Commission (now Texas Parks and Wildlife Magazine). That's probably when he met Snow, though it could have been earlier. One time when they both had business at the Black Gap Wildlife Management Area Wilke took a photo of Snow astride the mule he'd been using to access some of the rougher terrain on the 103,000-acre property bordering Big Bend National Park.

Both men had a good sense of humor, and that mule indirectly led to them becoming better friends. Each year, the game department magazine ran a photo spread showing all the wardens in the state. Wilke had repeatedly asked Snow to send him a photograph for that purpose, and Snow had been procrastinating. Finally, in a threat that worked, Wilke sent Snow a letter saying he planned to publish the picture of him on the mule. Only he'd be cropping out Snow's face and using the mule's mug instead. Snow soon sent Wilke the photo he needed.

The Demise of Grube

"Grube Making Long Strides In Development," San Angelo Standard-Times, Jan. 10, 1926.

"Grube Is Red Barn's Rival," San Angelo Standard-Times, Nov. 24, 1927.

"Bridge Pecos in Oil Field," San Angelo Standard-Times, Dec. 7, 1927.

"Jail 27 in Oil Town Raid; Chase Women," San Angelo Standard-Times, Jan. 18, 1928.

"El Masha Succeeds Oil Town of Grube," San Angelo Standard-Times, March 18, 1928. "Grube, Once Seen As Future City, Nearly Deserted," San Angelo Standard-Times, Nov. 27, 1928.

Pruning Glen Rose

Cox, Mike. "Texas Ranger Tales," Former Texas Rangers Association Straight Talk (November 2014).

Stranger at the Door

"Caller Attempts to Pay Mystery Debt to Widow of Slain Sheriff," Fort Worth Star-Tele gram, Oct. 14, 1927.

"Court Convenes at Carrizozo," Albuquerque Morning Journal, April 25, 1917.

"Fatal Shooting at Oscuro, New Mexico," El Paso Times, March 3, 1917.

"Fred Roberts Shot to Death at Oscuro," Carrizozo (New Mexico) Outlook," March 2, 1917.

"Mystery Man Showers Money On Widow," Austin American-Statesman, Oct. 13, 1927, p. 1.

Stephens, Robert. Texas Ranger Captain Dan Roberts: The Untold Story. Dallas: Privately published, 2009, pp. 218-225.

Four Bits to Watch My Back?

Author's interview with Phyllis Musgrove, recalling a story told by her late husband, Brewster County, Texas, April 25, 2009.

Author's interview with retired Ranger Lewis Rigler, Gainesville, Texas, Sept. 27, 2005. Tanner, Leon. Boots to Briefcases: Jack Borden Country Lawyer, Weatherford: Nebo Valley Press, 2003, p. 74.

Two Head Shots and a Smoke

Author's interview with Jim Wilson, Alpine, Texas, March 22, 2011.

Boessenecker, John, Texas Ranger: The Epic Life of Frank Hamer, The Man Who Killed Bonnie and Clyde, New York: Thomas Dunne Books, 2016, passim.

Modernization: 1935-2000

Ready for the Nazis

Author's interview with Brig. Gen. Matt Roberts (ret.), Austin, Texas, Sept. 5, 2000.

"Ex-Ranger, 88, Recalls Thrills of 'Fighting' Days/'Ran Indians to Death'" Austin Statesman, April 26, 1950, p. 16.

Sherrill, Bill, "Brady Visitor Recalls 'Judge'/W.H. Roberts of Llano Tells of Time Roy Bean Was Silenced by Rangers," Fort Worth Star-Telegram, July 8, 1941, p. 18.

The Two Noah Armstrongs

Marshall (Texas) Tri-Weekly Herald, June 30, 1877, p. 2.

Austin Daily Statesman, Sept. 27, 1877, p. 4.

"The Men Accused of the Murder of Sheriff Olive on Trial," Fort Worth Daily Gazette, Oct. 20, 1892.

El Paso Times, May 26, 1893, p. 2.

"The Train Robbery," Fort Worth Daily Gazette, May 27, 1893, p. 1.

San Saba County News, June 9, 1893.

Galveston Daily News, Sept. 24, 1893.

"Testimony in the Armstrong Case," Williamson County Sun, May 21, 1915.

Elizabeth Doyle, interviewer, "Noah Armstrong," U.S. Work Projects Administration, Federal Writer's Project, Life Histories 1936-1939, MSS55715; Box A734, Library of Congress.

Wright, Hamilton, "Thousands Throng Reunion for Festive Tribute to County's Early Settlers," Abilene Reporter-News, July 19, 1947, p. 3.

"Ranger, 97, Gets Bussed By Actress," Fort Worth Star-Telegram, May 17, 1949, p. 3.

Armstrong, Billy R., Sr., "Noah Armstrong" in A History of Coleman County and its People, Vol. 1, Coleman, Texas: Coleman County Historical Commission, 1985, p. 390.

Dillard, Jim, "The Murder of Sheriff John T. Olive," Focus on Georgetown (February 2011), p. 26.

Findagrave.com, "Noah Armstrong," Memorial ID 8135535.

Pain Never Did Bother Me Much

Bryan, Ann, "New Police Methods Talked At Runnels Lawmen Session," San Angelo Standard-Times, Feb. 25, 1957.

"Crusty Texas Ranger Dies; Burial Saturday in Austin," United Press International (UPI), Dec. 10, 1971.

Author's interview with Senior Ranger Capt. H.R. "Lefty" Block, Feb. 4, 1987.

Author's interview with retired Ranger Joaquin Jackson, Alpine, Texas, June 13, 2009.

Wilson, Jim, "Charlie Miller: A Unique Ranger," Shooting Times, Sept. 23, 2010.

Justice for Jane Doe

Cox, Mike. "Woman found shot to death on I-35 in Comal County," Austin American- Statesman, June 4, 1981, p. 26.

______. Cox and Susan Aschoff, "Unidentified woman found shot six times along I-35," Austin American-Statesman, June 5, 1981, p. 24.

Cox, Mike. "Deaths along I-35 frustrate sheriffs," Austin American-Statesman, June 7, 1981, p. 1.

Author's interview with retired Ranger Joshua Ray, July 5, 2023.

Author's interview with Ranger Trampas Gooding, July 5, 2023.

Loose Cartridges

Thrilling Episodes That Never Happened

Battle of the Painted Rocks

Cox, Mike. "Battle of the Paint Rocks: Scraping Off the Layers," West Texas Historical Association Year Book, Vol. LXXVIII (2002), pp. 151-169.

Battle of Bandera Pass

Cox, Mike. Gunfights and Sites in Texas Ranger History. Charleston,

NC: The History Press, 2015, pp. 81-82.

Enchanted Rock

______. Gunfights and Sites in Texas Ranger History. Charleston, NC: The History Press, 2015, p. 81.

"The Belle of San Antonio"

Crosby, David F. True West (January 1997), pp. 39-41.

"Captive Beauty, Miss King Rescued in Bloody Indian Fight (Logan Van Deveer Was Hero," Frontier Times (June 1938).

Posey, Mary Johnson. "Terrific Indian Fight With Knives in a Cave Gave Logan Van Deveer, Austin's First Owner, His Beautiful Bride," Austin American, Feb. 24, 1918, p. 17.

"Would Honor Man Who First Owned Land Austin Is Now Built On at Great Pageant," Austin American, March 5, 1915, p. 5.

Born in 1884, Mrs. Posey died at 76 in 1960. She had lived in Austin since 1910 but was returned to Burnet for burial in the Odd Fellow Cemetery there.

El Muerto

Dobie, J. Frank, "The Headless Horseman of the Mustangs," Tales of Old-Time Texas, Boston: Little, Brown and Co., 1955, pp. 147-154.

Herds, Lou Ann, "The Evolution of a Legend: The Headless Horseman of Texas," in Abernethy, Francis Edward., ed., Both Sides of the Border: A Scattering of Texas Folklore, Publications of the Texas Folklore Society LXI, Denton: University of North Texas Press, 2004, pp. 102-117.

Reid, Mayne. The Headless Horseman: A Strange Tale of Texas, London: Chapman and Hall, March 1865.

Forced to Dig Their Own Graves

Cox, Gunfights and Sites in Texas Ranger History, pp. 74-76

Wild Shootout on the King Ranch

Masterman, Patricia. "Horse Sense and Courtesy Mark Law Officer's 55-Year-Career," Amarillo Globe-Times, Feb. 17, 1958.

Tarnishing the Silver Star

'Destroy every bottle…'

Author's presentation, Texas Governor's Mansion docents, May 10, 2006.

No Cowboying on State Time

Undated newspaper clipping, author's collection.

'Ungentlemanly and Unsoldierly'

Dallas Daily Herald, Oct. 7, 1877.

An Ugly Incident

"Coleman Pioneer Recalls Concho as an Army Post," San Angelo Standard-Times, Feb. 2, 1940.

'William Tell' Jailed

Dallas Daily Herald, Feb. 28, 1880.

How One JP Viewed the Rangers

Hawley, C.A. "Life Along The Border." Sul Ross State College Bulletin. Alpine: West Texas Historical and Scientific Society. Vol. XLIV, No. 3, September 1964, p. 65.

The Ranger Who Investigated Himself

Author's interview with Harrison Hamer, Oct. 2, 2000.

Ranger Treasure Tales

Steinheimer's Millions

Author's presentation, Georgetown Heritage Society, Feb. 25, 2012.

Bertillion, L.D., "Steinheimer's Millions," Legends of Texas, Austin: Texas Folklore Society, 1924.

Dobie, J. Frank. "Steinheimer's Millions," Coronado's Children, Dallas: Southwestern Press, 1930, pp. 105-108.

Roberts, Bill, "Steinheimer's Missing Millions," Treasure World, (June-July 1974), pp. 24-27.

Roberts, Bill, "Steinheimer's Missing Millions," Treasure World, (June-July 1974), pp. 24-27.

Ranger Silver

"Buried Silver in Texas Dimly Traced," Corpus Christi Caller-Times,

Dec. 17, 1937, p. 18.

Cox, Mike. "Texas Tales," June 17, 2009.

Anecdotes and Apocrypha

"He'll Do to Ride the River With"

www.CoolNSmart.com, accessed April 26, 2023.

"He'll do to ride the river with," barrypopik.com, Nov. 1, 2015, accessed April 27, 2023.

Rangers and Rattlers

"San Saba Meet of Ex-Rangers Well Attended," San Angelo Morning Times, July 4, 1929, p. 10.

"Cattle Battle on Edwards Plateau in 1884," Frontier Times (March 1932), pp. 249-251.

Jobes, Harold D., "The Shoot Out at Green Lake," www.llanoriver.org/sin-

glepost/3015/12/04/the-shoot-out-at-green-lake, accessed June 27, 2023.

Author's interview with retired Ranger Joe B. Davis, Fredericksburg, Texas, June 26, 2023.

Coffee, Please

Author's interview with Joe B. Davis, July 28, 2023.

Let's Settle This Like Men

Author's interview with Jim Wilson, March 22, 2011.

Pardon Me, Ma'am

Author's interview with Joe B. Davis, June 15, 2000.

How the Rangers Got a New Man

Author's interview with retired Ranger Lewis Rigler, Gainesville, Texas, Sept. 27, 2005.

Author's interview with Jim Wilson, March 22, 2011.

Capitol Riot

Author's interview with Senior Ranger Capt. Bruce Casteel, n.d.

Acing the Promotional Exam

Author's interview with Capt. Mark Warren, DPS Training Academy, May 27, 1996.

What Older Rangers Talk About

Author's interview with Dave Duncan, Fort Davis, Texas Nov. 15, 2002.

Camp Chow

Captain Tobin's Legacy

Cox, Mike. "Ranger Tales," Former Texas Rangers Association Straight Talk, (November 2010).

Stout Enough to Float a Horseshoe

Fugate, Francis, Arbuckles: The Coffee That Won the West, El Paso: Texas Western Press, 1994, passim.

Cox, Mike. "Texas Ranger Tales," Former Texas Rangers Association Straight Talk (March 2017).

Ranger Cookies

Cox, Mike. "Texas Tales," March 31, 2016.

The Authorized Texas Ranger Cookbook. Hamilton, Texas: Harris Farms Publishing, 1994, p. 78.

The Rangers' Arlington

Author's interview with Joe B. Davis, June 23, 2023.

Block, Senior Capt. H.R. (Lefty). Remarks presented at Center Point Cemetery historical marker dedication. Aug. 22, 1987. Author's collection.

Cox, Mike. "Texas Ranger Tales," Former Texas Rangers Association Straight Talk, (March 2018).

Johnston, Jewel Dixon. "Texas Rangers of Kerr County." Kerrville Mountain Sun. Sept. 20, 1989.

Author' interview with Bobbie J. Powell, Center Point, Texas, Feb. 4, 1999. Townsend, Emmett C. to H.R. Block, July 23, 1987.

Witt, Gerald. The History of Eastern Kerr County, Texas. Austin: Nortex Press, 1986.

Another Conflict

"Texas Ranger statue at Love Field removed over concerns," Dallas Morning News, June 30, 2020.

Mort, John. "Mansfield Mob Routs Minister Amid Jeering," Fort Worth Star-Telegram, Sept. 5, 1956, p. 1.

Cox, Wearing the Cinco Peso, p. 15.

Boessenecker, Texas Ranger: The Epic Life of Frank Hamer, The Man Who Killed Bonny and Clyde, passim.

An elected member of the Texas Institute of Letters, Mike Cox is an award-winning author of more than 40 non-fiction books and hundreds of magazine articles, book reviews and newspaper columns.

He is the recipient of a Will Rogers Medallion and the A.C. Greene Lifetime Achievement Award for his extensive body

of work.

mikecoxauthor.com

Made in the USA
Columbia, SC
09 November 2024

0410509e-37e4-4006-b904-3e403e07058aR01